THE TROUBLED LIFE OF PETER BURNETT

The Troubled Life of Peter Burnett

OREGON PIONEER AND
FIRST GOVERNOR OF CALIFORNIA

R. Gregory Nokes

Oregon State University Press   Corvallis

Library of Congress Cataloging in Publication Control Number: 2018002730

0-978-0-87071-932-5

∞ This paper meets the requirements of ANSI/NISO Z39.48-1992
(Permanence of Paper).

First published in 2018 by Oregon State University Press
Printed in the United States of America

Oregon State University Press
121 The Valley Library
Corvallis OR 97331-4501
541-737-3166 • fax 541-737-3170
www.osupress.oregonstate.edu

*To my late father and mother, J. Richard Nokes and
Evelyn J. Nokes, who taught me the love of books
and inspired me to follow in my father's footsteps
as a journalist and writer of Western history.*

Contents

Preface

Here's what an enterprising young man could accomplish in just six short years in the early American West: He could organize his own wagon train; serve in Oregon's first elected government; be elected the territory's first supreme court judge; win election to Oregon's Territorial Legislature; blaze a wagon trail to California; join with young John Sutter to help develop the city of Sacramento; win election as the first governor of California; and, a few years later, serve on the California Supreme Court.

This was the life of Peter Hardeman Burnett—merchant, lawyer, emigrant, city planner, farmer, gold miner, politician, jurist, banker, author, and theologian. At first glance, it's an extraordinarily successful life. His résumé is the most impressive of any leader in the early American West. But for the Tennessee-born Burnett, saddled by decades of debt and personal failings, nearly every achievement brought disappointment. He would be staggered along the way by the tragic deaths of two of his children.

As a political leader, Burnett played a major role in organizing the first American governments in Oregon and California. But these accomplishments are overshadowed by a legacy of racism and advocacy of exclusion laws, aimed at prohibiting African Americans from settling on the Pacific Coast. As a member of Oregon's Legislative Committee, the first provisional legislature, he authored what became known as "Peter Burnett's lash law," threatening severe whipping of blacks who refused to leave. Also damaging to Burnett's standing in history was his ruling in the notorious Archy Lee slavery case as a member of the California Supreme Court in 1858.

Burnett's views on race seem extreme today, but at the time they represented one side of a debate over the role of blacks and minorities in the American frontier, a debate that has its parallel in today's arguments over admitting Muslims and Latinos into the United States. Burnett was successful in imposing some of his views in Oregon, less so in California. But in both jurisdictions, there were many who agreed with him that there was no room for African Americans. Like Burnett, many of the early settlers came from the South with conflicted feelings about blacks and slavery.

It is little remembered that Oregon voted in 1857 on whether to become a slave state. Although the proposal was rejected, nearly one-third of the electorate voted in favor. California, while established as a free state, nevertheless flirted with proslavery sentiments during much of its early history, and in 1852 enacted its own fugitive slave act.

On the other side of the debate were prominent leaders such as Jesse Applegate in Oregon and David Broderick in California, who argued the West should be open to all, and who blocked or overturned the more extreme proposals of Burnett and others.

Peter Burnett was blessed with good looks and natural charm. He was described in his mid-30s by a fellow emigrant as "a rather striking looking man of about ordinary height, with a very keen eye, a rather sloping forehead, light complexion and someone 'very ready of speech.'"[1] Photographs in his middle age reveal a strong resemblance to the late actor Paul Newman.

Burnett made an excellent first impression, and people turned to him for leadership. He was elected overwhelmingly as California's first governor in 1849. But his failure to exercise effective leadership, combined with a huge ego and some inexplicably tone-deaf policies, undermined his stature, and supporters soon abandoned him.

As governor, Burnett was ridiculed for such odd proposals as advocating execution for persons convicted of grand theft and robbery, and changing Thanksgiving from a Thursday to a Saturday. He resigned less than two years after being elected without giving any reason that made sense. A California newspaper commented that he had been so ineffective that nobody cared anyway.

Despite Burnett's prominence in western history, little has been written about him, and virtually nothing in depth. Burnett himself is the only source we have for his early life, and much of his later life as well. He tells his story in a rambling 488-page autobiography titled *Recollections and Opinions of an Old Pioneer*. Burnett finished it in 1880 when he was 73, fifteen years before his death in 1895. His memory occasionally failed him, and dates and places were sometimes confused.

As is the case with any autobiography, Burnett could be expected to put the best possible spin on his life, and he did this in spades. As interesting as what he included in his life story is what he left out. But he does tell us enough about his early experiences to reveal that he frequently felt humiliated by wealthy relatives, which made him distrustful and wary. It also fueled his desire for wealth and an "I'll show them" kind of resolve.

Burnett received little formal education, but he was extraordinarily well read. He wrote extensively, quoting at length from the works of economists, theologians, and political theorists. He seemed to have theories about everything, such as improving the US Constitution by requiring presidential appointment of state governors and lifetime election of US senators. Except for his later years as a banker, his entire career reflected a difficult struggle to practically apply his wide range of knowledge.

Burnett interacted during his life with some of the most prominent men of the time, among them Mormon leader Joseph Smith; pathfinder John Charles Fremont; missionary Marcus Whitman; Oregon Trail companion Jesse Applegate; Dr. John McLoughlin of the Hudson's Bay Company; John Sutter, on whose property gold was discovered in 1848; survivors of the ill-fated Donner Party; and Samuel Brannan, once the wealthiest man in the West, who brought Burnett into the banking career where he finally was able to excel.

Burnett's life in the West underscores the close ties that existed between Oregon and California during the early years of American settlement—the shared experience of often deadly struggles on the cross-continent emigrant trails, the movement of population between the two, and the similarity in attitudes toward American Indian tribes as well as immigrant Chinese and African Americans.

What follows is the story of a self-made man who achieved the fame he so desperately wanted and then ran from it, leaving a record of racism, frequently bizarre behavior, and jobs left undone.

Official portrait of Peter Hardeman Burnett, first governor
of California, from 1849 to 1851, in the California State
Capitol in Sacramento. Courtesy of the Building and
Property Management Branch of the Capitol Historic Region,
Department of General Services, State of California.

Chapter 1
Death of a Slave

For someone who would one day be elected governor of California, it was not an auspicious beginning: Peter Burnett shot and killed a man.

It was 1830 in Clear Creek, Tennessee. Burnett, then 23, had recently purchased a store, selling general merchandise to nearby cotton farmers. His goal was to get rich. But the store was losing money. In an attempt to stem his losses, Burnett purchased three barrels of Old Monongahela rye whiskey, "a favorite of those who loved whiskey," he would say. He sold it by the pint, quart, and gallon.[1]

Yet the whiskey's popularity attracted an unwanted imbiber. On arriving at the store one morning, Burnett found that a window shutter had been forced open. Assuming a burglary, Burnett spent the next night in the store with his rifle at his side, "determined to shoot the burglar if he should come and enter the store."

The shutter was normally secured by an iron bolt. But on this evening Burnett left it unlocked and fastened a string from the shutter to the handle of a tin coffee pot. The idea was that when the shutter swung open, the pot would fall to the floor and alert Burnett, hiding behind the counter, rifle in hand. He would then rise and shoot the burglar. But Burnett fell asleep. When he awoke, the coffee pot was on the floor, and the burglar gone. Burnett had slept through the racket, suggesting he must have been an extraordinarily sound sleeper.

Burnett tried a different strategy the following night. This time, he secured the window shutter with the bolt and fastened a string from the shutter to the trigger of the rifle, which he propped up on the counter—loaded, cocked, and ready to fire. And this time, he went home. He described the scene that greeted him the next morning: "I found a negro man lying on his back dead, with a mill-pick and jug by his side. He had broken open the window shutter with the pick, and the shot and one bullet had entered his forehead and produced instant

1

death."[2] The dead man was a slave, employed at a nearby mill. Burnett claimed to feel terrible at being the cause of the man's death. "The poor negro was fond of liquor, and wanted nothing else," he lamented.[3] An inquest was held, and the shooting was ruled a justifiable homicide.[4] Burnett said the owner of the slave might have sued him for damages but did not.

One might consider the odds that a random single shot from a propped-up rifle would strike the man squarely in the forehead, or—not inconceivably— whether Burnett had pulled the trigger and then been appalled by what he had done, concocting an alternative explanation. After all, he had intended to shoot the burglar the night before. And would Burnett really have gone home after just missing the burglar the previous evening? As for the victim, he must have been desperately thirsty to risk breaking into the store after being nearly caught the night before. But it's the story Burnett tells in his autobiography.

Whether the victim's race had anything to do with the shooting, the incident underscored two themes that would dominate Burnett's life: a refusal to accept African Americans as anything other than a subservient class, unworthy of equal treatment, and a constant preoccupation with money—desperate to make it, but more likely to lose it.

Peter Hardeman Burnett was born November 15, 1807, in Nashville, Tennessee, then just a hamlet on the American frontier. "I was born a pioneer in Nashville," Burnett would write, "and I was a pioneer most of my life."[5] He was the third of eight children of George and Dorothy Hardeman Burnet—five boys and three girls. His brothers were Glen Owen, George William, James White, and Thomas Smith; his sisters were Constantia, Elizabeth Ann, and Mary. While still in his teens, Burnett added a second "t" to his last name.[6]

Burnett's great-grandfather James Burnet emigrated from Ireland as a bachelor. Little else is known about James other than he was a farmer and died in Pittsylvania, Virginia, in 1765 at about age 60.[7] Burnett's father, George Burnet, was born in Pittsylvania County on September 16, 1770, one of four brothers. He was a farmer and a skilled carpenter who built several of Nashville's first buildings, including frame houses and log cabins. Burnett described his father as a "pretty good farmer" but also a poor businessman who was "often cheated."

Carpentry and farming didn't interest Peter, who had higher aspirations— although farming would later be thrust on him by necessity. He did emulate his father in one important respect: he proved to be a poor businessman, which kept him in a largely impoverished state during much of his early life.

Peter's mother, Dorothy Hardeman, was the daughter of Thomas Hardeman, one of the first settlers in Tennessee. Although also from a humble background, Hardeman became a wealthy landowner, accumulating more than 5,000 acres in the Nashville area. He was elected to the Territorial Legislature in 1794 and was a delegate to Tennessee's Constitutional Convention in 1796 along with a future president, Andrew Jackson, who was a neighbor and friend. Hardeman was elected to the new state legislature in 1798. Hardeman County, Tennessee, takes the family name.

Slaves made a significant contribution to Thomas Hardeman's wealth. When he decided to downsize his land holdings in 1809 and 1810, he sold seven male slaves for $500 to $600 apiece, about the average selling price of a male slave at the time.[8] A family biographer wrote, "Thomas's slaves had fulfilled their purpose for him, doubtless providing much of the well-being which he enjoyed." He also loaned slaves to his children.[9]

Peter weighed the merits of men in his family against the Hardeman men. His father was "raised poor and never went to school but three months in his life."[10] The Burnet men were "men of peace, very just, industrious, sober and piously disposed [who] cared very little for riches." But he seemed to most admire the Hardemans, who "were generally men of the world, first fond of fashionable pleasures, dress, and show, and afterward seekers of fortune. . . . They were generally good businessmen and good traders in such property as lands and stock." But they also, especially his young cousins, "wasted their patrimony . . . in fashionable life." Throughout his life, he would remain contemptuous of people who wasted their wealth.

The Burnets were influenced by, and perhaps jealous of, the Hardemans—certainly, Peter was jealous. When members of the Hardeman family moved from Tennessee to Howard County, Missouri, in 1816, the Burnet family followed a year later. Possibly they looked to the Hardemans for help, as the Burnets' first year in Howard County was difficult. The family lived in a one-room shack with a dirt floor and hole in the roof for a chimney, with whites on one side of the room and "the blacks" on the other.[11] Burnett didn't say the blacks were slaves, but he didn't have to—there wasn't another reasonable explanation.

The slaves were most likely a family of four. Burnett said there were fourteen people in the household. His parents and their eight children added to ten, leaving a possible four slaves. Burnett later mentioned the presence of an African American boy of about 6, and an adult male slave of about 40, whom he called "Uncle Hal." It seems odd that someone as poor as George Burnet would own slaves. Quite possibly the elder Hardeman loaned them to his daughter's family, or gave them as a gift.[12] A farmer without slaves, even a small farmer, was at a distinct disadvantage in a farm economy that depended on slaves to do the back-breaking work of harvesting hemp and tobacco, the region's major crops.

Although Burnett maintained in later years that he opposed slavery, he owned two slaves in Missouri, a male under age 10 and a female aged 10 to 23, according to the 1840 Census.[13] They may have been a mother and son, or brother and sister.

There is no record of what happened to Burnett's slaves, and he made no mention of them in his autobiography. But it seems likely that Burnett took one or both to Oregon in 1843, one of whom drowned en route.

Burnett expressed admiration for slaveholders in his autobiography. He said that his family generally treated its slaves well, and the slaves reciprocated with appreciative obedience. For example, the slaves of a close acquaintance, whom he didn't identify, "were exceedingly dutiful, and devotedly attached" to their master. Moreover, this owner claimed to have "never struck one of his children a blow in his life, and never but one of his slaves, and that *a little negro girl*."[14] Burnett seemed to overlook the possibility that the slaves might have felt differently.

In 1822, the Burnet family moved to Clay County in northwest Missouri, 250 miles up the Missouri River, settling on a farm of 160 acres. (Clay County is today in the Kansas City metropolitan area.) The move was partly inspired by illness among family members. Virtually everyone, including the slaves, fell ill. Burnett said he suffered from malaria, or ague—characterized by paroxysms of fever, chills, and sweating—during two successive winters at ages 12 and 13. He would be plagued by illness throughout his life, bedridden for weeks at a time.

Burnett received some schooling in Clay County—the basics in reading, writing, and arithmetic. It was his only formal education, although then and later he proved a quick study—he read religiously and was a prolific writer. During his career, he became known for excessively long speeches and letters.

In Clay County, a traumatic event occurred that "greatly distressed" the Burnet family. The teenage Burnett had gone on a "bee hunt" looking for honey with an uncle, whom he didn't identify, and his father's "faithful slave"

Uncle Hal.[15] They took the family's only wagon, riding across the state line into "Indian country."[16] Leaving the wagon at the edge of a prairie, they hiked with their horses into a wooded area looking for bees. They were gone several days. Typical of Burnett's style, he described the bee hunt in great detail before getting around to what had "greatly distressed our family." Among his observations, "Bees were generally hunted in the fall or winter, as the hives were then full of honey. In the fall the hunter would find the hives by seeing the bees coming in and going out; but in the winter he would discover the bee-tree by finding the dead bees on the snow at the foot of the tree. When a bee dies in a hive the living cast out his dead body, which falls to the ground. This is done during the few warm clear days in winter."

When Burnett and the others returned to the wagon, they found it a smoldering wreck. Fire had swept across the prairie in their absence. Uncle Hal broke down in tears. "He had always driven the team and was proud of it," Burnett said. While the tears weren't otherwise explained, the slave may have feared being blamed. Burnett's father couldn't afford another wagon and so replaced it with a homemade cart. Working a large farm without a wagon suggests the family was indeed in dire straits, even if they managed to keep slaves.

Burnett guessed the fire had been started by local tribes, who periodically set fire to the prairie to make it easier to hunt game. Digressing once again, he observed that "the fire extended into the thick underbrush that skirted the prairie, and cooked the ripe summer grapes on the vines that bound the hazel thickets together."

Soon after the loss of the wagon, Burnett left home to live with his sister Constantia and her second husband, William L. Smith, whom Burnett called Major Smith.[17] Burnett doesn't indicate whether he was pleased or displeased by the move to the Smith home, or whether he was being punished for the loss of the wagon. The new living arrangement lasted fifteen months, after which he returned briefly to his father's home. But he was soon to move again.

Sometime in 1826, a wealthy uncle, Constant Hardeman, and his wife came to visit, and "it was determined" that Burnett, then 19, should accompany them to their home in Rutherford, Tennessee. Before leaving, his father gave him a horse, saddle, camlet cloak, and $26, while his mother provided him with a "good suit of jeans."[18] The trip to Tennessee with the Hardemans was not a pleasant one. Burnett's horse couldn't keep up and fell behind, much to his embarrassment.

Burnett's few years with the Hardemans caused him to equate money with respect. In Rutherford, he didn't fit in. "Among my rich kin, I at once recognized my comparative poverty and ignorance," he wrote. Whether true or not, he felt "slighted by my relatives." Writing decades later, he said he decided then and there to follow the Hardeman's approach to life rather than his father's. "When I saw that my relatives were rich, and valued riches more than knowledge, I determined that I would employ my energies in the accumulation of a fortune."[19]

Burnett found a job as a hotel clerk in nearby Bolivar, the Hardeman County seat, earning a salary of $100 a year. He waited tables and served meals, including to some prominent leaders of the period, among them the frontiersman David Crockett and General Samuel "Sam" Houston, who led the fight for Texas's independence from Mexico. Burnett admired Houston's "eloquent style of oratory," speaking "slowly, emphatically and distinctly so that all could hear him, and all wished to hear him." By contrast, Crockett was "an off-hand speaker, full of anecdotes, and kept a crowd greatly amused."[20]

Although Burnett mostly enjoyed the five or six months he worked at the hotel, he was bothered that the owner's daughter and "two pretty stepdaughters" ignored him. "They considered themselves my superiors, and I never kept their company." Another humiliation was the loss of his hat, about which he goes into as much detail as any other personal recollection from this period. His prized fur hat was cut to shreds by someone at the hotel as a holiday prank. Lacking money for a new one, Burnett was resigned to going about bareheaded, evidently much ashamed. The importance of a hat may escape us today, but for Burnett it was obviously a big deal. "I was the subject of much jesting, was badly quizzed, and greatly mortified." After a week or so, his uncle helped him buy a new hat.[21]

It was sometime during his nineteenth year, while in Tennessee, that Peter added a second "t" to his surname. "My reason for the change was the opinion that the name would be more complete and emphatic when spelled Burnett."[22] Even so, his more emphatic name would bring no immediate change of fortune.

Throughout his long career, Burnett didn't waver in his determination to acquire wealth until later in his life, when a religious awakening led him to question his priorities. But that revelation came much later. In the meantime, he would find his pot of gold, but only after many detours and stumbles along the way.

Chapter 2
Sinking into Debt

Among guests at the hotel where Burnett worked was a Methodist minister, Reverend W. Blount Peck, known as "Parson Peck." Peck was opening a mercantile store in nearby Clear Creek, Tennessee, and hired Burnett to manage the store for $200 a year, twice his hotel salary.

Parson Peck's store was a log structure of 18 by 20 feet. Peck provided the merchandise, which he purchased in New Orleans, while Burnett handled sales and collected the bills. Most transactions were on credit, with bills payable in cotton, deposited before the end of the year at a nearby cotton gin—a common method of payment in the cash-short frontier. But neither Peck nor Burnett was up to the task of running a store. They quickly drove it into the ground, each blaming the other.[1]

Looking back on the experience, Burnett said it was doomed from the start. The failure caused a serious break between the two men, for which Burnett partially blamed himself. The major fault, according to Burnett, was that Parson Peck didn't have enough money to maintain his stock of goods. Peck, on the other hand, faulted Burnett for failing to collect bills due from customers. In retaliation for Peck's blaming him for the store's mounting debt, Burnett "censured" Peck for twice pledging the same debt to two different creditors. As a public rebuke, the censure probably embarrassed Peck. "These mutual charges led to a partial estrangement, which continued until I had left the state," Burnett said.[2]

Years later, Burnett regretted what he'd done. He realized Peck had probably made a simple bookkeeping error and "was entirely honest in his intentions." He wrote Peck, then living in Philadelphia, to apologize. "I desired to do him all the justice in my power, and to renew to him the reassurances of my esteem and gratitude. Whether he received my letter or not, I never knew."

One can guess the whole story is not being told, especially because of what happened next. Even though Burnett considered the venture doomed from the start, and even though he and Peck had had a falling out, Burnett purchased the store and its contents in 1829, paying Peck with a promissory note due in eighteen months. Peck, in turn, used Burnett's notes to pay off his creditors, which meant Burnett then owed the creditors.

While still working for Peck, Burnett met and wooed the woman who would become his wife, Harriet Rogers, one of two daughters of Peter Rogers, who had recently moved to a farm near the store. Burnett met Harriet through her brother, Hardin, for whom he expressed great affection. "He was a noble young man, with a fine face and beautiful black eyes, my favorite."[3] Peter and Hardin became inseparable friends, and studied law together. But Hardin fell ill with a fever that also afflicted Burnett. He recovered, but Hardin did not and died. "Poor fellow," Burnett wrote.[4]

As for Harriet, "the girl had won my heart." Parson Peck officiated at their wedding on August 20, 1828. Harriet was just 16.[5] Burnett built a small cabin near the Clear Creek store for the couple and the soon-to-arrive first of their six children, Dwight Jay Burnett, born May 23, 1829.[6] Five other Burnett children—Martha Letitia, Romietta Juett, John May, Armstead Lock, and Sallie Constantia—were born in Missouri. Peter's brother Glen would later marry Harriet's sister Sarah.

As a store owner, Peter Burnett was a bust, piling up huge debts. But as a marksman with a rifle, he was a sure shot. He once bragged he shot the heads off two turkeys at a considerable distance. So when he claimed it was entirely an accident that he shot and killed a black slave breaking into his store, one might wonder how much of an accident it was.

Looking back on the incident from the distance of fifty years, Burnett called it "a melancholy circumstance . . . which I have long deeply regretted." He claimed that because of this incident "the idea of shedding human blood is now terrible to me. I would rather bear almost any injury than take a human life."[7] But that statement of resolve didn't mean he wouldn't consider it, as he was soon to demonstrate.

It was also during this period that Burnett acknowledged that he enjoyed liberally dipping into his whiskey barrel during the day. It was only when the barrel was empty that he realized how much he "loved it." He resolved never to touch the stuff again. "I became satisfied that, if I indulged at all, I would be very apt to do some very tall drinking."[8]

Peter and Harriet Rogers Burnett in 1872 portraits. "The girl had won my heart," Burnett wrote. They married in Clear Creek, Tennessee, on August 20, 1828, and had six children. Courtesy of the Oregon Historical Society.

Burnett by this time was so heavily in debt that he lacked the money to replenish his stock. Nor could he sell what remained. It was a recipe for failure. His debts continued to accumulate without the means to repay them. He decided to return to Missouri, but he was faced with first closing his store and then making one last attempt to settle his debts. Harriet and their small son went ahead to Missouri to live with Peter's brother Glen, in Liberty, now a suburb of Kansas City. Burnett stayed behind in Tennessee and boarded with an uncle, William Hardin.

After thirteen months, "collecting all I could" but still owing a great deal, Burnett decided it was pointless to delay a move any longer. He said living apart from Harriet was "one of the hardest trials of my life."[9] While traveling on a Mississippi River steamer to join his family in Liberty, he was embarrassed to be "the most shabbily dressed man" on board, wearing a suit worn through the elbows.

He was beyond broke. He had just over 62¢ to his name and still owed $700 dollars to his Tennessee creditors. Moreover, he didn't have a job. At nearly 25, Burnett was no closer to acquiring a fortune than when he left Missouri for Tennessee six years earlier. Indeed, he had regressed.

Chapter 3
Burnett and the Mormons

If nothing else, Burnett was a quick study, adapting with little difficulty to new opportunities in his multilayered life. His next goal was to become a prosperous Missouri lawyer. Prior to Hardin Rogers's death, they had jointly purchased "a small library of law books."

While pursuing his legal studies, including reading the decisions of the Missouri Supreme Court, Burnett turned to the one job with which he had experience: running a store. He managed a Liberty mercantile store for Edward M. Samuel and Samuel Moor at pay of $400 a year. Although he considered it a good job, he quit after fifteen months, "having pretty well paid up [his] debts" and ready to begin a legal practice.

Burnett received his law license from Justice George Tompkins of the Missouri Supreme Court in 1834 and moved to Richmond, the Ray County seat, to hang his shingle.[1] But legal pickings were slim, especially for someone with virtually no experience. Burnett returned to the mercantile business, managing a store for James M. and G. L. Hughes on "very advantageous" terms, whereby he was to receive one-third of the store's profits. "I was still anxious to make a fortune, and this was the best opportunity."[2]

Burnett and the Hugheses had two good years, 1834 and 1835. In 1836, they took in a new partner, Colonel John Thornton—"one of the wealthiest men of Clay County"—who put up $5,000, raising the total capital to $13,000.[3] But in 1837, Burnett and Thornton evidently decided to go it alone. They bought out the Hugheses, a decision that did not turn out well. As part of the agreement, they had to vacate the Hughes-owned building, leaving them with the task of finding another location. If there were hard feelings involved, Burnett doesn't say.

The new partners agreed Thornton would build a new store in Liberty, while Burnett went to Philadelphia to purchase a stock of goods. He anticipated the new store would be ready when he returned, but it wasn't. The partners were compelled to find another building that was poorly located. The result was "a heavy loss to us," Burnett said. Adding to their difficulties was a nation-wide economic depression, known as the Panic of 1837, during which their customers lost money and jobs.[4] The two calamities were "enough to absorb all the profits of the former firm, and more than enough to swallow up those of 'Thornton & Burnett.' "[5]

What seems missing from Burnett's account is any explanation of Thornton's role in the store's demise. His failure to produce the promised store on time is puzzling. As "one of the wealthiest men in Clay County," he might have been expected to find another centrally located store, or to have bankrolled the store to see it through to more prosperous times. The likely explanation is that Thornton had given up on the business, and perhaps on Burnett as well.

Burnett's debts mounted from another business venture he mentions only briefly. "By the advice of others," he decided to build a sawmill and distill-ery near Liberty in 1837, and convinced his brother Glen and brother-in-law William Smith to join him. They borrowed $10,000 at an annual interest of 10 percent, payable in five years.[6] Predictably for Burnett, however, the enterprise soon failed and resulted in another heavy loss. Burnett offers no details of this business, except to say that years later he ended up covering most of the losses himself.

In just three years following his return to Missouri, Burnett had sustained combined losses of about $15,000. But however costly, he did learn one impor-tant lesson: "I have dread of steam saw-mills, steam distilleries, and the mercan-tile business generally."[7]

Burnett also edited a weekly newspaper in Liberty called *The Far West*, but he doesn't have much to say about this venture either. Online records from the University of Missouri show that eight issues of the newspaper were published from August 1836 to October 1836. It probably was in business much longer, but the newspaper's history has been lost. For the issues that have survived, Burnett's byline appears under the masthead as "Peter Burnet," with just one "t." The four-page newspaper listed his father-in-law, Peter Rogers, as proprietor.[8]

The choice of *Far West* for the newspaper's name is curious, as Far West was a town founded by members of the Church of Jesus Christ of Latter-Day Saints, or Mormons, 78 miles north of Liberty. It was the county seat of Caldwell County, established by the Missouri legislature in 1836 expressly for Mormons, who were then flooding into northwest Missouri from Ohio and elsewhere. Non-Mormons accused the newcomers of trying to take control of the region. The legislature sought to defuse unrest by containing the Mormons in an area separate from the non-Mormon population. There was an understanding the Mormons would not move beyond the Caldwell County borders. This understanding would not last.

The August 25th edition of *Far West* reported on a community meeting in Ray County at which residents approved a resolution condoning violence if Mormons insisted on settling in that county: "Resolved: That the emigrating Mormons cannot, must not, nor shall not settle in Ray County, peaceably if we can, forcibly if we must."[9] Subsequent editions carried virtually no mention of the controversy, even though the growing Mormon population was the dominant topic in the region. Given Burnett's opportunistic nature, he may have considered the Mormons a potential source of income and chose not to offend them with additional critical articles. If this was his strategy, it worked.

Conflict between the Mormon and non-Mormon populations erupted almost as soon as Mormons began arriving in Missouri in 1831, responding to a prophecy from their prophet, Joseph Smith, that Independence in Jackson County was the true site of the Garden of Eden. Smith directed his followers to build a new Jerusalem at Independence to await the second coming of Jesus. A cornerstone was laid for a temple, which although never completed became known as "Temple Lot," a revered site for many Mormons.

Among issues dividing Mormons and non-Mormons, and there were many, was slavery. Mormons generally did not keep slaves, and ambiguous comments regarding slavery by church leaders led to suspicion they might promote abolition in Missouri or stir up rebellion among slaves and Native Americans. By 1833, there were 1,200 Mormons in Jackson County, equal to a third of the population. Fearing loss of political control, a committee of Jackson County residents issued a statement in July 1833 harshly denouncing the Mormon presence.

> We believed them deluded fanatics, or weak and designing knaves, and that they and their pretensions would soon pass away; but in this we were deceived. The acts of a few designing leaders amongst them have thus far succeeded in holding them together as a society; and since the arrival of the first of them, they have been daily increasing in numbers;

and if they had been respectable citizens in society and thus deluded, they would have been entitled to our pity rather than to our contempt and hatred. . . . We have every reason to fear that, with but very few exceptions, they were of the very dregs of that society from which they came, lazy, idle and vicious.[10]

The committee went a step further at a meeting on July 16, ordering Mormon settlers to sell their land and leave Jackson County, an edict that became known as the "Mob Manifesto." With armed vigilantes threatening to enforce the edict, the Mormons relocated to the new legislature-established Caldwell County. Despite the understanding they would stay put, the fast-growing population—estimated at about three thousand—was soon spilling into neighboring counties, especially Daviess County to the north. Joseph Smith designated a new holy site in Daviess County called Adam-odi-Ahman, commonly called Diahman, where he claimed Adam had retreated after being expelled from the Garden of Eden. [11]

The events that embroiled the Mormons in conflict in Jackson County were soon to repeat themselves in Daviess, with abuses mounting on both sides. The Mormons formed a secret army known as the Danites, named for a passage in the book of Daniel.[12] Events moved quickly. On October 18, 1838, several hundred Danites torched non-Mormon homes and buildings and seized property throughout Daviess County, in reprisal for property taken from them in Jackson and Carroll Counties. They virtually destroyed the Daviess County seat of Gallatin. Authorities blamed Smith for the violence and issued a warrant for his arrest. Smith turned himself in, after which he was released on bail.[13]

Depredations continued. On October 24, a contingent of Mormons attacked a Missouri militia unit at Crooked River in Ray County, immediately south of Caldwell County, forcing the militia to flee. The militia casualties were one dead and six wounded, while Mormons casualties were three dead and seven wounded.[14]

Responding to appeals from local leaders, Governor Lilburn Boggs issued what became known as the notorious "Mormon extermination order" on October 27, 1838. The order accused Mormons of "open and armed defiance of the laws" and of making "war upon the people of this state." Boggs declared: "The Mormons must be treated as enemies and must be exterminated or driven from the state, if necessary for the public peace—their outrages are beyond all description."[15]

The bloodiest of several clashes occurred at a small Mormon settlement known as Haun's Mill in eastern Caldwell County on October 30. A Mormon named Jacob Haun had built a new mill and refused advice from church leaders to flee for his own safety. About two hundred local militiamen attacked about thirty-five defenders, killing as many as thirty-one—the casualty figure was in dispute—with seven militiamen wounded.[16]

To end what he saw as a rebellion, Governor Boggs ordered his officers to raise 1,400 troops, in addition to the already established militias, for a total armed force of about 2,500.[17] He placed them under the direct command of General John B. Clark, who marched on Far West with orders to expel the Mormons, defended by a Danite force of about 800. Burnett was among Clark's hastily assembled militia. While marching to Far West, Burnett recalled crossing the Crooked River battlefield in Ray County. "The dead and wounded had all been removed; but the clots of blood on the leaves where the men had fallen were fresh and plainly to be seen. It looked like the scene of death. Here lay a wool hat, there a tin cup, here an old blanket; in the top of this little tree hung a wallet of provisions; and saddles and bridles, and various articles of clothing lay around in confusion."[18]

General Clark's forces surrounded Far West. The closest Burnett came to combat occurred one night when a sentry sounded the alarm that "a body of armed men" was approaching from the direction of the town. "A fearful impulse came over me, such as I had never felt before," Burnett said. "I knew that it was most probable that the victorious Danites would be upon us." Why victorious, he didn't say—it's not clear the Danites prevailed in any battle. Nevertheless, Burnett said he volunteered with others to confront the apparent enemy, riding forward with "my gun in my right hand," only to discover the intruders were friendlies, a militia unit coming to join them. "Thus ended this alarm."[19]

Faced with overwhelming odds, Joseph Smith surrendered without a fight on November 1. Smith and several other Mormon leaders, including Danite leader Lyman Wight, were promptly court-martialed and found guilty of treason. Their sentence was death. Major General Samuel Lucas, who presided over the court-martial, ordered General Alexander W. Doniphan to execute Smith and the others in Far West's public square at nine o'clock the following morning.[20] But Doniphan refused to carry out the order. In a note to Lucas, he said, "It is cold blooded murder. I will not obey your order. My brigade shall march for Liberty tomorrow morning at 8 o'clock; and if you execute these men, I will hold you responsible before an earthly tribunal, so help me God![21] If not for Doniphan, Burnett said, "I think it most probable that the prisoners would have been summarily tried, condemned and executed."[22] Doniphan, a prominent lawyer, had previously represented Mormon interests, and as a member of the Missouri legislature, had been instrumental in establishing Caldwell County. Burnett became a lifelong admirer of Doniphan, who brought Burnett into his law practice. Burnett dedicated his autobiography to him.

As wars go, the casualties in the 1838 Mormon War, as it became known, were modest. Twenty Mormons were killed and about the same number wounded, with one militiaman killed and a dozen wounded.[23]

Doniphan was hired to defend Smith, Wight, and other Mormon leaders against charges of treason, arson, and robbery. He brought in Burnett and another attorney, Amos Rees, to aid in the defense. Doniphan already knew Burnett and had confidence in his abilities, having served with him on a committee that sent a successful proposal to Congress in 1835 in support of Missouri's annexation of an area to the northwest known as the Platte Country.[24] Another member of the committee was David Atchison—a future US senator.

During a contentious preliminary hearing for Smith and the others in Liberty in March, Burnett said the attorneys felt threatened by an angry anti-Mormon crowd. Burnett delivered the opening remarks, while Doniphan responded to the prosecution's case. Doniphan and Burnett had armed themselves, and when Doniphan rose to speak, Burnett told him not to worry about the threats because he would "kill the first man that attacks you."[25] Burnett's pledge a few years earlier to do anything to avoid shedding another man's blood was in jeopardy.

Burnett recalled that Doniphan gave "one of the most eloquent and withering speeches I ever heard," while a crowd of a hundred or so raged behind them. "All the time I sat within six feet of him, with my hand upon my pistol, calmly determined to do as I had promised him." But there was no gunplay. The defendants were bound over to the grand jury, meeting in Gallatin in Daviess County on April 8.

Judging from Burnett's description, Gallatin must have resembled a war-torn city. But Burnett had no sympathy for the non-Mormons in Daviess County, calling them backwoodsmen, "rude and ungovernable." He accused them of provoking the crisis by preventing Mormons from voting in the 1838 election.[26]

Because the Daviess County courthouse had been virtually destroyed, the grand jury convened in a log schoolhouse along a road knee-deep in mud. Joseph Smith and the other prisoners arrived on a Saturday to await the court opening on Monday. Burnett shared a bed with Amos Rees in one corner of the mud-splattered schoolhouse—he said no one slept much during the next five days. Smith and Wight passed the time by talking almost constantly. Although Smith didn't drink, he arranged for a bottle of whiskey to be brought to the guards in a successful effort to befriend them.

During the downtime between court sessions, Burnett said Smith did such an effective job of befriending others that townspeople came to talk with him. Burnett claimed to have heard—although did not witness it himself—that Smith was challenged to a friendly wrestling match and won. "In the short space of five days he had managed so to mollify his enemies that he could go unprotected among them without the slightest danger."[27]

Burnett was impressed by Smith, whom he called "more than an ordinary man." The Mormon prophet, who would live only a few more years, "possessed the most indomitable perseverance, was a good judge of men, and deemed himself born to command, and he did command."[28]

But no amount of fraternizing with former adversaries could save Smith from being indicted on all the charges. When the grand jury's indictment came down, Burnett applied for a change of venue. The court agreed and ordered the trial moved to Columbia in Boone County, well away from the turmoil involving the Mormons. The prisoners left on the trip of 150 miles, escorted by Daviess County Sheriff William Morgan and four deputies.

There are different accounts of what happened next. What isn't in dispute is that Smith and the others escaped on April 16. One version of the story is that Smith offered Sheriff Morgan $800 "to take a nap," and Morgan complied.[29] While the sheriff denied complicity, he nonetheless was blamed. Upon Morgan's return to Gallatin, angry townspeople forced him to ride through town on an iron bar. His injuries were so severe that he died soon thereafter.[30] Burnett's account of his affiliation with the Mormons ends with Smith's escape.

There was a great deal more to the story, however. Virtually the entire population of Mormons—once as high as ten thousand—had departed Missouri by the end of May 1839, many resettling in Nauvoo, Illinois. A good number were destitute, or nearly so, having sold their Missouri land and property at giveaway prices.[31] Smith also found his way to Nauvoo, which he pronounced the new

Kingdom of God.[32] The town became a thriving religious community protected by a well-armed militia called the Nauvoo Legion. It was in Nauvoo that Smith took up the practice of polygamy, taking as many as forty wives.[33]

In 1844, Smith declared himself a candidate for president of the United States, even as he faced severe criticism from both Mormons and non-Mormons for his polygamist practices. Rapidly unfolding events that would lead to his death were soon to follow. On June 7, 1844, a dissident Mormon newspaper, the *Nauvoo Expositor*, issued a strong denunciation of Smith "and those who practice the same abominations and whoredoms."[34] Smith's followers retaliated by breaking into the newspaper's offices and smashing the printing press. When non-Mormons threatened their own retaliation, Smith declared martial law and mobilized the 5,000-member Nauvoo Legion. He backed down from an armed conflict, however, in the face of a threat by Governor Thomas Ford to mobilize the Illinois militia against him.

Ford ordered Smith to surrender and face charges of destroying the newspaper's press. The governor promised to personally guarantee his safety. Smith gave himself up and was jailed with eleven others in Carthage, the Hancock County seat, on June 25. Despite the governor's guarantee of safety, a mob broke into the jail on June 27, and, with the apparent complicity of the guards, attacked Smith.[35] Trapped in an upstairs room, Smith was shot several times and killed, along with his brother Hyrum.

Burnett, meanwhile, had been gaining status and respect as an attorney, even as his business losses mounted. He was enrolled as one of the first attorneys in the new Platte County by circuit court judge Austin King on March 25, 1839. Others enrolled at the same time included Doniphan and Atchison.[36] Governor Boggs also appointed Burnett as district attorney for a new five-county judicial district comprising the counties of Platte, Clinton, Andrew, Buchanan, and Holt. Burnett moved his family to the county seat of Platte City, where he served three one-year terms as district attorney, twice appointed by the governor and once elected. Atchison was the district's presiding judge.[37]

Burnett's cases as district attorney—his title was circuit attorney—ran the gamut: gambling, grand larceny, counterfeiting, and unlawfully selling whiskey to Native Americans. He felt overwhelmed at times by the sheer number of cases, as many as one hundred in Platte County alone during a single court term. "I do not remember to have been so often utterly worn out as I was while district attorney in Judge Atchison's district," he wrote.[38] While the travel from county to county proved exhausting, Burnett took satisfaction from his work. "I was a vigilant, but candid prosecutor. If I became satisfied that the prisoner was innocent, I told the jury so, but if I thought him guilty, I prosecuted him with all the energy and ability I possessed, and was generally successful."[39]

But Burnett was not making the money he desired and was still bedeviled by the debts from his failed business ventures. Although he managed payments of about $1,000 a year, his debts plus accumulating interest would still require many years to pay off. It was about this time he learned of a substantial amount of free land for settlers in far-off Oregon. It might be the panacea for his problems. In 1843, he resigned as district attorney and resolved "to go to Oregon."[40]

Following his death in 1895, Burnett would be warmly remembered by Platte County historian W. M. Paxton. "The enterprise, hardihood, intelligence and devotion of Peter H. Burnett have blessed and benefitted four states of our union," he wrote in 1897. "He was our first prosecuting attorney, and discharged the duties of his office with marked success."[41]

Chapter 4
Fleeing Debt on the Oregon Trail

Peter Burnett approached each new venture with high hopes it would turn his life around and bring him the wealth he'd so long desired. And so it was with Oregon. He helped organize the first major wagon train of 121 wagons, which left Independence, Missouri, on May 21, 1843, on the 2,000-mile journey.

Called the Oregon Emigration Company, the wagon train included nearly 900 settlers—men, women, and children—who would more than double the white population of Oregon. The settlers took with them 698 oxen, 296 horses, and 973 cattle.[1] As the first of the major wagon trains, it would go down in history as the Great Migration of 1843.

Oregon in 1843, then known as the Oregon Country, stretched from the Rocky Mountains to the Pacific Ocean, and from Russian Alaska on the north to Mexican California on the south. It was a vast region jointly occupied, and contested, by Great Britain and the United States. To the degree there was any government at all, it was provided by the Hudson's Bay Company, the British fur-trapping enterprise based at Fort Vancouver, across the Columbia River from present-day Portland. Aside from fur trappers, a few explorers, missionaries, and a handful of early settlers, the Oregon Country was unknown to most Americans prior to the 1830s. But that was about to change.

Several coincident developments propelled Oregon into the national consciousness. Missionaries, including Marcus and Narcissa Whitman in 1836, had successfully crossed the continent for a decade. In the 1830s, Oregon emigration societies, promoted by the Methodist Church, organized in cities throughout the country, where members shared information on Oregon and contemplated the possibility and challenges of emigrating.[2] There was also a growing allegiance to the concept of Manifest Destiny—that the United States was preordained to expand from coast to coast.

Map of emigrant trails in Oregon and California. Courtesy of Stephan Smith, Smith Creative Group, Portland.

A leading adherent of this concept was Missouri Senator Thomas Hart Benton, who would declare on the Senate floor on June 3, 1846, "I look upon the settlement of the Columbia river by the van of the Caucasian race as the most momentous human event in the history of man since his dispersion over the face of the earth." He debunked the notion that the Oregon Country was a wasteland. "It is not a worthless country, but one of immense value, and ... will be occupied by others, to our injury and annoyance, if not by ourselves for our own benefit and protection."[3]

But there was no bigger spotlight on the West than the widely read two-hundred-page report by explorer John Charles Fremont, the renowned "pathfinder," describing his five-month expedition to the Rocky Mountains in 1842.[4] Not only was the West suitable for settlement, he said, but the Continental Divide should not pose a major barrier to cross-continent travel. He wrote of the ease of passing through a 20-mile-wide gap over the divide in present-day Wyoming. "I should compare the elevation which we surmounted immediately at the pass to the ascent of the Capital Hill, from the Avenue, at Washington [DC]."[5] Known as South Pass, future emigrants were said to be scarcely aware they had crossed the divide until they noticed streams flowing west instead of east.[6]

The crossing of the divide by white women established in the public mind the feasibility of entire families traveling overland to the West Coast. The first white American women to cross were missionary wives Eliza Spalding and Narcissa Whitman in 1836. Spalding made note of the crossing in her journal entry for July 4 without palpable excitement. "Crossed ridge of land today, called the Divide, which separates the waters that flow into the Atlantic from those that flow into the Pacific, and camped for the night on the headwaters of the Colorado."[7]

Also setting the stage for a major migration was the introduction of legislation by Senator Lewis F. Linn of Missouri that would give free land to settlers. Linn's goal was to secure the region for the United States by populating it with Americans. Linn was greatly encouraged when he learned of the successful crossing by white women. In a speech on the Senate floor on June 6, 1838, he declared: "Thus has vanished the great obstacle to a direct and facile communication between the Mississippi Valley and the Pacific Ocean."[8] Of course, Native American women had been crossing the divide for thousands of years.

Once-doubtful newspapers soon were spreading an epidemic of "Oregon Fever" that, over the next two decades, would lure 53,000 emigrants to Oregon, and more than 200,000, including gold miners, to California.[9]

Emigrants had a long list of incentives for heading west in the 1840s and 1850s. Among them was the prospect of free land, of course, but also the opportunity for economic betterment for those hurt by the 1837 depression. The expectation of a healthier climate also drew people west—malaria was a constant threat in the Mississippi Valley. Moreover, many nonslaveholders wanted to escape the turmoil surrounding slavery. There was also patriotic fervor and, for some, the pure adventure of it all. And there was gold!

Would-be emigrants were egged on by boosters making exaggerated claims about a region they'd never seen. The late trail historian John D. Unruh Jr. said that emigrants anticipated "a veritable utopia" in the American West. "They viewed the new and fabled lands of Oregon and California as regions of rebirth and hope, where upward mobility was not merely possible but virtually certain," Unruh wrote in *The Plains Across*, published posthumously in 1993.[10]

Burnett's prominent role in organizing the 1843 emigration was reported in newspapers of the day, including the *Ohio Statesman* of March 14, 1843, which reprinted an article from a Missouri newspaper, the *Platte Eagle*:

> The people are again in motion here in relation to the emigration to Oregon this spring. Peter H. Burnett, Esq., one of our most estimable citizens is among the foremost here in exciting a laudable spirit in relation to the settlement of that desirable country. On Tuesday evening Mr. Burnett delivered a very able lecture upon this subject, in which was embodied a vast fund of information calculated to impress all who had the pleasure of hearing him with the advantages attendant on an early settlement of our western demesne [acquisition of land]. The American eagle is flapping his wings, the precursor of the end of the British lion, on the shores of the Pacific. Destiny has willed it.[11]

A month later, on April 16, 1843, the Ohio newspaper told its readers: "The Oregon fever is raging in almost every part of the Union. Companies are forming in the East, and in several parts of Ohio, which added to those of Illinois, Iowa and Missouri will make a pretty formidable army. The larger portions of these will probably join the companies at Fort Independence, Missouri, and proceed together across the mountains. It is reasonable to suppose that there will be at least five thousand Americans west of the Rocky Mountains by next autumn."[12]

Among those joining the 1843 wagon train were members of an emigration society of churchgoing Christians in the Iowa Territory who left Iowa City on May 12 to join other wagons at Independence. They included Burnett's future business partner, Kentucky-born Morton M. McCarver. Not unlike other emigrants, the Iowa contingent adopted rules of the road, listing the food, weapons, and other equipment they would need. Among weapons were a "rifle gun, to carry from thirty-two to sixty bullets to the pound, and a tomahawk and knife." Also, "Every man ought to carry with him a Bible and other religious books, as we hope not to degenerate into a state of barbarism." Reflecting the prejudice and hostility toward African Americans that prevailed even in free territories and states, they resolved, "No negroes or mulattoes shall be allowed to accompany the expedition under any pretenses whatever."[13] Nevertheless, the Burnett wagon train included several African Americans.

One emigrant lured to Oregon by Burnett's speeches was David Thomas Lenox, who lived a few miles from Burnett in Missouri. His son Edward remembered his father taking him to hear Burnett speak. Burnett stood atop a box on the sidewalk in front of his store in Weston, and pictured "in glowing terms the richness of the soil, the attraction of the climate and then, with a twinkle in his eye, he said, 'they do say, gentlemen, that out in Oregon the pigs are running about under the great acorn trees, round and fat, and already cooked, with knives and forks sticking in them, so you can cut off a slice whenever you are hungry.' " Discounting the pig story, Lenox's father was "so moved" by Burnett's description of an Oregon neither had ever seen that when Burnett invited his listeners to sign up for the trip, his father was among the first to sign.[14]

In 1842, Burnett had moved to Weston, where along with his duties as a circuit attorney he was part owner of a general store. "I purchased an interest in the place," Burnett said. Most likely, with a wife and six young children to support, he found it necessary to renege on his pledge to put the mercantile business behind him.[15] Weston was a small port on the eastern bank of the Missouri across from Fort Leavenworth, 43 miles northwest of Independence. It was described "as a busy little town" where "drinking and gambling were the chief employments," along with hemp and tobacco.[16]

As for his motives for going to Oregon, Burnett, then age 36, recalled: "I saw that a large American community would grow up, in the space of a few years, upon the shores of the distant Pacific; and I felt an ardent desire to aid in this most important enterprise." He also sought a healthier climate for Harriet, who had been in failing health for several years. "It was all we could do to keep her alive through the winter in that cold climate," Burnett said. "Her physician said the trip [to Oregon] would either kill or cure her."[17]

Health was a major consideration for another Missouri family, that of Daniel Waldo of St. Clair County. While it was usually the men who decided to emigrate, Daniel's wife, Melinda, made the decision for her family. According to an Oregon neighbor and future governor, Theodore T. Geer, Daniel Waldo had changed his mind about joining the 1843 wagon train, in part because of worry over possible attacks by the Native American tribes. But he was overruled by Melinda, whom Geer quoted as saying, "Well, Dan Waldo, if you want to stay here another summer and shake your liver out with the fever and ague, you can do it; but in the spring, I am going to take the children and go to Oregon, Indians, or no Indians."[18]

Senator Linn's land law, introduced in the Senate in December 1841, would have allocated 640 acres—one square mile—to each adult settler, plus 160 acres for each child. It was a powerful magnet for small farmers and others struggling in Missouri's depressed economy. The bill passed the Senate but failed in the House. Even so, Burnett, along with many others, was confident it would eventually pass. Adding up the possible allocations for his family of six children, he envisioned as much as 1,600 free acres.

Burnett explained to his creditors what a windfall of 1,600 acres could mean for all concerned. "If Dr. Linn's bill should pass, the land would ultimately enable me to pay up." He might profitably grow crops and pay what he owed. "There was at least a chance," he said. On the other hand, "In staying where I was, I saw no reasonable probability of ever being able to pay my debts." He claimed his creditors consented.[19] Left unsaid was the obvious: that in the event he couldn't repay, it would be much more difficult, if not impossible, for creditors to collect from 2,000 miles away.

A version of Linn's bill would finally pass in 1850 as the Oregon Donation Land Claim Act, which set the maximum for a family at a still considerable 640 acres, half in the husband's name and half in the wife's. A single male was entitled to a maximum of 320 acres.[20]

The patience of Burnett's creditors would have its limits. His brother-in-law William Smith sued Burnett in Clay County Circuit Court on August 4, 1847, seeking payment of $12,011. Smith claimed the money was owed him from their joint mercantile business. From what we know about Burnett's early fortunes in Oregon, or lack thereof, he may not have made any payments at all in the four years after leaving Missouri. Also named in Smith's suit were Burnett's brothers Glen and George. All were ordered to appear in court or else a judgment would be rendered against them.[21]

Most certainly, none of the Burnetts appeared. They were all in Oregon. Along with a third brother, James, they emigrated in 1846. They also all followed Burnett's lead by adding a second "t" to their surnames. Burnett eventually settled the debt. Years later, he wrote to George that Glen still owed him money from the settlement.

Burnett and his family left Weston for Oregon on May 8, 1843, with two ox-pulled wagons, one small two-horse wagon, four yoke of oxen, two mules, and a supply of provisions. They arrived nine days later at the wagon train's rendezvous 12 miles west of Independence. Burnett had no parents to leave behind. His mother died two months earlier, on March 17, 1843, in Platte County. His father died in Clay County on February 22, 1838.

Independence, Missouri, in 1843 was a frontier town with a population of about seven hundred. It would soon grow to two thousand, as it became the major departure point for the emigrant wagon trains.[22] A future Oregon judge and author, J. Quinton Thornton, described the streets of Independence in 1846 as filled with "African slaves, indolent dark-skinned Spaniards, profane and dust-laden bull whackers, going to and from Santa Fe with their immense wagons, and emigrant families bound for the Pacific."[23] Other western Missouri towns, notably St. Joseph and Westport–Kansas City, experienced similarly rapid growth as departure points.

Burnett was elected captain of the wagon train on June 1 after giving what was described as a rousing speech to the assembled emigrants. Recalling the speech years later, James W. Nesmith, a future US senator from Oregon, called Burnett "a smooth-tongued advocate" for what the emigrants could accomplish once they reached Oregon. With some tongue-in-cheek, Nesmith gave this account of Burnett's speech: "He appealed to our patriotism by picturing forth the glorious empire we would establish upon the shores of the Pacific. How, with our trusty rifles, we would drive out the British usurpers who claimed the soil, and defend the country from the avarice and pretension of the British lion, and how posterity would honor us for placing the fairest portion of our land under the dominion of the stars and stripes." The meeting ended with "three cheers for Captain Burnett and Oregon."[24]

The Canadian-born Nesmith, 23 and single, took it all with a grain of salt. What people were saying about Oregon, he said years later, was a "mixture of fiction and perverted fact that contained no definite information of the country and its resources." Nesmith was elected the wagon train's quarterly sergeant, whose responsibilities included maintaining a roll of the emigrant men, although not the women and children.[25]

The emigrants hired John Gantt, a former fur trader and US Army captain, as their guide—the early wagon trains typically hired fur trappers familiar with the region.[26] Gantt agreed to lead them for a dollar per person as far as Fort Hall in present-day southeastern Idaho, where he would turn south to California.[27] Assuming only male heads of household were counted, Gantt's pay would have amounted to about $125. Guides charged more to later wagon trains.

The process by which Burnett and others were elected to leadership positions with the wagon train greatly amused Matthew C. Field, an editor of the *New Orleans Picayune* who was returning from a reporting trip to the Rocky Mountains. Field wrote that the candidates for each position would march off at a given signal, followed by the settlers who favored them. "Every candidate flourished a sort of tail of his own, and the man with the longest tail was elected." Field called it "a curious mingling of the whimsical with the wild." The process was repeated until all positions were filled.[28]

An important addition to the leadership was missionary Marcus Whitman, who was on a return trip to the mission he and Narcissa established in 1836 at Waiilatpu, near present-day Walla Walla, Washington. Marcus had gone to New York to consult on mission business with the American Board of Commissioners, while Narcissa remained at the mission.

Whitman was more familiar than most with the trail to Oregon, as it was his third trip across the continent. His first was in 1835 to scout possibilities for a mission; the second was in 1836 when he and Narcissa established the mission. Traveling with the Whitmans in 1836 were the missionary couple, Eliza and Henry Spalding, and the cabinetmaker and future Oregon historian William H. Gray from New York. Gray, Spalding, and Burnett would soon have a lot to say to one another.

Overlooking Whitman's vast experience, Burnett wrote in his autobiography that "None of us knew anything about a trip across the Plains, except our pilot Captain Gantt." In a thinly veiled complaint about his own situation, he said Gantt had traveled previously with "disciplined men, who knew how to obey orders."[29]

Obeying orders was important to Burnett. As wagon train captain, he had promulgated a list of rules that he tried to enforce. But he ran into trouble almost immediately, unwilling or unable to compromise when his orders were challenged or disobeyed. Burnett attributed the resistance "to the fact that our emigrants were green at the beginning." Moreover, he was beset by "ten thousand little vexations," such as "at one time an ox would be missing, at another time a mule, and then a struggle for the best encampment, and for a supply of wood and water." He seemed especially annoyed by the teamsters, who raced one another in their wagons. The teamsters were in turn frustrated by Burnett's insistence they travel single file.[30] His difficulties as wagon train captain were a harbinger of shortcomings that would plague him as a future political leader.

Morton McCarver cited a dispute over the loose cattle during the trip as an example of Burnett's inflexible rules. "Those without cattle refused [Burnett's orders] to stand guard at night over cattle belonging to others." There were also complaints that the cattle consumed most of the forage when the emigrants camped together, leaving too little for the oxen and other working livestock.[31]

Burnett resigned as captain on June 8, just seven days after accepting the position. In an essay for the *New York Herald* in 1845, Burnett blamed his resignation on "consequences of ill health," although nowhere else did he mention an illness during the trip.[32] Whatever the reason, his resignation was evidently welcomed by most of the emigrants. There would be many resignations for Burnett in years to come, but none quite so quick as this one.

After Burnett stepped down, a solution to the cattle-guarding issue was found. The leadership was divided, with Virginia-born William J. Martin, most recently of St. Clair County, Missouri, taking charge of seventy wagons traveling with few cattle, while Jesse Applegate, also of St. Clair County, led the remaining sixty or so wagons of those with more numerous cattle.[33]

Once the wagon train had been divided, wagons and cattle stretched for nearly a mile. Applegate, with about two hundred cattle of his own, called his wagons "the cow column." Writing years later, Applegate said, "Those not encumbered with or having but few loose cattle attached themselves to the light column; those having more than four or five cows had of necessity to join the heavy, or cow column." Managing so many cattle was not easy. "The large herd of horned beasts that bring up the rear [are] lazy, selfish and unsocial," he said. "It has been a task to get them in motion, the strong always ready to domineer over the weak, halt in the front and forbid the weak to pass over them.... They seem to move only in the fear of the driver's whip."[34]

Applegate gave Whitman most of the credit for the success of the wagon train: "His constant advice which we knew was based upon a knowledge of the road before us, was, 'Travel, travel, travel; nothing else will take you to the end of your journey; nothing is wise that does not help you along; nothing is good for you that causes a moments delay.'" According to Applegate, it was "no disparagement to others to say that to no other individual are the emigrants of 1843 so much indebted for the successful conclusion of their journey as to Dr. Marcus Whitman."[35]

Burnett appeared to accept his diminished status with equanimity, even relief, and made the rest of the trip with comparative peace of mind. He seemed to pay little attention to the other settlers, few of whom he named. He instead filled this section of his *Recollections* with detailed descriptions of the terrain and wildlife, along with his own exploits. He told how he killed a buffalo, congratulating himself on his skill in maneuvering the buffalo into a position where he could fire the fatal shot through the animal's lungs.[36]

Harriet's health must have improved significantly, as Burnett reported that they traded off sleeping and driving the family wagon. It was one of the few mentions of his wife during the journey. The trip must have been difficult for Harriet, as care of the children fell to the women, although she may have had the help of a slave.

Burnett exulted in what he perceived as his wisdom and foresight. One example occurred on June 14 at Fort Laramie, a trading post on the North Platte River in present-day eastern Wyoming, when "a foolish, rash young man . . . wantonly insulted" a Cheyenne chieftain. Burnett took credit for avoiding a possible clash with the Cheyenne tribe.

> Though the chief did not understand the insulting words, he clearly comprehended the insulting tone and gestures. . . . I saw there was trouble coming, and I followed the chief, and by kind earnest gestures made him understand at last that this young man was considered by us all as a half-witted fool, unworthy of the notice of any sensible man; and that we never paid attention to what he said, as we hardly considered him responsible for his language. The moment the chief comprehended my meaning I saw a change come over his countenance, and he went away perfectly satisfied. He was a clear headed man; and, though unlettered, he understood human nature.[37]

The wagon train more or less followed the trail blazed by fur-trapping parties during the previous twenty years. The trail, familiar to Gantt and Whitman, would soon become known as the Oregon Trail. It proceeded west from Independence, northwest along the south bank of the Platte River, followed the North Fork of the Platte through Nebraska into Wyoming's Sweetwater River country, to reach South Pass and the Continental Divide on August 7. Once across the divide, Burnett stopped to drink from "a large pure spring," the beginning of rivers draining into the Pacific.[38] But with a thousand miles still to go, there was little celebrating.

The wagons continued to Fort Hall, the junction of the Oregon and California trails. From here, the Oregon-bound wagons would proceed north-west toward the Columbia River, while the California wagons would turn southwest across Nevada to follow the Humboldt River toward the Sierra Nevada crossings into California.

Fort Hall was an important stop for rest and resupply for emigrants on both trails. An American, Nathaniel Wyeth, established Fort Hall in 1834 to support the American fur trade. But he gave up in the face of stiff competition from the Hudson's Bay Company, which acquired the trading post from Wyeth in 1837.

Narcissa Whitman was unimpressed with Fort Hall when the missionaries stopped there in 1836. In her journal entry for September 1, she wrote, "The buildings of the fort are made of hewed logs, with roofs covered with mud brick, chimneys and fireplaces also being built of the same; no windows, except a square hole in the roof, and in the bastion a few port holes large enough for guns only. The buildings were all enclosed in a strong log wall."[39]

Smaller groups of travelers, including the Elijah White party in 1842, had abandoned their wagons at Fort Hall, believing the terrain ahead was too difficult, and continued on horseback. McCarver said the 1843 emigrants were urged by the Hudson's Bay chief trader at Fort Hall, Richard Grant, to forgo Oregon and detour to California. Oregon, they were told, was less than advertised—poorer soil, inferior timber, and abysmal climate. But Whitman assured the emigrants none of this was true and they could safely take their wagons as far as the Columbia River.

The trail from Independence to Fort Hall had been comparatively smooth— "perhaps the finest natural road" to be found anywhere, Burnett wrote. His widely published remarks would later give him cause to regret.[40] He was unaware the most difficult part of the journey lay ahead: deep canyons, basalt rock cliffs, steep, heavily forested mountains, and the treacherous rapids of the Columbia.

Gant left the wagon train at Fort Hall to head to California as planned, followed by some of the emigrants. Whitman took over as guide for the Oregon wagons and was paid $80 to lead them the next 500 miles to his Waiilatpu mission.[41] He rode ahead, leaving notes along the trail with directions for the settlers to follow.[42]

From Fort Hall, the emigrants proceeded nearly 300 miles to Fort Boise, another trading post, after which they forded the Snake River and followed the Burnt River into northeastern Oregon, where travel became appreciably more difficult. "The road up this stream was then a terrible one," Burnett recalled, "as the latter runs between two ranges of tall mountains, through a valley full of timber, which we had not the force or time to remove." It was September 21, late in the year with mountain travel still ahead.

On October 2, they started a five-day ordeal through the Blue Mountains. Heavy snowfall made it difficult to keep track of their cattle. Even worse, according to emigrant Nineveh Ford from North Carolina, was the fallen timber scattered through the forest. Cutting through the windfall was especially difficult with axes dulled from frequent use.[43]

The wagons reached the Whitman mission at Waiilatpu on October 10, where they rested four days and purchased needed provisions.[44] Burnett came to Whitman's defense in the face of complaints that Whitman gouged the emigrants with high food prices.

Whitman, he said, should have received gratitude for the assistance he provided the emigrants but was instead "most ungenerously accused by some of our people of selfish motives. . . . This foolish, false, and ungrateful charge was based upon the fact that he asked us a dollar a bushel for wheat, and forty cents for potatoes." Although Whitman's prices were significantly higher than prices the settlers charged for their own crops at home, the emigrants failed to realize that Whitman, at the isolated mission, paid double for his supplies.[45]

The complaints prompted Burnett to philosophize about his fellow travelers. "The exhausting tedium of such a trip and the attendant vexations have a great effect upon the majority of men, especially upon those of weak minds"—clearly, Burnett didn't count himself among the weak minded. He continued, "Men, under such circumstances become childish, petulant and obstinate."[46]

After Waiilatpu, most of the settlers followed the south bank of the Columbia River toward The Dalles in their wagons, while Burnett, the Applegates, and a few others proceeded downstream on rafts, leaving their wagons and cattle at Fort Walla Walla to be sold or retrieved at a later date. Fort Walla Walla was another Hudson's Bay trading post, also known as Fort Nez Perce, 25 miles west of Waiilatpu.

The wagon train broke up at The Dalles, with the emigrants separately making their way the final 80 miles of their journey down the Columbia River toward Oregon City and the Willamette Valley, the destination for most. The Dalles served as a convenient rest stop before the arduous and perilous journey on the Columbia. A Methodist mission allowed the emigrants to purchase a limited supply of foodstuffs—potatoes, dried peas, and a maximum 8 quarts of flour. The mission was established in 1838 to minister to local tribes; the crops were grown by Native Americans workers. In 1850, as more and more wagon trains passed through The Dalles, the US Army established Fort Dalles,

The Surgeon's Quarters, now part of the Fort Dalles Museum, is the only remaining building from Fort Dalles, built in 1856 to protect emigrants from raids by native tribes. The Dalles was the final rest stop for Oregon-bound emigrants on the Oregon Trail. Photo by the author.

assigning several hundred troops to protect the emigrants from—and sometimes fight with—the region's tribes.

The emigrants had already learned of the dangers in the river that confronted them. Immediately upriver from The Dalles was a spectacular 9-mile complex of rapids and falls remembered today as Celilo Falls. Here, basalt outcroppings compressed the mile-wide Columbia into narrow channels, perhaps 40 feet across in places, through which the river thundered in mountains of white froth, at points turning back on itself in dangerous whirlpools.

Two children of the large Applegate family, 9-year-old cousins Edward and Warren, drowned at Celilo Falls on November 6. Edward was Jesse's son; Warren was the son of Jesse's brother Lindsay. The Applegate family—three brothers, Jesse, Lindsay, and Charles, and their families—were among those who left wagons and cattle at Fort Walla Walla and set out downriver in rafts, with Native American guides. Approaching The Dalles, the raft with the two cousins upended into a whirlpool.

The tragedy was recalled years later by yet another of Lindsay's sons, also named Jesse, who was 7 at the time. He had been in a separate raft with the two fathers—who were steering—and their wives. He told in dramatic detail of watching the second raft founder in rapids on the far side of the river:

> This boat now near the south shore, it would seem, should have followed our boat as the pilot was with us, and this was a dangerous part of the river. But there was little time to consider mistakes, or to be troubled about what might be the consequences, for presently there was a wail of anguish, a shriek, and a scene of confusion in one boat that no language can describe. The boat we were watching disappeared and we saw the men and boys struggling in the water. Father and Uncle Jesse, seeing their children drowning, were seized with frenzy, and dropping their oars sprang up from their seats and were about to leap from the boat to make a desperate attempt to swim to them, when Mother and Aunt Cynthia, in voices that were distinctly heard above the roar of the rushing waters, by commands and entreaties brought them to a realization of our own perilous situation, and the madness of an attempt to reach the other side of the river by swimming. . . . The men returned to the oars just in time to avoid, by great exertion a rock against which the current dashed with such fury that the foam and froth upon its apex was as white as milk.[47]

Sucked into the whirlpool, the cousins' raft disappeared. The boys' bodies were never recovered. Also lost was Alexander "Mac" McClellan, said to be

Celilo Falls near The Dalles, a perilous passage for emigrants. Jesse and Lindsey Applegate each lost a son here during the 1843 emigration. The falls were an important fishery and gathering place for tribes from throughout the Northwest for thousands of years, until inundated behind The Dalles Dam in 1957. Courtesy of the Oregon Historical Society.

steering the raft. Lindsay's 11-year-old son Elisha managed to swim to safety. The helplessness and the horror of watching their sons drown would prompt Lindsay and Jesse three years later to develop an alternate overland trail into Oregon that avoided the river.

Celilo Falls, or "Sound of Water upon the Rocks," had been an important village, fishing site, and trading center for Native Americans for thousands of years, bringing together tribes from throughout the Pacific Northwest. The emigrants must have watched in awe as tribal fishermen stood on rocks and platforms using dip nets to catch yard-long salmon at the base of the falls. The salmon clustered in the churning current to conserve energy before attempting to leap over the falls on their way from the distant Pacific to spawning sites further upriver. The salmon still swim the river today, albeit in much diminished numbers. However, the falls no longer exist. They were inundated behind The Dalles Dam, built by the US Army Corps of Army Engineers in 1957.

> "I can't be diplomatic about it," said Mary Burslie Mertz Davis, a docent at the Surgeon's House, the last remaining building at Fort Dalles. "I have to say we ruined a way of life."[48] Davis was just 12 when the dam gates closed on March 10, 1957. She watched from high ground with her father and hundreds of others, whites and Native Americans alike. Some of the tribespeople had tears streaming down their faces, some with backs to the river as the mighty Columbia flooded behind the dam into a huge reservoir. Davis said it took just six hours to completely submerge the rapids, covering what had been an important source of food and a cultural foundation for tribes for thousands of years. Still ingrained in her memory is the echo of the roar of the rapids that never stopped.[49]

Some of the 1843 emigrants, not wanting to risk the remaining rapids, left their wagons and continued overland by pack train. Others dismantled their wagons and loaded them onto rafts, hiring Native Americans to guide them on the river and portage them around difficult rapids.[50] Cattle were trailed along the river or left at The Dalles to be fattened and retrieved the following spring.

There was yet another drowning. This time it was a young African American woman, or girl, who was possibly one of Burnett's slaves. Nineveh Ford said the unidentified female fell into the river and disappeared while filling a bucket near a rapid known as the Cascades, about 50 miles below The Dalles. Ford said she "had been a servant, attached I think, to Burnett or his brother-in-law's family."[51] Young Jesse Applegate also recalled the drowning, although he remembered the African American as a girl: "During the late evening, a man from Peter Burnett's camp came to ours and said that a little Negro girl was lost. She had been sent to the river where the boats were to get a bucket of water. The storm had continued and the boats on the beach were wildly rocked and tossed by the waves. Some thought the girl had entered one of the boats to dip up the water and had been thrown into the river and was never found."[52]

The woman, or girl, may have been one of Burnett's two slaves recorded in the 1840 Census. There was no mention of Burnett's male slave, but possibly he was brought along as well.[53] It would hardly be surprising that someone who had grown up in a home with slaves in Tennessee and Missouri wouldn't at least consider bringing his slaves to help with the substantial amount of work facing the family in Oregon. Burnett employed five drivers for his wagons; typically, such help were hired teamsters, trading work for the opportunity to seek their fortune in Oregon.

There was one identified slave in the wagon train, Rachel Belden, a slave of Daniel Delaney, a former plantation owner from Tennessee.[54] There may have been others, but nobody kept track of the slaves on the Oregon Trail.

During the long journey to Oregon, James Nesmith tallied seven deaths among the adult males, including McClellan, Clayborn Paine, and a Mr. Stevenson, who was not otherwise identified. Paine died on August 4, Stevenson on August 9, both succumbing to illness and buried along the trail.[55] Another death was of Miles Ayres, or Eyers, who drowned while crossing the Snake River near Idaho's American Falls, swept away in the swift current when his mule lost its footing.[56] Also lost were Daniel Richardson, who died on the Sweetwater River; C. M. Stringer, of unknown causes; and William Day, who succumbed to illness after reaching Fort Vancouver. Of the 294 men over age 16 who started the journey, 267 reached Oregon, 7 died, 5 turned back, and 15 detoured to California.[57]

Nesmith didn't record deaths of women and children, as he kept records only of men age 16 and over. Thus his list didn't include the drownings of the Applegate cousins or the young African American servant. Nor did he mention 6-year-old Joel Hembree, crushed under a wagon wheel after falling from the family wagon on July 19.[58] The boy was one of eight sons of Joel and Sara Hembree from McMinnville, Tennessee, and was buried along the trail in a dresser drawer. The Hembree gravesite in Converse County, Wyoming, is said to be the oldest identified grave on the Oregon Trail.

Young Hembree was not the first to perish in a mishap on the Oregon Trail. That dubious honor may have gone to an emigrant named Stockwell, who accidentally shot himself near Ash Hollow, Nebraska, while traveling with the 1841 Bidwell-Bartleson Party to California. John Bidwell, who would be elected to Congress from California in 1865, recalled that Stockwell was killed "while in the act of taking a gun out of the wagon, drew up the muzzle toward him in such a manner that it went off and shot him in the heart."[59] Deaths from other causes, including childbirth, were not infrequent in the primitive conditions of the wagon trains.[60]

James Nesmith would regret in later years that he hadn't maintained records of women and children, but at the time he hadn't considered it one of his responsibilities.[61] Some male emigrants took the position that women were of little help on the trail. John M. Shively of St. Louis, a member of the 1843 wagon train, wrote later that "However much help your wives and daughters have been to you at home, they can do but little for you here." He said "herding stock, through either dew, dust or rain, breaking brush, swimming rivers, attacking grizzly bears or savage Indians, is all out of their line of business. All they can do, is to cook for camps, etcetera."

One trail historian found that women played a much bigger role than Shively suggested. "Far beyond merely performing domestic chores such as cooking, cleaning and overseeing the children, women sometimes drove wagons, helped with their repair, engaged in trading with Indians, attended ill sojourners, assisted at river crossings, and helped clear the land on which the family ultimately settled."[62]

A day or so following the drowning of his brother and cousin, young Jesse Applegate stumbled onto a Native American burial ground strewn with the bones and remains of the Indian dead. "We passed a pond or small lake on which were floating many rafts made of logs on which were dozens of dead bodies rolled in blankets or . . . mats." Others reported that the remains were watched over by small statues they called "little wooden devils."[63]

The trail from Missouri ended at Oregon City, the only town in the Oregon Country, 18 miles south of today's Portland. The 1843 emigrants would have tramped into Oregon City through streets that were a sea of mud—rain fell nearly daily that fall and winter. They would have passed a ramshackle collection of crude buildings clustered along the eastern bank of the Willamette River at the foot of a sheer 200-foot basalt rock cliff. Immediately upriver were the horseshoe-shaped Willamette Falls, a spectacular 40-foot plunge over a basalt ledge. Dr. John McLoughlin, the chief factor for the Hudson's Bay Company at Fort Vancouver, had harnessed the power of the falls for a sawmill in 1830, and a flour mill was soon to follow. McLoughlin had claimed the entire area as his own in 1829, but his claim wouldn't last.

The falls was a traditional fishing ground for salmon and lamprey eel for tribes from throughout the Pacific Northwest. The area was part of the home-land of the Clackamas tribe and the Clowewalla band, both of the Chinook people, known for the practice of flattening their heads. The Clowewallas controlled the falls from their village on the west side of the river. Among the tribes regularly fishing at the falls were the different bands of the Kalapuya, who populated the Willamette Valley.[64]

Even before the advent of the major wagon trains, the Chinooks, Kalapuyas, and other tribes were depleted by the diseases brought by trappers and early settlers. The arrival of thousands of additional settlers only worsened their plight. In 1853, while posted with the US Army at the Columbia Barracks near Fort Vancouver, the future president Ulysses S. Grant wrote sympathetically of the Chinooks: "This poor remnant of a once powerful tribe is fast wasting away before the blessings of civilization—'whisky and Small pox.' "[65]

In 1843, Oregon City had several dozen houses, most of them built by McLoughlin for his workers. The region's first hotel opened that year, although it was little more than a shelter where men slept on the floor.[66] Other structures included a blacksmith shop and a Methodist church—a Catholic church would arrive in 1845.[67]

Some of the 1843 emigrants may have shopped for supplies at the new store of Philip Foster, who arrived by ship from Maine in 1843 and built a two-story building with a store on the ground floor, selling goods imported from the Sandwich Islands. While the emigrants probably welcomed the sight of civilization, such as it was, it's doubtful many would have waited long before dispersing to claim land for their new farms in the fertile soils of the Tualatin and Willamette Valleys.[68]

Competition for the best land was predictably intense. A new provisional government, organized only months earlier, entitled a settler up to a square mile of land—first come, first served. All the settler had to do was stake his claim—an axe mark on a tree might suffice—and start farming. The 1850 Donation

One of the earliest photographs of Oregon City, at the end of the Oregon Trail, from the early 1850s. Oregon City was the first incorporated city west of Rockies and capital of Oregon's provisional and territorial governments. From here, emigrants dispersed into the Willamette and Tualatin Valleys to claim their new farms. Courtesy of the Oregon Historical Society.

Land Claim Act, passed by Congress, upheld the provisional claims. By 1855, the last year of the act, the Oregon City Land Office had recorded 5,289 claims for various-sized parcels.[69]

Oregon City was to soon experience rapid growth from the thousands of settlers flooding into Oregon during the next two decades. It was the first incorporated city west of the Rocky Mountains in 1844, and would become capital of both Oregon's provisional government in 1843 and the territorial government in 1848, by which time it counted a population of nearly a thousand. Over the years, however, Oregon City was eclipsed by the faster-growing cities of Portland, Eugene, and Salem, the state capital.[70]

Burnett did not go directly to Oregon City with the others. Leaving his family in The Dalles, he traveled on a 40-foot Hudson's Bay Company boat to Fort Vancouver, arriving on November 7. McLoughlin was expecting him. McCarver had gone ahead with a letter of introduction from Burnett, and also a request for help for the near-destitute emigrants still at The Dalles.[71] McLoughlin sent two boatloads of provisions to The Dalles, to be sold or given to the emigrants, according to need and ability to pay, and a separate supply for Burnett.[72]

A stickler for detail, Burnett noted in his *Recollections* that he had traveled 2,000 miles in the nearly seven months since leaving Missouri, averaging over 11 miles a day.[73] The goal for later wagon trains would be a much shorter trip,

starting in mid-April to arrive in Oregon or California in mid-August, a journey of five months by averaging 15 miles a day.[74] Not all wagon trains met that
goal—the speed of travel was greatly influenced by the weather. But it was risky
to arrive later than early October, after which mountain snows imperiled travel,
as the California-bound Donner-Reed Party tragically discovered in 1846.

Burnett remained several weeks at Fort Vancouver, enjoying McLoughlin's
hospitality. Presumably, he found the fort as pleasant as Narcissa Whitman had
in 1836. She spent several weeks as McLoughlin's guest while Marcus scouted a
site for their mission. In her journal entry for September 1, Narcissa wrote, "We
have every comfort we can ask for here, enough to eat and drink and are as well
provided for as we should be in many boarding houses in the States."[75]

The fort was surrounded by 20-foot walls of upright timbers, encompassing
an area larger than two football fields. The most prominent of the fort's many
buildings was the two-story governor's house with an exterior double stairway
leading to a main hall on the upper floor. Also within the walls were a schoolhouse, chapel, office buildings, hospital, bakery, blacksmith, shops, and apart-
ments for company officers and clerks. Three cannons protected the governor's
house, one a 24-pounder, all pointing toward the main gate. Bastions at the corners of the fort provided cover for ships in the nearby Columbia. The gardens,
fields, sawmill, and other buildings were outside the walls.[76]

Burnett was singularly impressed, especially on seeing two square-rigged
vessels and a steamboat moored in the Columbia. "My very heart jumped as I
set eyes on these familiar objects, and for the first time in four months I felt as if
I had found substantial evidence of civilization." Orchards and fields extended
for 5 miles along the river, all "fenced into beautiful fields, a great portion of
which is already under cultivation and is found to produce the grains and veg-
etables . . . in remarkable profusion."[77]

After three weeks at the fort, during which Burnett said he sought
McLoughlin's views of conditions in the Oregon Country, he left to retrieve
his family in The Dalles. He traveled with John Fremont, then on his second of
his four western expeditions. Fremont was returning to The Dalles to rejoin his
crew after obtaining supplies at Fort Vancouver for the next leg of his explora-
tions into California. It took Burnett and Fremont ten days to reach The Dalles,
slowed by the swift river current and drenching rain.

Burnett made his usual excellent first impression, as Fremont wrote glow-
ingly: "This gentleman, as well as the Messrs. Applegate, and others of the emigrants whom I saw, possessed intelligence and character, with the moral and

intellectual stamina, as well as the enterprise, which gave solidity and respect-ability to the foundation of the [American] colonies."[78] Typical of Burnett, he basked in his association with someone he regarded as important. He called Fremont an excellent traveling companion, whose "bearing toward me was as kind as that of a brother."[79]

Peter Burnett has received little credit for his major role in helping to organize the 1843 wagon train. There are several reasons why, but foremost was prob-ably his personality. As noted, he made a positive first impression, so much so that people almost automatically turned to him for leadership. He savored com-mand, but he seemed unable to effectively exercise it. Too many people came away disappointed, including those who would write the history of the Oregon Trail.

William Gray, who traveled west with the Whitmans in 1836, failed to mention Burnett in connection with the wagon train in his *History of Oregon*, written in 1870. Gray detested Burnett, calling him "a very ambitious man—smooth, deceitful and insinuating in his manners," although acknowledging he "was unquestionably the most intelligent lawyer then in the country." Gray gave Marcus Whitman the credit for the success of the 1843 wagon train.[80] John Unruh mentions Burnett only in passing in his history of the Oregon Trail. Nevertheless, as to the importance of 1843 wagon train, Unruh left no doubt.

> The approximately nine hundred persons who reached Oregon in the "great migration" of 1843 provided the necessary manpower for the organization of a provisional government, putting the Hudson's Bay Company on the defensive and thereby "saving" or "winning" Oregon from Great Britain. The 1843 overlanders also served history, it has been said, by demonstrating that wagons could be taken successfully to The Dalles, a necessary occurrence if there was to be ever-increasing family emigration and thus eventual American occupation of the Pacific Coast. . . . There is no denying the far-reaching significance of this first large and successful transcontinental emigration.[81]

Another prominent chronicler of the Oregon Trail, John Merrill Mattes, ascribed to Whitman the leadership of the 1843 wagon train, although he cited Burnett as among the "fine leaders" who were the "real heroes of the migra-tion." Mattes also applauded Burnett's recommendation that migrants use oxen to pull their wagons rather than horses, which were less durable.[82] Another contemporary historian, David Alan Johnson, mentioned Burnett as simply "a fellow overland immigrant" when writing about another emigrant. Johnson paid greater attention to Burnett's later activities in land sales and politics in California.[83]

One who did give Burnett full credit was English-born John Minto, who traveled to Oregon in 1844 in a wagon train led by a former Missouri sheriff and military leader Cornelius Gilliam. The Gilliam wagon train was one of two major wagon trains in 1844; the second was led by another former Missouri sheriff and slaveholder, Nathaniel Ford.[84] Minto wrote that "no other single individual exerted as large an influence in swelling the number of home-building emigrants to Oregon in the years 1843 and 1844 as Peter H. Burnett." Minto, who served four terms in the Oregon legislature, said Burnett made speeches wherever he could find an audience "and succeeded beyond his own expectations."[85]

There had been earlier wagon trains of much smaller numbers. The first party of emigrants to travel with covered wagons was the Bidwell-Bartleson party, which left from Westport, Missouri, in May 1841 with fifteen wagons and sixty-nine emigrants. About half of these continued to Oregon, while nine wagons and about thirty emigrants followed Bidwell to California. They abandoned their wagons during a difficult crossing of the Great Salt Lake Desert and finished their journey on foot and horseback, crossing the Sierras over the 9,600-foot-high Sonora Pass and arriving in the San Joaquin Valley in late October.[86]

One emigrant in the Bidwell party, Nancy Kelsey, wrote of witnessing a horrific incident when Mexican soldiers chased "a runaway negro" near their camp soon after they arrived. She said they shot him four times and then ran their swords through him, explaining this brought them "good luck."[87]

Another party of sixteen wagons and about one hundred emigrants traveled to Oregon in 1842, led at the start by the future Indian agent Elijah White. The 1843 Burnett party, however, was by far the largest of the early wagon trains, and the first to take wagons to the Columbia River. It is awe-inspiring today to consider how nearly a thousand people came together in a short period of time, bidding adieu to homes, farms, family, and friends, to embark on a journey into the unknown.

Chapter 5
Marcus and Narcissa
DYING FOR A CAUSE

Peter Burnett had a short fuse when he or his interests were attacked. This was the case when he rushed to defend the Catholic Church, which he'd recently joined, against accusations that Catholic priests had encouraged the 1847 Whitman massacre.

The accusations were made from the pulpit by missionary Henry Spalding, who had narrowly escaped the November 1847 slaughter at Waiilatpu, which was blamed on rogue members of the Cayuse tribe. Marcus and Narcissa Whitman and eleven others were killed. Forty women and children were taken captive.

Burnett had been among those who praised Whitman's "services" to Oregon, saying they "were practically more efficient than those of any other person, except perhaps those of [Missouri Senator Lewis] Dr. Linn. . . . I am in doubt as to which of these two men did more in effect for Oregon."[1]

The Whitmans and Spaldings had been assigned by the Boston-based American Board of Commissioners of Foreign Missions to convert the Native American tribes to Christianity. The Whitmans located their mission to the Cayuse at Waiilatpu along the Walla Walla River in high-desert country 8 miles west of present-day Walla Walla, Washington, just north of the Oregon state line. The Spaldings placed their mission to convert the Nez Perce at Lapwai, 120 miles to the northeast, in the Idaho panhandle. Henry Spalding was not a favorite of Narcissa's, to whom he had once proposed and been rejected.[2]

The Whitmans had little success in converting the more resistant Cayuse, while the Spaldings worked among the friendlier Nez Perce with better results. But the Whitmans also provided valuable services to wagon trains passing through—food, rest, and medical care. They also took in nearly a dozen children, among them seven orphans whose parents, Henry and Naomi Sager of Platte County, Missouri, had died on the trail in 1844.

One has to wonder what Marcus was thinking when he took Narcissa to Oregon in the first place, or why she agreed to go. They left on their mission only days following their marriage on February 18, 1836, in New York. Narcissa was ill suited for a missionary's life, living thousands of miles from her family in New York.

Narcissa's long, plaintive letters home reveal her to be lonely, frequently ill, exhausted, and afraid. An agonizing two years would lapse between letters from her family, a cause of constant complaint. She frequently voiced fear she would never see them again. And she would not.

When a daughter, Alice Clarissa, was born to Narcissa on March 14, 1837—only months after settling at the mission—it gave her hope that mission life might be endurable. Two years later, however, Alice wandered from the house and stumbled into the Walla Walla River. A Cayuse worker at the mission found her body.

The death of her only child plunged Narcissa into a deep depression from which she never fully recovered. She questioned in one letter home whether God was punishing her for loving her daughter more than "the Savior," and predicted she would "soon go to her."[3]

Narcissa lived in frequent fear of the Cayuse, most of whom resisted the missionaries' efforts to convert them. They would frequently enter uninvited into the Whitman home and demand food or other favors. Narcissa wrote of one especially terrifying experience in a letter to Marcus on October 2, 1842, while he was on the East Coast.

About midnight I was awakened by some one trying to open my bedroom door. At first I did not know what to understand by it. I raised my head and listened awhile and then lay down again. Soon the latch was raised and the door opened a little. I sprang from the bed in a moment and closed the door again, but the ruffian pushed and pushed and tried to unlatch it, but could not succeed; finally he gained upon me until he opened the door again and as I supposed disengaged his blanket at the same time I [was] calling John [probably one of the Sager children], and ran as for his life. The east dining room door was open. I thought it was locked, but it appears that it was not. I fastened

the door, lit a candle and went to bed trembling and cold, but could
not rest until I had called John to bring his bed and sleep in the kitchen.
... Had the ruffian persisted I do not know what I should have done. I
did not think of the war club, but I thought of the poker.[4]

Narcissa occasionally seemed inspired by their missionary work and exhibited genuine fondness and concern for members of the tribe. In a letter to her
mother on July 4, 1847, Narcissa expressed sympathy at the dual challenges
facing the Cayuse—the white-introduced diseases devastating their tribe, and
their understandable alarm and fear at the sight of the parade of immigrant wagons crossing their lands every fall.

> For the last two weeks immigrants have been passing, probably 80 or
> 100 wagons have already passed and 1,000 are said to be on the road.
> ... The poor Indians are amazed at the overwhelming numbers of
> Americans coming into the country. They seem not to know what to
> make of it. Very many of the principal ones [tribal members] are dying,
> and some have been killed by other Indians. ... The remaining ones
> seem attached to us, and cling to us the closer; cultivate their farms
> quite extensively, and do not wish to see any Sniapus [Americans]
> settle among them here; they are willing to have them spend the winter
> here, but in the spring they must [want them to] all go on.[5]

News of the massacre came from William McBean, the chief Hudson's Bay
trader at Fort Walla Walla. McBean wrote to his Vancouver headquarters on
November 30 that "about thirty souls of the Cayuse tribe" had died of fever
and dysentery, and the tribe "believed the doctor poisoned them. ... As far as I
have been able to learn, this has been the sole cause of the dreadful butchery."[6]
McBean learned of the slaughter from a man who escaped and fled to the trading post "half-naked and covered with blood."[7]

The immediate reaction in the Willamette Valley settlements was fear that
the attack foreshadowed a wider uprising aimed at all white settlers. The provisional legislature quickly organized a mounted militia of fifty volunteers, called
the Oregon Rifles, to occupy and protect the Methodist mission at The Dalles,
and block a feared invasion of the Willamette Valley. The self-financed Oregon
Rifles, the region's first military unit, rode out of Oregon City on December 9 to

Gravesite of Marcus and Narcissa
Whitman and many of the other
thirteen people massacred at the
Whitman Mission at Waiilatpu near
Walla Walla, Washington, on November
29, 1847. Photo by the author.

the celebratory "firing of cannons and the cheers of assembled citizens," according to the *Oregon Spectator*. "It speaks well for our city that in less than twenty-four hours this detachment was raised and had started for the scene of action."[8]

The legislature also authorized a larger force of five hundred volunteers, under the command of Colonel Cornelius Gilliam, "for the purpose of chastising the Indians engaged in the recent horrid massacre at Waillatpu [*sic*]."[9] Gilliam, however, would accidentally kill himself weeks later while returning to Oregon City for reinforcements. Searching for something in his wagon, he tugged on a rope in which a rifle was entangled. It discharged, and he was instantly killed.[10]

Burnett indicated he helped organize the volunteers, writing without elaboration, "We raised an army of some five hundred brave and hardy men, and marched them into the enemy's country."[11] He evidently did not join them, although the muster rolls listed a P. H. Burnette (with an "e") as a private in Company A of the Second Regiment.[12] Able-bodied men were routinely listed on muster roles to be called to duty if needed. Burnett's brother George did serve. He was captain of a company of about eighty-five men from Yamhill and Tualatin Counties that was assigned to The Dalles.[13]

The Oregon volunteers, later backed by two companies of the US Army's Mounted Riflemen from Fort Leavenworth, pursued the Cayuse into the Snake River country at the start of a long and inconclusive war lasting nearly a decade. Cayuse chieftains attempted to resolve the conflict in 1850 by surrendering five members of the tribe, said to be among the killers. They included the long-sought Chief Tiloukaikt. When asked why he gave himself up, the chief reportedly replied, "Did not your missionaries teach us that Christ died to save his people? Thus die we, if we must, to save our people." He refused food. "What hearts have you to offer me of your food, whose hands are red with your brother's blood?"[14]

The five were tried for murder at a two-day trial in Oregon City on May 21. They professed their innocence—one account said they were turned in by other chiefs simply to relieve pressure on the tribe. Although there was little evidence they were involved, Judge Orville Pratt of the Territorial Supreme Court instructed the twelve-member jury of white men that their surrender was proof enough. The Cayuse were found guilty following a two-day trial. Judge Pratt refused to allow a last-minute reprieve to allow time for an appeal to the US Supreme Court, and the men were hanged June 3, 1850, and buried in unmarked graves.[15]

The captives from the mission had been freed by the Cayuse months earlier with the help of the new chief factor at Hudson's Bay, Peter Skene Ogden, who negotiated a ransom of blankets, shirts, guns, ammunition, and tobacco.[16]

Although the Cayuse were undoubtedly responsible for the massacre, there were unfounded accusations, apparently originating with Spalding, that they had been encouraged by Catholic missionaries. Spalding had narrowly escaped the massacre, while his daughter Eliza was among the women and children taken captive.

Spalding alluded both in a sermon and in print to a "universal suspicion" that Catholics were involved. The threads of evidence ranged from flimsy to nonexistent. But Spalding had no compunction against weaving the threads into a plot. "It is said that Catholics [missionary priests] took part in the murders and in the distribution of the plundered goods [and] that during the massacre. . . . They were passing and repassing [the mission] in company with the murderers." As further evidence, he said, "Not a Catholic has been injured or disturbed . . . all of which strongly imply that there was a previous understanding between Catholics and the murderers."[17]

Burnett, who converted to Catholicism in 1846, rushed to the church's defense. He challenged Spalding to debate "the grave and solemn charges [Spalding had made] against others from the pulpit." Spalding declined to debate, and instead proposed an exchange of letters in the *Oregon Spectator*. But the editor refused to get involved. Instead, each man wrote his views in a publication called the *Oregon American*, after which Burnett apparently dropped the matter. No evidence was ever offered of Catholic complicity in the massacre.

Chapter 6
A Short Oregon History
ASTOR'S DEBACLE

Peter Burnett never doubted the Oregon Country would come under the American flag. "We knew to a moral certainty, at the moment we brought our families, cattle, teams, and loaded wagons to the banks of the Columbia River in 1843, the question was practically decided in our favor. . . . We could bring into the country ten immigrants for every colonist Great Britain could induce to settle there."[1]

The Treaty of 1818, signed in London on October 20, provided for joint occupancy of the Oregon Country by Great Britain and the United States. Both nations had competing claims but cooperated in administering the vast region with its valuable resource of fur-bearing animals, especially beaver.

The arrival of the 1843 wagon train had been the second of a one-two punch aimed at asserting the American claim. At about the time Burnett departed Missouri for Oregon, a handful of earlier settlers, fur trappers, and missionaries were meeting on May 2, 1843, at Champoeg in the Willamette Valley to consider establishing a provisional government. The vote was close: fifty-two in favor, fifty against. The Hudson's Bay Company, which represented British interests, was represented by fifty-two men, largely former French-Canadian trappers then living in the Tualatin Valley. Two defected to the American side.

Establishment of the provisional government was a rebuke to the British and to the Hudson's Bay Company, whose chief factor, Dr. John McLoughlin, had been tasked by his London headquarters with keeping American settlers out of Oregon. McLoughlin opposed the establishment of an American-aligned provisional government, favoring instead a government independent of both the United States and Great Britain.[2]

However, the new provisional government mollified McLoughlin by limiting its jurisdiction to the settled areas of the Willamette Valley. Historian Frederick V. Holman said there was "a tacit understanding" that Hudson's Bay Company would control the country north of the Columbia. It wasn't until August 15, 1845, that McLoughlin agreed to join the provisional government with the stipulation that the company would only pay taxes on goods sold to the American settlers, not on its other operations.[3]

The competing claims to the Oregon Country had some origins in the fur trade. Americans planted their flag when Jacob Astor, the wealthy New York–based merchant, developed a fur-trading post at the mouth of the Columbia River in 1811, a few years after the Lewis and Clark Expedition of 1804-06 left the region. Called Fort Astoria, the post was to serve as the base of operations for Astor's Pacific Fur Company.

Astor, who never set foot in Oregon, had sought to elbow aside the British and dominate the fur trade in the entire region west of the Rocky Mountains. But the New Yorker's strategy failed for a combination of reasons, including bad timing, bad management, and bad luck.

Astor sent two expeditions to establish his new outpost. One group sailed aboard Astor's ship, the square-rigger *Tonquin*, from New York around Cape Horn, a 12,000-mile voyage. The ship, with a crew of twenty-three plus twenty-six passengers, was under the command of Captain Jonathan Thorn, a career naval officer. The second expedition was an overland journey of sixty men and one woman, led by Wilson Price Hunt. Both expeditions lost lives.[4]

The overland expedition met with near-disaster after Hunt miscalculated its position and traded the party's horses for canoes when they reached the Snake River in Wyoming's Grand Teton Mountains. He mistakenly believed they could travel by canoe down the Snake and Columbia Rivers to Fort Astoria—an impossibility. They were soon stymied by rapids and falls and were forced to abandon their canoes. They traveled the remaining 800 miles on foot. Starving and exhausted, they arrived at Fort Astoria long behind schedule.[5]

Astor's ships fared even worse. The *Tonquin*, the first of the trading ships, was blown to smithereens at Clayoquot Sound on the west coast of Vancouver Island in Canada in June 1811. Captain Thorn had anchored near the village of Opitsatah to trade with the Clayoquot tribe. The Clayoquots, however, were poised to exact revenge for an attack two decades earlier by American sea captain Robert Gray, who, in a dispute with the tribe, leveled the village and its two hundred homes with cannon fire in 1792.[6] Such transgressions were not forgotten.

Although forewarned about the potential for retaliation, Thorn chose to sail into Clayoquot waters anyway, anxious to start trading for furs. Under a pretense of preparing to trade, members of the tribe boarded the *Tonquin* and slaughtered twenty-seven of the unsuspecting crewmen. Among those killed were Thorn and Alexander McKay, the well-known Scottish trader.[7]

When the natives returned the following day to loot the ship, a surviving member of the crew ignited 9,000 pounds of powder in the ship's magazine. The explosion killed an estimated two hundred Clayoquots, along with the remaining crewmen. The ship's native interpreter witnessed the explosion from shore, and gave his account of events in later years.[8]

Another Astor ship, the *Beaver*, was damaged in a storm off the coast of Alaska and sailed to the Sandwich Islands (Hawaii) for repairs. Hunt, whom Astor had put in charge of the fort, had joined the *Beaver's* crew and was stranded in the islands. He was still there when the War of 1812 broke out. A third ship, the *Lark*, sent by Astor from New York to defend the fort, was badly damaged in yet another storm and sank off the island of Maui. The crew of a fourth ship, the *Forester*, refused to sail to Astoria and remained in the Sandwich Islands.[9]

With the American leaders dead or far away, those remaining at the fort sold out to the British North West Company in October 1813, thus ending Astor's Oregon venture. The British gave the post a new name, Fort George. The North West Company, in turn, merged with the Hudson's Bay Company in 1821, which abandoned the fort after building Fort Vancouver as a replacement in 1825.

Astor's considerable investment was a total loss after just over two years. Nevertheless, the short-lived settlement at the mouth of the Columbia River helped establish an American claim to the Oregon Country.

The United States and Great Britain resolved their dispute over Oregon under terms of the Oregon Treaty, signed in Washington, DC, on June 15, 1846, which gave the United States jurisdiction over the region south of the present-day boundary with Canada. Britain gained control of what is today British Columbia. Congress established the Oregon Territory on August 14, 1848. It encompassed the vast area from the Rocky Mountains to the Pacific, south to the border with California and north to Canada.

Senator Linn's strategy of encouraging American settlement with free land had worked. But Linn would not live to know of its success. He died on October 3, 1843, at age 89, a month before the 1843 wagon train reached Oregon City.

Chapter 7
Burnett's Not-Going-to-Happen Big City

Peter Burnett could be faulted for many things, but lack of ambition wasn't one of them. He set out for Oregon intending to acquire a huge tract of free land. But once in Oregon, he switched gears. He was going to build and develop the region's first major port city.

Perhaps Burnett changed his mind because he didn't know what he would do with so much free land. After all, he never wanted to be a farmer. Or perhaps it was because the new provisional government had limited the free land to one square mile per family—not as much as Burnett envisioned, although still a great deal of land. Or perhaps he saw an opportunity to make that fortune, and show the snooty Hardemans back home he was no slouch when it came to making money.

While other settlers began staking out their claims, Burnett teamed with fellow immigrant Morton McCarver to lay out a port city on the Willamette River, named Linnton in honor of Senator Linn. McCarver picked the location, five miles south of the river's confluence with the Columbia. The two men "supposed it" to be the farthest up the Willamette that oceangoing vessels could safely go. McCarver had previous experience at town-building, helping lay out Burlington, Iowa, in the mid-1830s.[1]

Burnett and McCarver built a wharf and a warehouse for their new city, and cleared a crude wagon road across the heavily forested Tualatin Mountains into the fertile Tualatin Valley, then known as Tualatin Plains.[2] They anticipated that farmers would bring their crops over the road to load onto ships for distant markets. A supremely confident Burnett wrote, "I have no doubt that this place will be the great commercial town in the territory." They would sell lots for $50, "and sell them fast at that," he predicted.[3]

Burnett built a cabin for his family in Linnton. But he was preparing for a bonanza that never came. Burnett and McCarver soon discovered they could

Morton McCarver partnered with
Peter Burnett in an unsuccessful
attempt to develop the town of
Linnton as a major Willamette River
port. McCarver traveled to Oregon
with Burnett in the 1843 wagon train.
A McCarver descendant later said
the two men had a falling out over
development plans for Sacramento City
in California. Courtesy of the Oregon
Historical Society.

only wave at the ships passing them by, headed to the new Portland, which had the advantage of being closer to the farms of the Willamette Valley.[4]

When it became obvious they couldn't sell enough lots to cover expenses, Burnett was forced to admit failure. "I soon found that expenses were certain and income nothing." It must have been a bitter pill to swallow, as it added to the narrative that he was a failure at business. Burnett next decided "to make me a farm." It wasn't what he wanted, but he had seven mouths to feed. McCarver had already covered his bets by taking out a square-mile land claim in Tualatin Plains. But although Burnett and McCarver gave up on Linnton, it would not be the last attempt at city-building for either man.[5]

In April, Burnett moved his family to the Tualatin Plains, 20 miles west of Portland in today's Washington County. He presumably traveled over his newly built road, today known as the steep and winding Germantown Road, which is within the Portland city limits. Burnett purchased 250 acres of farmland plus 10 acres of nearby timber. The timber cost him $25—he didn't say what he paid for the farm, purchased from an unnamed farmer, or give its location. He also filed a claim for the settlers' right to a square mile of land. His claim, number 39 in the county's land claim records, is dated April 16, 1846. Washington County Recorder J. S. Long made a note that Burnett "holds [the land] by personal occupancy."[6]

Burnett's description of his new farm suggests he fell in love with it. "The plain was beautiful, and was divided from the plains adjoining by living streams of water flowing from the mountains, the banks of which streams were skirted with fir and white cedar timber." The land "was gently undulating. . . . The rows of green ash in summer give the plain a beautiful appearance."[7]

The former Burnett claim is still farmland, protected from development in a state-designated agricultural zone. US Highway 26, the main east-west highway from Portland to the Oregon coast, cuts diagonally across the property. The town of North Plains abuts the property to the north, while a half mile to the northwest is the Pumpkin Ridge Golf Course, the site of several major golf tournaments. There are two small landing strips on the property, one for gliders. Large oak trees are at two corners, with county land claim markers nearby, were easily located by a surveyor friend, Tim Kent of Vancouver, Washington. A migrant workers' camp was located along the southern embankment of Highway 26. Although posted, I was not stopped when I visited the camp to ask several Spanish-speaking workers if anyone knew the history of the property. None did.

A lumber mill producing wood chips for fiber board was at the westernmost edge of the property. Crops in evidence were corn, alfalfa, red clover, and a hazelnut orchard, while another large field had been left fallow. Aged stumps of oak trees, 4 feet across, indicated that the hazelnut orchard had earlier uses. The creek Burnett mentioned is probably McKay Creek, named for another settler.

Peter Burnett's 1846 donation land claim in Washington County, formerly Tualatin County, about 25 miles west of Portland. Still designated for agricultural use by the state, the square-mile property includes a hazelnut orchard and a chip mill. The mountains of the Coast Range are in the distance. Photo by the author.

Burnett admitted knowing little about farming. He hadn't engaged in any manual labor during all of his seventeen years as a merchant and a lawyer in Tennessee and Missouri. Nevertheless, he "did succeed well" on his new farm. He planted potatoes and 3 acres of wheat that first May, working in his bare feet after wearing out his boots. He later made ill-fitting shoes for the family out of tanned deerskin, a skill learned from his father.[8]

Burnett's first home in the Tualatin Plains was a borrowed cabin belonging to David Lenox, who joined the 1843 wagon train after hearing Burnett's sidewalk appeal in Missouri. Lenox made it a condition that Burnett allow the newly organized West Union Baptist Church to hold Sunday services in the cabin. Lenox organized the church six months after arriving in Oregon.

Church records show that the congregation met at least once in "the house of Peter H. Burnett" on December 14, 1844, although Burnett's name was not listed in the membership rolls. To Burnett's considerable embarrassment, he attended services barefoot, complaining, "I was worse off than I was when without a hat in Bolivar, Tennessee."[9]

Lenox would later donate 2 acres of his mile-square donation land claim for a permanent church in 1853 where his home once stood. Thirty miles west of Portland, the church was still in use in 2017 and was said to be the oldest church building west of the Rockies. Lenox, who died in 1874, and his wife, Louisa, are buried in the adjacent church cemetery.[10]

The Lenox land claim appears on maps of donation land claims. Burnett's, however, does not. The 1850 Oregon Donation Land Claim Act affirmed the claims of the first settlers. To secure ownership, however, a settler was required to live on the land and farm it for four years, a process called "proving up." Burnett would not have met the requirement, having departed for California in 1848.

The property ended up with Thomas R. Cornelius, an 1845 emigrant from Howard County, Missouri, for whom the nearby town of Cornelius is named. Cornelius, who served in Oregon's territorial and state legislatures, registered the claim on March 6, 1848.[11]

Before leaving for California, Burnett sold his second property, the 240 acres he purchased outright, to a John Smith for $5,250. The price included a herd of cattle. Harriet and their young children presumably continued living on this property before joining Burnett in California. Burnett expressed doubt in a letter to a friend on June 29, 1849, that Smith, "a drunkard," would ever take possession.[12] He also expressed interest in buying it back if Smith didn't take

The West Union Baptist Church near Hillsboro, Oregon, is said to be the oldest Protestant church building west of the Rockies. Before the church was built in 1853, the congregation met at least once in Peter Burnett's home. Photo by the author.

possession. It isn't known whether Smith did take ownership, but there's no indication Burnett bought the property back.

Two of Peter Burnett's brothers who followed him to Oregon took out claims that appear on land claims maps. George, a farmer, local judge, and officer in Oregon's volunteer militia, located his square-mile claim in Yamhill County.[13] Glen, a preacher, took out a claim in Polk County, where he organized Bethel Church and helped establish the former Bethel College.[14]

Times were difficult for the Burnett family those first couple of years. "We were frequently without any meat for weeks at a time, and some times without bread, and occasionally without both bread and meat," Burnett wrote. "If we had milk, butter and potatoes, we were well content." He recalled a day in May 1845 when there was no food at all in the house. Harriet saved the day—or a hungry night—when she suggested digging up potatoes left in the ground from the previous year, which Burnett had forgotten. They "sufficed us for a meal, though not very good."[15]

By the following year, 1846, the family had gained its footing. They were "secure of a good living" on their farm of "excellent land . . . well stocked with domestic animals and fowls." Burnett attributed their well-being to "the industrious and sober habits of myself and family."[16] He failed to mention until later in his autobiography that he had been elected by the provisional legislature in 1845 to the relatively lucrative post of supreme judge, which must have made at least a modest contribution to his "good living."

One unanswered question during this period: Where did Burnett get his money? He wrote that when the family arrived in Oregon "we were poor." Their oxen and horses were too worn out to be useful for farm work until the following spring. But for someone who set out from Missouri $15,000 in debt, and arrived in Oregon as a self-described poor man with a large family, he found enough money to cover some rather considerable expenses. These included his trip across the plains and the cost of the oxen, wagons, food, and other provisions for the six-month trip.

The estimated cost of a basic trail outfit was $600 to $800. A yoke of oxen at Independence cost $25 in 1846. Mules were priced about the same. Moreover, Burnett brought more than the basic outfit—three wagons, four yoke of oxen, and two mules. Once in Oregon, he faced the not insignificant upkeep of his large family, plus the cost of developing the wagon road over the rugged Tualatin Hills. There was also the cabin at Linnton, and his purchase of the farm and timber in Tualatin Plains. McCarver, who apparently came away with some money from his Iowa ventures, may have footed much, or even all, of the cost of the Linnton project, although that's only a guess.

Assistance in the form of loans, or even gifts, may have come courtesy of John McLoughlin, the first person Burnett wanted to meet in Oregon. Burnett said he became "an intimate" friend of McLoughlin, and, assuming this is true, he may have had access to McLoughlin's generosity. McLoughlin, in turn, may have sought to win the favor of an influential American who might be sympathetic to his interests.

No individual loomed larger in the Oregon Country when the first settlers arrived than Dr. John McLoughlin. Known to tribes throughout the Northwest as "the White Headed Eagle," he stood at the extraordinary height for his day, six feet four inches, with shoulder-length prematurely white hair. He carried a gold-headed cane and ruled the Oregon Country almost as his personal fiefdom for more than twenty years. One historian opined that he carried himself with the dignity and authority "of a baron in feudal times."[17]

The Canadian-born McLoughlin was viewed with suspicion, even hostility, by many settlers, largely because he represented British interests, but also because he was Roman Catholic; most settlers were Protestants. Yet the settlers' dislike was usually in the abstract, and those who met him were frequently won over by his charismatic personality. The late Frederick V. Holman, author of a notable 1907 biography, said McLoughlin was "the great and noble autocrat of

Dr. John McLoughlin, chief factor of
the Hudson's Bay Company at Fort
Vancouver. Known to native tribes as
"the White Headed Eagle," he helped
Peter Burnett get established in the
Oregon country. Courtesy of the
Oregon Historical Society.

the whole Oregon Country, it's ruler and protector." According to Holman, he
was "by nature a great leader and captain of men."[18] Burnett was among those
who lavished praise on McLoughlin, calling him "one of the greatest and most
noble philanthropists I ever knew . . . a man of superior ability, just in all his
dealings, and a faithful Christian."[19]

McLoughlin was born October 19, 1784, at Rivière-du-Loup in Québec. As
a youth, he trained in medicine. Although he lacked a medical school education, he was hired as a physician by the North West Company at its fur-trading
post on Lake Superior. He also had a knack for trapping and soon became a
fur trader of some considerable success and ability. After the Hudson's Bay
Company emerged as the successor to the North West Company, he was promoted in 1824 to chief factor at Fort George—soon to be reconstituted as Fort
Vancouver. This placed him in charge of British fur-trading interests throughout the Pacific Northwest, including twenty-two trading posts. He married
Marguerite Wadin McKay, a Native American of the Cree tribe and widow of
Alexander McKay, who was killed in the 1811 *Tonquin* massacre.

In attempting to execute the policy of the Hudson's Bay Company to dis-
courage American settlers and redirect them to Mexican California, McLoughlin
was placed in an impossible position. He was unwilling to withhold assistance
to the emigrants who came anyway, many without food or resources, exhausted
from their 2,000-mile journey. "How to act, so as to secure the approbation of

the directors and stockholders in England, and at the same time not to disregard the most urgent calls of humanity . . . no possible line of conduct could have escaped censure," Burnett wrote.[20]

McLoughlin did Burnett a favor the first time they met. Burnett had been urged by a company representative at Fort Walla Walla to leave his trail-worn cattle there and obtain new cattle in exchange at Fort Vancouver. But Burnett quoted McLoughlin as saying the cattle at Fort Vancouver were inferior "Spanish cattle." McLoughlin sent orders to Walla Walla to care for Burnett's cattle until he could retrieve them.[21]

McLoughlin also traded properties with Burnett, exchanging two lots in Oregon City for two lots in Linnton. Burnett got the better of the deal, as the Oregon City lots were valued at $200 apiece, four times what Burnett charged for properties in Linnton.[22] Burnett didn't say whether McLoughlin had helped him in other ways, although it's a fair assumption he did. William Gray said as much, although without offering specifics.

McLoughlin was soon to learn, however, that Burnett was not always eager to repay favors. Under pressure from his London office, and with his authority and income reduced, McLoughlin resigned from Fort Vancouver in 1845 and moved across the river to Oregon City, where he appealed to Burnett, then judge of Oregon's Provisional Government Supreme Court, to award him US citizenship. Burnett declined, explaining that because Oregon was not officially an American territory, his hands were tied.

Burnett was drawn into a controversy over McLoughlin's Oregon City claim. He took the odd position for a lawyer that a voter-approved law might be changed without submitting the change to voters. The debate involved "claim jumping" on a large tract of McLoughlin's riverfront property. An emigrant named A. J. Vickers claimed 274 acres of McLoughlin's claim in 1846, contending it was improperly registered and therefore up for grabs.

McLoughlin had claimed the property as early as 1829. His expansive landholdings included Oregon City, Willamette Falls, and a small island—later named Abernethy Island after the provisional governor, George Abernethy. McLoughlin asserted his claim in a letter on July 21, 1840, granting permission to the Methodist missionary, Jason Lee, to build a store:

> I beg to inform you that in 1830, as is well known to most of the old
> settlers in the Wallamette, I took possession of the side of the falls on
> which I got a mill race blasted, from the upper end of the falls across to

the Clackamas river and down to where the Clackamas falls into the Wallamette including the whole point of land and the small island in the falls on which portage is made and which I intend to claim when the boundary line is drawn. . . . Of course this is not to prevent your building the store, as my object is to establish my claim.[23]

But Vickers and others ignored McLoughlin, and made claims of their own. Lacking citizenship, McLoughlin found himself in a difficult position. Over the years he had given conflicting accounts as to whether he had claimed the land for himself or for the Hudson's Bay Company, which as a foreign corporation could not lawfully claim the land after the British yielded authority over the region to the United States in 1846.[24]

Compounding McLoughlin's plight was his failure to comply with a voter-approved requirement in 1845 that land claims had to be reregistered within a year.[25] The issue escalated, and a public meeting was called to discuss claim-jumping, to which Burnett was invited to speak. Without publicly taking sides, Burnett argued that if the registration requirement proved cumbersome and unfair, it should be changed. He obviously felt it was unfair, even though he had helped write the requirement into Oregon's provisional constitution, called the Organic Laws of Oregon. Public sentiment was on McLoughlin's side, and Vickers's claim was denied. But McLoughlin would lose title to the land in 1850 when the Donation Land Claim Act specifically excluded his claim.

With the arrival of the first wave of settlers, McLoughlin concluded that the British strategy of excluding the Americans was doomed to fail. Instead, he assisted the settlers, sending boats to The Dalles to transport some of them down the Columbia, for a price, and extended credit for food, seeds, and farm implements to help them start their farms. Burnett said some settlers unfairly complained that the Hudson's Bay Company gouged them with high prices. "Many of our immigrants were unworthy of the favors they received, and only returned abuse for generosity."[26]

Oregon historian Charles Henry Carey wrote that McLoughlin's "kindness and humanity" to the settlers didn't earn him any plaudits from his London headquarters, where he was "severely criticized." Conversely, "some who were beneficiaries of his kindness [in Oregon] failed to repay, or even joined in a movement against him."[27] One estimate put the number of settlers who owed McLoughlin money at the time of his death in 1857 at two hundred.[28]

Of course, it would be naïve to think McLoughlin's motive for helping the settlers was purely altruistic; he also surely anticipated the settlers would be future customers—the Hudson's Bay Company was the only store in town. William Gray interpreted McLoughlin's every action, no matter how benign, as part of "the long premeditated baseness of the Hudson's Bay Company in their efforts to get rid of all American missionaries and settlers."[29]

While the American settlers were generally anti-Catholic, Burnett came to embrace Catholicism, having been introduced to it at a Christmas Eve mass in 1843 at Fort Vancouver. Although he was a member of the Disciples of Christ, he said the mass made "the deepest impression upon my mind."[30]

Burnett formally converted to Catholicism in June 1846 at a ceremony administered by Father De Vos, a Jesuit missionary.[31] Burnett must have known it would tarnish his popularity in Protestant Oregon, but his new faith was deeply rooted. He later wrote that "nine-tenths of the people of Oregon were at that time opposed to my religion."[32] Most of the few Catholics in the Oregon Country were Canadians associated with the Hudson's Bay Company. Harriet, formerly a Methodist, also converted.

Gray saw only self-interest in Burnett's conversion. He contended Burnett had sought a religion that "would pay the best," alluding to his connections to McLoughlin and the Hudson's Bay Company.[33] Gray held McLoughlin in as much contempt as he did Burnett. Notwithstanding Gray's early history of the region, however, he wasn't entitled to the final word on Burnett, McLoughlin, or, for that matter, much of what else transpired in Oregon history. Gray was vindictive to a fault toward those he didn't like, which was quite a long list. Wrote one historian: "Gray was ambitious, always striving for a status in life higher than for what he was qualified."[34]

Most historians have considered McLoughlin as a stabilizing force in the Northwest prior to the arrival of the American settlers. Charles Carey wrote that during the twenty-two years McLoughlin was in charge at Fort Vancouver, "there were no wars; travel was safe, thefts were rare."[35] James Nesmith called McLoughlin "a public benefactor" and predicted the people of Oregon would someday erect a statue in his honor.[36] And so it happens that a statue of Dr. John McLoughlin, complete with shoulder-length hair, today represents Oregon in National Statuary Hall in the US Capitol.[37]

Chapter 8
Rewriting Oregon

It should come as no surprise that among the first great rush of immigrants were many of the West's future leaders. Prominent among them was Burnett, who was elected on May 14, 1844, to the nine-member Legislative Committee, Oregon's first elected legislature, and later as the first governor of California.

Others who rose rapidly to political leadership in Oregon included Jesse Applegate, Morton McCarver, Daniel Waldo, James Nesmith, Nathaniel Ford, and Cornelius Gilliam. Waldo and McCarver served with Burnett on the Legislative Committee.

Almost immediately after his arrival, Burnett became a huge booster for the Oregon Country, writing long letters filled with unrestrained hyperbole about the region's wonders to friends and newspaper editors across the country. He would later lavish the same praise on California.

Probably before he had put a single seed in the ground, Burnett wrote, "Perhaps there is no country in the world where a man can live so well upon so little labor."[1] In another letter, he wrote, "Our country is most beautiful, fertile and well-watered with the most equable and pleasant climate." His favorable assessment of life in Oregon included a 125-page letter to the *New York Herald*, sent while he was still in Linnton.[2]

The purpose of his letters—and other early emigrants sent them, too—was to lure more settlers to Oregon. More settlers meant more farms, more markets, more stores, more buyers, more roads, and, not to be discounted, more voters. There was a patriotic interest too, as more settlers strengthened the American claim to the region. When Burnett referred to settlers, he of course meant white settlers.

To enjoy the comfortable and prosperous life that awaited them, Burnett said all an emigrant had to do was load up a wagon or two, and set out overland for 2,000 miles. Burnett offered advice and encouragement—use oxen, not horses; travel in small groups to make it easier to find forage for livestock; and bring as few belongings as possible, save for food and clothing.

Women were in short supply, and Burnett advised men to find a wife before they started, and, once in Oregon, avoid leaving them alone for extended periods of time. It was not clear what Burnett had in mind, but it suggested a danger of wife-stealing. It was also advice Burnett himself ignored when he left his wife alone for six months upon departing Oregon for California. His one complaint was that Congress had so far failed to extend territorial status, although it would soon do so.[3]

But Burnett found himself on the defensive for his widely published remark about the ease of wagon travel to Oregon. He had written from the Sweetwater River in western Wyoming that "up to that point, the road we had traveled was the finest natural route, perhaps, in the world." When he wrote that letter, however, the most difficult part of the journey was still ahead. Burnett insisted his comment was misconstrued "as a description of the entire route," with the result that settlers in later wagon trains "whenever they came to any very bad road, they would most commonly say, 'This is more of Burnett's fine road.'"[4]

Burnett was also accused of understating the prices settlers could expect to pay in Oregon, such as claiming feathers cost ¢37 a pound. But when they arrived, the price was more than ¢62. Burnett explained, "I told you what the price then was, and not what it would be two or three years later."

But whether Burnett had or hadn't exaggerated the attractions of Oregon, he and others accomplished their purpose. The flow of overland emigrants to Oregon soon became a flood. There were other factors, too. The very success of the 1843 emigration itself was enough to lure others to follow.

The number of emigrants on the Oregon Trail increased from 875 in 1843 to 2,500 in 1845, and to 4,000 in 1847. The emigration would shift massively in favor of California after gold was discovered at Sutter's Mill in 1848. The total overland emigrants to Oregon during the twenty-year period 1840–60 was estimated at 53,062. The estimate for California was 200,235.[5] Thousands more arrived by ship.

When Burnett arrived in Oregon, he didn't think a provisional government was either needed or appropriate, given the divided jurisdiction between Great Britain and the United States. He conveniently chose to overlook that such a government had already been in place for a year, administered by the appointed Legislative Committee. But once he concluded a government was needed, he claimed it as his idea, and decided he was the obvious choice to lead it. "As we could not with any exact certainty, anticipate the time when the conflicting claims of the two contending governments would be settled, we determined to organize a provisional government for ourselves."[6]

Burnett was elected one of nine members of the 1844 Legislative Committee, receiving thirty-two votes to represent Tualatin County.[7] Although several other members received more votes in other counties, Burnett appeared to take charge effortlessly.

The elected committee proceeded to rewrite the laws approved a year earlier by the appointed committee, whose members included William Gray.[8] The laws had been adopted by a handful of settlers and others on July 5, 1843, while Burnett was still en route to Oregon. It also authorized the election at which Burnett was elected.

The 1843 laws had been intended to stand "until such time as the United States of America extend their jurisdiction over us." Among other provisions, it flatly banned slavery and guaranteed freedom of worship, trial by jury, habeas corpus, and the sanctity of private contracts. These weren't sufficient for Burnett, however. Historian Charles Carey wrote that the Burnett-led committee "took the liberty of destroying the charter from which it derived its own powers."[9] Gray was furious, complaining that "no regard was paid to any previous laws, or constitutional provisions."[10]

But Burnett and his supporters faced little opposition, in part because they had brought a majority of Oregon's potential voters with them. The Burnett-led committee also was acting at least partly at the recommendation of an independent three-person executive committee, which had urged the "adoption of some measures of a more thorough organization."[11] The executive committee briefly functioned as the provisional government's chief executive.

The Burnett committee recommended the election of a governor to succeed the executive committee—George Abernethy, formerly of New York, won election as Oregon's first governor in 1845.[12] The committee also proposed evolving into a thirteen-member Provisional Legislature. It validated the claims of the settlers to a square mile of land but eliminated the huge allocations of land, up to six square miles, allotted to the Catholic and Methodist missions. The committee levied a modest property tax and prohibited alcoholic beverages, although Governor Abernethy later vetoed the alcohol ban.

The property tax legislation carried a unique enforcement penalty, which Burnett owned as his idea. A taxpayer was given the option of not paying the tax but faced a partial loss of civic rights. As Burnett explained in a letter to the *Platte Argus* of Missouri: "if he did not pay, being able, we disbarred him from suing in the courts as plaintiff." He said it "worked like a charm. . . . Nearly all the population paid without hesitation." Burnett claimed the Legislative Committee's achievements as mostly his. "I had most of the business to do," he wrote.[13]

One piece of business Burnett addressed in this period was to help former fur trappers with their land claims. Congress was considering an early version of a territorial bill for Oregon, backed by Representative James M. Hughes of Missouri, that would have reserved land claims exclusively for Caucasians. Burnett wrote Senator David Atchison, his former law partner in Missouri, on December 8, 1844, pointing out that the fur trappers, many of them French-Canadian and former employees of the Hudson's Bay Company, had fathered children with Native American wives. Some of these families were his neighbors in the Tualatin Plains. Referring to the wives and children of a deceased husband and father, Burnett wrote, "Any law that would take from them their farms, the labor of years, would most deeply mortify all persons in this country."[14] His letter got results. The Donation Land Claims Act, enacted by Congress in 1850, validated the claims of "American half-breed Indians." It excluded African Americans, however.

None of the changes the Burnett committee made in the laws would be more controversial, or have more far-reaching consequences, than Burnett's exclusion law and its "lash law" companion, banning African Americans from settling in Oregon.

Chapter 9
The Lash Law
"DISGRACE AND INFAMY"

Peter Burnett's place in history will forever be tarnished by his advocacy of laws to prevent African Americans from settling in the new states and territories on the Pacific Coast. He was successful in winning enactment of such a law in Oregon in 1844, but unsuccessful in California.

Article Five of Oregon's original 1843 organic law declared: "There shall be neither slavery nor involuntary servitude in said territory, otherwise than for the punishment of crimes, whereof the party shall have been duly convicted." The wording was adopted from Article Six of the Northwest Ordinance of 1787.[1] The organic law said nothing about excluding blacks or anyone else from the Oregon Country, although it denied blacks the right to vote.

According to historian Henry Carey, however, the provision banning slavery outright had been "unsatisfactory to many."[2] While Carey didn't mention the reason, the obvious explanation was that some influential settlers wanted slaves to help work their square-mile claims.

Burnett's Legislative Committee substantially altered the antislavery law at its first session in June 1844. Instead of banning slavery outright, the committee allowed slaveholders a three-year grace period to free their slaves. After three years, freed slaves were required to leave Oregon. Moreover, any free black who arrived in the region after enactment of the law was required to turn around and leave.

The exclusion law included an especially onerous feature. It provided for severe whipping for a free black man or woman, or a newly freed slave, who refused to leave Oregon within a prescribed period of time—two years for a man, three years for a woman. Section 6 provided: "if any such free negro or mulatto shall fail to quit the country as required by this act, he or she may be arrested upon a warrant issued by some justice of the peace, and, if guilty upon trial before such justice, shall receive upon his or her bare back not less than twenty nor more than thirty-nine stripes, to be inflicted by the constable of the proper county."

Known to Oregon history as "Peter Burnett's lash law," the whipping penalty may never have been enforced; at least, there's no record of enforcement. But the law stands as a reflection of the attitude of many early Oregonians toward people of color.

The vote on the committee in favor of the exclusion law and slavery grace period was six to two. Voting with Burnett were McCarver, Waldo, Thomas Keizer, Matthew Gilmore, and Robert Newell. All but Newell had traveled with Burnett to Oregon. The opposing votes were cast by Asa Lovejoy, a future law partner of Burnett's, and David Hill, who had cast one of the fifty-two votes at Champoeg in favor of a provisional government.[3]

Burnett sought to explain his support for an exclusion law in a letter to a Missouri newspaper: "The object is to keep clear of that most troublesome class of population [blacks]. We are in a new world, under the most favorable circumstances, and we wish to avoid most of those evils that have so much afflicted the United States and other countries."[4] This attitude might explain the exclusion law, but not Burnett's motive for relaxing the law against slavery. The reason may have been as simple as extending a favor to friends and settlers who wanted slaves, perhaps even himself.

Another council member who had been a slaveholder in Missouri was Daniel Waldo.[5] Descendants of a former slave named America Waldo contend that Waldo fathered America with her slave mother in Missouri and brought America to Oregon as a small girl in 1843. But Waldo's white descendants deny this claim, and say America might have come with, and been fathered by, Daniel's brother Joseph, who emigrated from Missouri in 1846. Descendants of both families agree that after arriving in Oregon America grew up in the Daniel Waldo household near Salem.[6]

The exclusion law's whipping penalty was too much for the three-member executive committee. It was also too much for Gray, who called the whipping penalty "an inhuman act . . . which should stamp the names of its supporters with disgrace and infamy."[7] The executive committee urged the Legislative Committee to expunge whipping, although it did not question the exclusion law itself.

The committee at its second meeting in December 1844 substituted a forced labor penalty for whipping. A free African American who stayed longer

Legislative chambers in
Oregon City for Oregon's
provisional and territorial
governments. Courtesy of the
Oregon Historical Society.

than allowed would be hired out to the lowest bidder for a fixed period of time, after which he or she would then have to leave Oregon. The new penalty, while eliminating whipping, seemed to condemn a free black to a condition of servitude not unlike slavery. Burnett would later say it was his decision to drop the whipping penalty, which was not true.

Gray was not mollified by the change. "The principles of Burnett's bill made it a crime for a white man to bring a negro into the country, and a crime for a negro to come voluntarily, so that, in any case, if he were found in the country, he was guilty of a crime, and punishment or slavery was his doom."[8]

When a new committee was elected in June 1845, Burnett was no longer a member. The de facto leader was Jesse Applegate, who proceeded to write the exclusion law out of the 1843 organic laws so that they once again flatly prohibited slavery.[9] Applegate had denounced the whipping penalty as not only cruel, but also potentially fatal. "Any poor Negro so unfortunate as to be compelled to come here by his master was to be whipped every six months . . . until he ran away or died under his infliction."[10]

The Applegate committee submitted the new organic laws to voters, who ratified them by a vote of 255 to 22 on July 25, 1845. Except for the expunged exclusion law, the laws were largely written by the Burnett committee.[11]

The precedent set by the short-lived exclusion law would resonate in an antiblack attitude that prevailed during most of Oregon's early history. There would be two more exclusion laws. The second was enacted by the Territorial Legislature in 1849 and remained in place until 1854. The third was a voter-approved clause written into Oregon's 1857 constitution, making Oregon the only free state admitted into the Union with an exclusion clause in its constitution. It was approved by an all-male white electorate and not removed until 1926. The framers of the constitution also proposed a clause to establish Oregon as a slave state. While this was rejected by a vote of 7,727 to 2,645, the vote indicated significant proslavery sentiment.

While most settlers opposed slavery, they appeared unconcerned by the presence of the small number of slaves. The prohibition against slavery was largely ignored by slaveholders until tested in court in 1852 in *Holmes v. Ford*, in which a former slave, Robin Holmes, sued his former owner, Nathaniel Ford, for the freedom of three of his children. Ford, a former sheriff of Howard County, Missouri, was an 1844 immigrant who brought six slaves from Fayette, Missouri, including the Holmes family. They arrived during the slavery grace period, presumably allowing Ford to keep his slaves for up to three years, until 1847. He kept them much longer, however.

Under pressure from a small but growing abolitionist movement, Ford finally freed Robin Holmes and his wife, Polly, in 1850, but he kept three of their children. Ford argued in court that he had brought the children to Oregon at his own expense when they were too small to do any work, but now that they were older, he was entitled to benefit from their labor.

Holmes, illiterate and raised in a slave culture, demonstrated a great deal of courage in bringing a suit against Ford in a region generally hostile to blacks. Ford, meanwhile, was gaining considerable influence in Oregon—he would serve five terms in the Provisional and Territorial Legislatures. Despite the odds, Holmes prevailed. On July 13, 1853, Judge George Williams, chief justice of the Territorial Supreme Court returned the children to the Holmeses in a ruling that determined once and for all that slavery was unlawful in Oregon.[12] Williams later explained:

> Whether or not slaveholders could carry their slaves into the territories and hold them there as property had become a burning question, and my predecessors in office, for reasons best known to themselves, had

declined to hear the case. This was among the first cases I was called upon to decide. Mr. Ford contended that these colored people were his property in Missouri from which he emigrated, and he had as much right to bring that kind of property to Oregon and hold it here as much as he had to bring his cattle or other property here and hold it as such; but my opinion was, and I so held, that without some positive legislative enactment establishing slavery here, it did not and could not exist in Oregon, and I awarded the colored people their freedom. . . . So far as I know this was the last effort made to hold slaves in Oregon by force of law. There were a great many virulent pro-slavery men in the territory, and this decision, of course, was very distasteful to them.[13]

The ruling against slavery did not translate into enforcement, however, and one of the Holmes children, Mary Jane, remained in the home of a Ford relative until her marriage to another former slave in 1857, at which time Nathaniel Ford was said to demand $700 as compensation for her value as a slave.[14]

The ambivalence toward slavery was also underscored in a handwritten document from Maria Scott, one of two slaves brought to Oregon over the Applegate Trail in 1846 by Richard Linville, who last lived in Missouri. The document is dated August 2, 1851, and addressed to Polk County, Oregon Territory. "Received of Richard Linville the sum of two hundred dollars in full for the money and property which I paid him for my freedom as we then thought I was not free having been a slave of his in the United States and brought to Oregon by him and whereas it is now thought that it will be a free state the aforesaid Richard Linnville has paid me back the aforesaid two hundred dollars which two hundred dollars I promise to pay back to the said Richard Linville if in case it should be a slave state."[15]

Burnett went to great lengths to explain the reasons for many of his actions over the years, yet he could never explain away his policies of exclusion toward African Americans. But he tried. Perhaps the lamest of the many excuses he gave to avoid being blamed for the lash law was this: "Neither myself nor the other members who voted for the original bill are responsible for the objectionable features of the measure because we ourselves corrected the error. I maintain as true this general proposition that a person who commits a mistake, and then corrects it himself, before anyone suffers in consequence of it, deserves commendation rather than censure."[16] As vacuous and slippery as that statement was, it conveniently overlooked that the Legislative Committee made the change at the recommendation of the Executive Committee. This proclivity toward hyperbole, exaggeration, self-justification, and evasiveness— all distinguishing traits of Burnett's life in Missouri and Oregon—would also characterize his experience in California, although on a much larger playing field. Nothing would so blemish Burnett's political career as his hostility toward people of color.

Chapter 10
Considering His Options

Burnett did not seek reelection to the 1845 Legislative Committee, now named the Provisional Legislature, perhaps because he had his eye on a larger prize. On August 18, 1845, he was elected by the Provisional Legislature to a four-year term as the supreme judge for Oregon's Provisional Supreme Court.

Supreme judge was the most lucrative government position in Oregon at the time, with pay of up to $500 annually.[1] The position was first offered to Nathanial Ford, but Ford turned it down. For Burnett, the income no doubt contributed greatly to the comfortable life he was then living.[2]

Incomplete court records indicate most of the judicial work was fairly routine, swearing in new attorneys and dealing with cases of dueling and assault. Perhaps the most prominent of the cases was upholding the conviction of John Watson for attempted murder on September 14, 1845, and sending him to jail for two years.[3]

Burnett resigned in 1846, before his term was completed, to join a law practice in Oregon City in partnership with Asa Lovejoy, a Massachusetts native who joined the 1843 wagon train and ran unsuccessfully for governor in 1847.[4] Burnett's resignation before his term was finished evidently didn't subject him to criticism, as the *Oregon Spectator* praised him for performing his judicial duties in "a most able, faithful and satisfactory manner . . . [and] the bench loses one who was eminently qualified to give it honor."[5]

An early history of the Willamette Valley suggested that Burnett resigned after learning that a new circuit judge, Alonzo Skinner, an 1845 immigrant from Ohio, was being paid more than he was—$800 a year.[6] If true, this is not mentioned in any other Oregon history.

Burnett was generally highly regarded in early Oregon, his status reflected in his selection as the main speaker at the region's first Fourth of

July observance in 1846. Following a thirty-one-gun salute and a procession to Oregon City's Methodist Church, Burnett spoke at length, praising the American form of government as the envy of the world and which "operated like a piece of perfect machinery—harmonious in every part."[7] In years to come, however, he would assess that machinery differently.

Burnett returned to politics in 1848, seeking and winning election to the new Territorial Legislature after Congress gave Oregon territorial status. He received 129 votes, all from Tualatin County.[8] Two months later, however, he resigned. He was revealing himself to be someone who did not feel obligated to fulfill his public responsibilities. It was an attitude he would take with him to California.

Although Burnett was frequently attacked for his leadership of the 1844 Legislative Committee, he never wavered in his insistence that—aside from the exclusion law—the committee's work preserved Oregon's provisional government and paved the way to territorial status. "It is my solemn opinion that the organization [government] could not have been kept under the laws of 1843," he said.[9]

But Burnett's nemesis, William Gray, found nothing to applaud, even though he had benefited from the changes, as he was elected to the new Provisional Legislature in 1845. What seemed to anger him most was that Burnett disregarded the work of the 1843 committee without so much as a nod of appreciation for having organized the initial government.

Burnett did contribute to a much-improved governmental structure for early Oregon. It was unlikely the three-person Executive Committee could have long functioned without fracturing into division and stalemate. Moreover, the new thirteen-member legislature was more representative of the growing population. Providing secure financing was essential for the provisional government to function.

Gray included his frustrated denunciations of Burnett in his *History of Early Oregon*, published in 1870, although Burnett didn't learn of them until eight years later, while living in San Francisco. Despite the lapse in time, the thin-skinned Burnett responded as if Gray had just written his criticisms.

While Burnett had once pledged never to "engage in newspaper controversies or personal squabbles," Gray's criticisms necessitated an exception. "I must depart from my usual course to notice certain charges against me by W. H. Gray," he wrote in his *Recollections*. Taking "notice" involved an extraordinary thirty-eight pages in a chapter titled "Misstatements of W. H. Gray."[10] In those thirty-eight pages, Burnett gave insight into his character to a degree he surely never intended. He came across as boastful, self-important, and defensive, willing to bend the truth to his liking. Gray's criticisms had amounted to a single page.

Gray had written that the Burnett-led changes in the 1843 organic laws "seemed only to mix up and confuse the people, so much so that some doubted the existence of any legal authority in the country." He suggested Burnett had exercised undue influence on other committee members to achieve his aims.

Burnett acknowledged he had ignored the organic laws but said the 1843 committee had accomplished little of any lasting importance. As for influencing other council members, he claimed, "My influence arose from the fact of my qualifications and my good character." One can almost envision him thrusting out his chest as he wrote: "Waldo, McCarver, Gilmore and Keizer had traveled with me across the Plains and had seen me fully tested in that severe school of human nature." He didn't mention that he flunked out after just ten days in that school.

He took particular umbrage at an assertion by Gray that he had emigrated to Oregon "to seek his fortune." Even though Burnett had several times acknowledged his desire to be a wealthy man, he now wrote that by the time he emigrated, he had "ceased to pursue riches, and my only business object was to make a decent living for my family, and pay what I owed." He neglected to mention he had by this time made a sizable fortune in California.

Burnett claimed to never have sought any position in Oregon's provisional government, nor ever asked anyone to vote for him—which was surely not true. He said all his elected and appointed positions were attained "without any serious effort on my part." He went on to boast, "I have been a candidate before the people six times; once in Missouri, twice in Oregon and three times in California, and I was successful in every case." In other words, he both sought office and didn't seek office.[11]

Gray wasn't alone in criticizing the actions of the 1844 Legislative Committee under Burnett's leadership. Jesse Applegate wrote to his brother Lisbon on February 15, 1846, in a letter heavy with sarcasm, that "gentlemen of such high political pretensions" on the Burnett committee "without even examining the tattered bits of paper which they had sworn to support[,] or consulting the people[,] went to work on a Constitution to suit themselves."[12]

Hubert Howe Bancroft, in his comprehensive 1886 *History of Oregon*—much of it written by his colleague Frances Fuller Victor—was among the harshest critics. According to Bancroft, the committee had undertaken "to remodel the organic law itself to an extent amounting to subversion."[13]

While still in Oregon, Burnett also got into an angry exchange of letters with David Hill, who had served with him on the Legislative Committee and cast one of the two votes against Burnett's exclusion law. Hill had also served on the 1843 committee.

In a letter printed in the *Weekly Tribune* in Liberty, Missouri, Burnett quoted Hill as complaining in another Missouri newspaper, the *Boonville Weekly Observer*, that the 1844 committee was dysfunctional. In a stinging rebuke clearly aimed at Burnett, Hill had called the 1844 committee a collection of "broken down merchants . . . or lawyers who could not make a living by their practice and who had sold themselves to the Hudson's Bay Company for the privilege of buying a few goods on credit."[14]

Burnett responded with unrestrained vitriol, calling Hill "a childish old widower upon whose mind nature has bestowed no extravagant gifts, and education has been more sparing." As if that were not insulting enough, Burnett said Hill "had all the vulgar prejudices and low suspicions to be found in the most ignorant minds." He also accused Hill of reneging on his debts to the Hudson's Bay Company.[15]

Burnett also got into a public dispute with Elijah White, the former American Indian agent, over whether Burnett had charged White $10 to testify before the Legislative Committee against a law, supported by Burnett, to ban alcoholic beverages. Burnett said it was White who, as a nonmember, offered to pay $10 to speak, which he was allowed to do. According to Burnett, the money wasn't collected, and he blamed the disagreement on White's "ardent feelings and great ranting."[16]

Burnett usually prevailed in his public spats, at least in the opinion of those whose support counted most to him, especially newspaper editors. Even though Burnett had departed Missouri mired in debt from his multiple business failures, the *Tribune's* editor told readers in an introduction to Burnett's letter concerning Hill that Burnett was "a gentleman well known to the people of Clay County and the state generally, as a man of truth; therefore this letter may be relied upon as correct in everything it relates to."

Burnett used his facility with words to good effect. If he wanted to cajole, he cajoled. If he wanted to dismiss, he dismissed. If he wanted to evade, he evaded. And he wrote a lot of words. His letter to the *Tribune* filled seven columns of type over two days, with three of those columns on the August 15 front page. In his letter, Burnett improbably apologized for not writing more often because of other demands on his time. "I have written a great deal, as much as I could . . . and yet I find my friends complaining I have not written enough." No records have survived of any such complaints.

Burnett's bias against African Americans had its parallel in his attitude toward Chinese, expressed years later in California. He was more charitable toward Native Americans. In perhaps the most poignant passage in his *Recollections*, he referred to the callousness with which settlers treated the native inhabitants. He said the settlers "came, not to establish trade with the Indians, but to take and settle the country exclusively for ourselves. . . . [We] went anywhere we pleased, settled down without any treaty or consultation with the Indians, and occupied our claims without their consent. . . . Every succeeding fall they found the white population about doubled. . . . They instinctively saw annihilation before them."[17]

The American Indian population of the Oregon Country was estimated at about 100,000 in the early 1820s, about the time John McLoughlin took charge of Hudson's Bay Company operations and before the tribes were devastated by malaria and epidemics spread by fur trappers, seamen, and early settlers.[18] The impact was most severe along the lower Columbia River, where entire villages were wiped out.[19] The several Kalapuya bands which occupied the Willamette Valley were diminished to a few thousand at most.[20] Those who remained were too few and too weakened to resist the settlers moving onto their traditional lands.

David Harrelson, a Kalapuya, cited in an interview "reasonable" estimates by others indicating as much as 90 percent of some Kalapuya bands may have been wiped out between 1750 and 1850. But he said they had regained strength and status as members of the Confederated Tribes of the Grand Ronde. Today the Grand Ronde operates the highly popular Spirit Mountain Casino, which opened in western Oregon in 1995. Harrelson, 31, the tribes' cultural resources manager, said the day before our interview a member of the tribe had caught the first salmon at Willamette Falls—using a traditional dipnet—in more than a century. The tribes had only recently received support from the Oregon Department of Fish and Wildlife to resume salmon fishing at the falls on a restricted basis. Lamprey fishing was already

*permitted at certain times of the year. "The falls are the last place with eels in abun-
dance, and it brings tribes from throughout the Northwest, much as it was before the
settlers came," Harrelson said.*[21]

Chapter 11
Those Darned Debts Again

Peter Burnett was not one to be left behind. Although he insisted he was no longer interested in seeking a fortune and was making "a good living" on his Tualatin Valley farm, he nevertheless joined the gold rush to California in 1848.

Once again, old debts motivated him. Paying those debts, Burnett said, was "sacred with me."[1] Burnett had been paying a little at a time from his work in Oregon and "had not the slightest interest in leaving" Oregon. That is, until the major gold discoveries in California.

Whether his debts were the whole story, Burnett's decision to join the gold rush changed his life, as it did tens of thousands of others, and it shaped the future of California itself. He would never return to Oregon.

Gold was discovered at John Augustus Sutter's sawmill on the South Fork of the American River on January 24, 1848. Coincidentally, this discovery occurred a week before Mexico formally surrendered its claim to California, along with much of the rest of the American Southwest, in the Treaty of Guadelupe Hidalgo, which ended the Mexican-American War. The treaty was signed on February 2, 1848.

Oregonians were among the first outside California to learn of the discovery. The news apparently was leaked by a Captain Newell of the brig *Honolulu*, which stopped at Fort Vancouver in July to purchase picks, shovels, and other mining equipment before heading to California. Newell first said the equipment was for coal miners, but revealed the discovery of gold before weighing anchor.[2] "This extraordinary news created the most intense excitement throughout Oregon," Burnett wrote.[3]

The response was immediate. An estimated three thousand Oregon men headed for the gold fields, fully two-thirds of the territory's able-bodied males.[4] Farmers abandoned their crops; workers quit their jobs; pack trains were organized. The *Oregon Spectator* suspended publication for a month because its printers joined the exodus. Even members of the new 1848 Territorial Legislature couldn't resist. Twelve of the twenty-two elected members, Burnett among them, left for California, some failing even to give notice.[5] Lacking a quorum, the legislature was unable to convene until the following year.

Not only were Oregonians among the first outside California to hear about the gold strikes, but they also had the advantage of being closer to the gold fields. While California was just a pack train away for Oregonians, albeit a rugged one, a New Yorker faced one of three options, all of them challenging. One was to travel by ship, a five- to eight-month voyage around Cape Horn. The second was to traverse the Oregon and California trails, a route that was not any faster. The third was to cross the 52 miles of the Isthmus of Panama, cutting months off the trip, but risking accident, sickness, banditry, and exhaustion. Crossing the Isthmus involved a voyage to the eastern coast of Panama—then part of Colombia—followed by a boat on the Chagres River for half the distance, then travel by mule or on foot to the Pacific. On the Pacific side of the isthmus, the traveler would look for another ship for the final leg of the trip to San Francisco. Most miners from the East came by ship, and most sailed around Cape Horn.[6]

President Polk announced the discovery of gold to the country on December 5, 1848, igniting the gold rush. California's nonnative population soared from 8,000 in 1840 to more than 100,000 in 1850, and nearly 400,000 in 1860.[7] By June of 1850, there were 635 abandoned ships in San Francisco Bay, deserted by their gold-seeking crews.[8]

Burnett was skeptical about the significance of the gold discoveries "until I had evidence satisfactory to me." He received confirmation that the discoveries were real and substantial in a letter sent by the former Missouri governor, Lilburn Boggs, then living in California, to his brother-in-law in Oregon, Alphonso Boone.[9] Boggs had survived a serious assassination attempt at his home in Independence, Missouri, on May 6, 1842, that left him near death. He was shot four times in the neck and head; Mormon president Joseph Smith was widely suspected of ordering the assassination.

With no longer any "reasonable cause to doubt" the abundance of gold, Burnett convinced his wife that he should go to California to take advantage of "the only certain opportunity to get out of debt within a reasonable time." He said he made the decision reluctantly, because they had promised one another following their earlier long separation in Missouri and Tennessee they would not again separate. But Burnett considered the abundant gold in California to be "a new and special case . . . and I thought it my duty to make the effort." It apparently didn't give him pause that he had just been elected to the Territorial Legislature—for Burnett, resignation was nothing new. Moreover, President Polk was soon to appoint him to Oregon's first Territorial Supreme Court; Burnett said he didn't learn of the appointment until he was in California. He declined the appointment, again citing the need to "pay my debts."[10]

Looking back on his life, Burnett would say that in California he "succeeded beyond my expectations."[11] But when he left Oregon, he couldn't yet have imagined the circumstances that would enable that success.

Burnett demonstrated once again his ability to persuade, organize, and take charge—this time successfully. He wasn't content to travel as other Oregonians had, loading belongings on the back of a mule and plodding southward into the mountains over a pack trail. Assured by John McLoughlin of the feasibility of wagon travel to California, Burnett went into "the streets of Oregon City" to recruit for a wagon train—much as he'd climbed atop a box on a Missouri sidewalk to recruit emigrants for Oregon. It took just eight days, he said, to recruit 150 travelers, mostly men, with forty-six wagons and ox teams. It was an incredibly short time to convince men to drop everything, leaving family and farms behind. But it demonstrated the powerful lure of gold to people throughout the Willamette Valley. Most who made the trip with Burnett would return after a year or so, many with gold in their pockets.

While Burnett liked to be first at whatever he did, he couldn't be first in the gold fields. But he knew he could be the first to take wagons from Oregon to California by clearing a wagon road through the rugged mountains separating the fast-growing regions. Burnett traveled with two wagons and ox teams, two horses, and six months of provisions, enough to survive the winter if they became trapped by mountain snows. He also carried enough lumber to build a rocker for placer mining. As usual, he had done his homework.[12] He was joined on the trip by his brother-in-law, John Rogers, and a nephew, Horace Burnett, his brother Glen's son. Not surprisingly, Burnett was elected captain of the wagon train, and, on this occasion at least, he would see the job to completion.

The distance from Oregon City to the gold fields in the Sacramento Valley was roughly 500 miles. Burnett had the benefit of two other trails, one known as the Applegate Trail and the other later called the Lassen Cutoff. Burnett had predicted to an acquaintance in Missouri the previous March that the southern

Sign near Tulelake, California, indicating the road developed by Peter Burnett to the California gold fields in 1848. Known as the Burnett Cutoff, it was the first wagon road between Oregon and California. Photo by Deston Nokes.

Oregon portion of the Applegate Trail had great potential as "a wagon way to California."[13] Burnett took as his guide the veteran fur trapper Thomas McKay, son of John McLoughlin's wife, Marguerite.

The Applegate Trail was mapped and crudely developed in 1846 by brothers Jesse and Lindsay Applegate and Levi Scott, an 1844 emigrant from Illinois. It was intended as an alternate route into Oregon to avoid the Columbia River, where Jesse and Lindsay had each lost a son in 1843. A dozen others worked on the trail, among them famed fur trader and trail guide Moses "Black" Harris. The Applegate crew had started from the Willamette Valley, working south across the Calapooya Mountains, through Umpqua Canyon and the Umpqua range, into southern Oregon and the Rogue River Valley. From near present-day Ashland, Oregon, they angled eastward across the northern tip of California into Nevada, where they crossed the arid Black Rock Desert to intersect the California Trail coming south from Fort Hall.

The Burnett Party brought tools to rebuild the most difficult portions of the trail, including through the steep and rugged Umpqua Canyon, where in 1846 the first party of approximately five hundred emigrants to use the Applegate Trail struggled to survive. Only about twenty out of one hundred wagons reached the Willamette Valley.[14] Many were wrecked or abandoned in the Umpqua Canyon, forcing the emigrant families to continue on foot. One man died and was buried in the canyon, and a child was badly burned and disfigured.[15] At least a dozen other settlers died at points along the trail. Rescue parties sent from the Willamette Valley saved many others.

One of those who recalled the struggle through the canyon in 1846 was J. Quinton Thornton, who became a fierce critic of the Applegates for over-promising the ease of travel. Thornton and his wife waded for 3 miles in the canyon's icy stream, fording the stream thirty-nine times, while slogging amid "a great many cattle that had perished and were lodged against and among the rocks." Rain was constant. Thornton feared losing his wife when she temporar-ily lost her sight and collapsed while wading in the freezing waist-deep water.[16]

The last of the Applegate emigrants reached the Willamette Valley after Christmas, two months later than those who took the Columbia River route. The Applegate emigrants had traveled nearly 1,000 miles from Fort Hall, while the Columbia route, including a new emigrant road over Mt. Hood called the Barlow Trail, was about 700 miles.

Burnett didn't mention whether he encountered any appreciable difficulty in the canyon, although it couldn't have been easy. The Applegate Trail, also known as the southern route, would later become an acceptable and well-used trail into Oregon.

The Burnett wagons followed the Applegate Trail from the Willamette Valley as far as Klamath Lake near the Oregon-California border, where they turned south near present-day Klamath Falls, breaking their own trail as they went. A sign near trail ruts south of Tulelake, California, identifies them as a portion of the Burnett Cutoff, also called the Burnett Road. Clearly visible on the western horizon is the snow-covered peak of 14,179-foot Mt. Shasta in the southern Cascade Mountains. The road steers east of the lava beds where about fifty Modoc Indians, led by Captain Jack, would fight off the US Army for months in the 1872–73 Modoc War until finally killed and captured.

"Watch out for rattlesnakes!" warned Erin Stedman, a clerk at Don's Deli in Tulelake, California, where my son, Deston, and I stopped to ask directions to the Burnett trail sign. I wanted a picture of this sign for my book, as there are few signs or anything else with Burnett's name on it. We had driven for a half hour up and down California Highway 139 in a fruitless search for the sign. We'd passed the entrance to the Tulelake encampment, where Japanese Americans were interned during World War II, but no Burnett sign. We hadn't gone far enough, Stedman said. "Look for the tree with some shoes hanging from the branches" (she didn't know why there were shoes hanging from the branches). Following her directions, we found the tree, although it was shoeless this day, and behind it, the sign. The sign also told us there were trail ruts nearby. Warned of the snakes—thank you, Ms.

Stedman—Deston plunged his brand-new Lexus down a sagebrush-clogged dusty dirt road until we found the ruts, clearly marked with a sign that also quoted from Burnett's Recollections: *"We travelled twenty miles toward a heavy body of timber in the distance (Timber Mountain). Peter Burnett Oct. 1848."*

Their path took them across a dry prairie and into a forest of "beautiful pines"—the giant orange-barked ponderosas that thrive in the high desert, although extensive logging has greatly thinned the once-thick forests. Water and game were scarce, and on one occasion their only fresh meat was a large badger, which they roasted. The badger's meat inspired Burnett to lapse into a claimed expertise in his *Recollections* on exotic animal body parts that made especially good eating. Among them were "the foot of the badger, the tail of the beaver, the ear of the hog," and "the foot of the elephant." He had never actually eaten an elephant's foot, but he knew of its delectability from good authority.[17]

The party encountered a lone Native American on the trail and surrounded him at rifle point.[18] The native was "about sixty years old, was dressed in buckskin, had long coarse hair and dim eyes and his teeth were worn down to the gums," clearly not a threat to anyone. Harmless as he seemed, however, one of the men proposed killing him. Burnett talked him out of it, suggesting that if he wanted to kill him, he should do so in a fair fight, which "he promptly declined." They let the man go. But in a comment typical of whites' feelings of superiority, Burnett added, "We considered this mode of treating the Indians the most judicious, as it displayed our power and at the same time our magnanimity."[19]

The wagons continued on their new trail for about 50 miles when, near the Pit River, they encountered "to our utter surprise and astonishment" an unknown trail—the Lassen Cutoff—which they turned to follow for the next 150 miles.

The cutoff was a project of Danish-born Peter Lassen, who in 1844 had become a Mexican citizen and received a land grant of 22,000 acres in Tehama County in the northern Sacramento Valley. Lassen was leading a small group of emigrants in ten wagons in a roughly southwest direction at the same time as Burnett approached from the north. The Lassen Party emigrants had left the California Trail in Nevada, following the Applegate Trail into California before turning southwest along the North Fork of the Pit River, with Lassen breaking new ground as they went. He was leading them to his ranch on Deer Creek,

Wagon ruts near Tulelake on the Burnett Cutoff to California. The sign quotes Burnett's diary: "We traveled over prairie some twenty miles toward body of timber in the distance." Photo by the author.

near its confluence with the Sacramento River.[20] He strategized that the emigrants might settle in a town he was planning called Benton City.[21] But while Lassen touted his cutoff as a shortcut, he hadn't previously explored it, which soon became evident.[22]

The Burnett wagons followed Lassen through mountains, which Burnett identified as the Sierra Nevada, but were actually the southernmost spur of the Cascades, which includes 10,400-foot Mt. Lassen, or Lassen Peak, as it's named today. They crossed the northern slopes of Mt. Lassen as they turned southwest toward the Sacramento Valley. Moving at a faster pace, Burnett caught up with the Lassen Party in a pine forest. By this time, half of Lassen's wagons had been abandoned and the other half converted into carts to more easily maneuver through the heavy timber. Burnett said members of the Lassen Party were near starving, having been "without any bread for more than a month."

Burnett gave them food and invited them to follow him the rest of the way. According to Burnett, sixty to seventy axe-wielding men—or ten to fifteen, mentioned in an earlier correspondence—cut a road through the timber, working nearly as fast as the wagons could follow. Again water was scarce, and they tied their oxen to wagon wheels at night to keep them from wandering off.

One of the most difficult challenges was getting past a barrier on a narrow ridge near a place known as Steep Hollow. Burnett described the challenge of navigating this ridge. "I came to an immense mass of rock, which completely straddled the narrow ridge and totally obstructed the way. This huge obstacle could not be removed in time, and the wagons had to pass around it. They were let down the left side of the ridge by ropes to a bench, then passed along the bench to a point beyond the rock, and were then drawn up to the top of the ridge again by double teams."[23]

The wagons finally emerged from the forest on a bluff overlooking what Burnett described as "the magnificent valley of the Sacramento, gleaming in the bright and genial sunshine" with "the grand blue outlines of the Coast Range" in the distance. Following a difficult descent into the valley, the party began to break up, with some wagons rushing ahead, impatient to reach the gold fields. Burnett and others rested at Lassen's ranch, south of present-day Red Bluff, near the small town of Vine. There is nothing left of the ranch buildings today, but at the time the ranch was the northernmost white settlement in California.[24] After resting—he didn't say how long—Burnett would have followed established wagon roads south through the Sacramento Valley for another 200 miles to the gold fields on the western slopes of the Sierras north and east of present-day Sacramento.

The Burnett wagons had traveled 500 miles in little more than a month. Typical of Burnett, he sought public recognition, announcing his arrival in a letter to the *California Star* in San Francisco on November 8 and printed on December 2. "I am one of the wagon party just arrived from Oregon. . . . You are no doubt aware of the fact that our wagons were the first ever brought through from Oregon to this country."[25] He predicted many more wagons would follow. Burnett had an eye on winning support for his future aspirations, always looking for the next opportunity.

Burnett had an agenda.

Chapter 12
Lusting for California Gold

It was a scene Peter Burnett would not forget: his first look at a mining camp from a hillside overlooking Long Bar on the Yuba River on November 5, 1848.[1] "Below, glowing in the hot sunshine, and in the narrow valley of the lovely and rapid stream, we saw the canvas tents and the cloth shanties of the miners. . . . Here we promptly decided to pitch our tent."[2]

Burnett counted eighty men, three women, and five children in the camp, although it would soon grow to hundreds. Long Bar was in Yuba County, about 60 miles north of today's Sacramento, and one of many productive mining sites on rivers and streams in the Sacramento Valley. An 1850 sketch revealed Long Bar as an island in the middle of the narrow river. Mining activity appeared concentrated on the long, sloping riverbank on the west side of the river.[3]

No one paid much attention as Burnett and his companions descended the hillside in their wagon—would-be miners arrived daily. That first evening, Burnett introduced himself and found old acquaintances from both Missouri and Oregon. Among the Missourians were John P. Long, for whom the bar was named, and his brother Willis.[4] The Longs were related to Burnett by marriage— another brother married Burnett's youngest sister, Mary. The connections Burnett was making with old friends would serve him well in California politics.

With his brother-in-law and nephew, Burnett purchased a claim for $300, to be paid in gold dust at the going rate of $16 an ounce. Their claim extended 20 feet along the river and 50 feet back. After assembling their rocker box, they began mining. Working as a team, Burnett shoveled promising sand and gravel onto a zinc sieve atop the box, while Rogers dumped buckets of water over the shoveled material and Horace rocked the device back and forth. If all worked as planned, gold dust and small nuggets would wash through the sieve and sink to the bottom of the box. The lighter sand and gravel washed out the lower open end of the box.

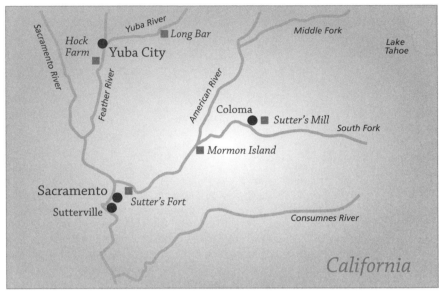

Mining areas around Sacramento. Gold was discovered in 1848 at Sutter's Mill at Coloma, on the south fork of the American River. Courtesy of Stephan Smith, Smith Creative Group, Portland.

Burnett said their claim proved its worth, daily producing $20 of gold apiece, and they soon paid off the claim. But it was back-breaking and tedious work. Recalled Burnett: "We rose by daybreak, ate our breakfast by sunrise, worked until noon; then took dinner, went to work again about half-past twelve, quit work at sundown, and slept under a canvas tent on the hard ground."[5] They arrived at the end of each day exhausted. Burnett lasted six weeks. There was more money for less work elsewhere.

Burnett left his claim on December 19, joined by six other unnamed miners, presumably including John and Horace. Again, Burnett cited his debts as the reason for what amounted to another resignation from a job not finished. "It would take me many long years to make enough in the mines to pay my debts," he explained.[6]

Burnett intended to go to San Francisco to set up a law practice but stopped en route at Sutter's Fort, the inland fortress and trading post built by John Sutter, at whose nearby sawmill gold was discovered months earlier. And at Sutter's Fort Burnett stayed, his fortunes about to change.

When Burnett arrived to begin his new adventure, California was in the midst of an uneasy transition from Mexican rule to an undefined status under the

American flag. Mexico surrendered its control in 1846 over what it knew as Alta California, a vast area extending east from the Pacific, across the Sierra Nevada, to present-day Utah. The region had been under Mexican rule since Mexico won its independence from Spain in 1821.

But Mexico had never seemed to know what to do with the sparsely settled region. The late Kevin Starr, prominent California historian, wrote that the last decade of Mexican rule "was a confusion of revolution, counterrevolution, graft, spoliation, and social disintegration" as Northern and Southern factions struggled for supremacy.[7]

Whereas land in Oregon had been essentially free for the taking—after Native American tribes were pushed aside—this was not the case in California. Under Spanish and Mexican rule, large tracts of the best land had been ceded to favored recipients. Much of these so-called "ranchos" remained undeveloped and unoccupied but were still off-limits to settlers. The Treaty of Guadelupe Hidalgo upheld the validity of these grants. The treaty also gave Mexican residents a year to decide whether to remain and become US citizens—many did.

Another difficulty facing Americans were Mexican laws. Although the Mexican government was gone, its laws and customs remained in place. These included the alcalde system—confusing to Americans—under which municipal governments were administered. An alcalde was roughly equivalent to a mayor, but with greatly expanded powers, combining the roles of judge, jury, and chief executive. Laws were still written in Spanish, a language unknown to most newly arriving Americans.

During the period from the conquest in 1846 to statehood in 1849, California was loosely administered by a series of appointed American military governors who enforced the Mexican laws and otherwise left things pretty much as they found them. This led to rising discontent that there was not yet an accountable American government administering American laws. The situation was wide open for the ambitions of men such as Peter Burnett.

Burnett arrived at Sutter's Fort on December 21, 1848, where he once again met up with old friends, among them Dr. William M. Carpenter, who Burnett learned was making $600 a week treating the injuries and illnesses of the inexperienced miners. Convinced there was ample room on what was fast becoming a gold-fueled gravy train, Burnett decided to stay. He turned again to lawyering, moving in with Carpenter and splitting the rent. They slept in the same bed, and ate meals prepared by workers in the fort's kitchen. Burnett cut wood and made the fire; Carpenter swept the office and made the bed. The arrangement worked out well. A schematic of the fort's layout identifies a doctor's office next door to Sutter's office in the two-story administrative building in the center of the fort complex. The shared doctor's office was ideally located for Burnett to become acquainted with the Sutters.

Being in the right place at the right time seemed always to apply to Burnett. He had been at the fort only a few days when he was approached by Sutter's son, John Augustus—recently arrived from Switzerland—with an offer Burnett couldn't refuse. Young Sutter, known as August, said he needed someone to handle his finances, and Burnett came recommended "as a man of highly respectable character." August wanted Burnett to help him execute a scheme to pay off his father's substantial debts before his creditors seized Sutter's land holdings and other assets, including Sutter's Fort. It's of no little irony that one man's debts enabled Burnett to be relieved of his.

John Sutter bore many similarities to Peter Burnett. Both had emerged from humble origins with limited education. They shared a mutual hunger for prestige and wealth. Like Burnett, Sutter struggled with debt, and, like Burnett, he seemed unable to refrain from sabotaging his substantial achievements.

The two men also spoke with silver tongues and were able to speak with authority, although their words too often rang hollow. One biographer described the elder Sutter as "a born raconteur."[8] But the two men may have been too much alike, relating like oil to water. Sutter would develop a strong dislike for Burnett. A year after they first met, they would run against one another for governor of California.

There were also important differences. Sutter was impetuous and careless in his decision-making, and lacked Burnett's more thoughtful understanding of the events shaping the American West. Also, while Burnett appeared genuinely motivated by patriotism—along with acquiring wealth and prestige—Sutter seemed interested only in wealth and prestige. His actions showed it didn't matter to him whose flag flew over California.

Sutter was born in 1803 in Kanden, Germany, a village near the Swiss border, where his father and grandfather worked as foremen in a paper mill. He and his wife, Annette Dubeld, would have four children. John Augustus Sutter Jr. was the eldest, born October 25, 1826, only a day following his parents' wedding, in what must have been a major scandal.[9] In business for himself in a dry

Sutter's Fort in Sacramento. Peter Burnett opened a law office here in 1848 after tiring of gold mining. Working with John Sutter Jr., he became wealthy selling property for the new Sacramento City in 1849, much to the displeasure of the elder John Sutter, who favored a town he named Sutterville. Photo by the author.

goods store, Sutter quickly fell into debt, largely because of his affinity for a flamboyant lifestyle. He fled to the United States in 1834 ahead of a possible date with debtor's prison, leaving his family behind.

In America, Sutter reinvented himself. Instead of being from a working-class family, he claimed to be the son of a Lutheran clergyman. Rather than being poorly educated, he claimed to be a graduate of a prominent military academy at Thun, Switzerland, where one of his classmates was Louis-Napoleon Bonaparte, the future French emperor. Rather than running a business into the ground, he became Captain John Sutter, veteran of the elite Swiss Guard of the French king Charles X.[10]

Sutter arrived in California in 1838 after a circuitous route that took him from Missouri to Oregon to the Sandwich Islands. There, he borrowed heavily to finance a planned colony in California, over which he could rule. A letter from the US consul in Honolulu, James C. Jones, helped Sutter gain an audience with the Mexican governor of California, Juan Bautista Alvarado, who bought into his scheme. The attraction for Governor Alvarado was that Sutter's project would help secure Mexico's authority over more of the region.[11]

Sutter picked a site for what he would call New Helvetia in the Sacramento Valley at the confluence of the American and Sacramento Rivers, 80 miles

John Sutter, originally from
Germany and Switzerland,
established Sutter's Fort in
1839 and ruled on behalf
of Mexico over much of the
Sacramento Valley. Gold was
discovered during construction
of his mill on the South Fork
of the American River in 1848,
igniting the California gold
rush. Courtesy of the California
History Room, California State
Library, Sacramento.

inland from San Francisco, at the time a small village called Yerba Buena.
To get started, he purchased still more goods on credit, including several
vessels.

In developments that would later benefit Burnett, Governor Alvarado on
June 18, 1841, gave Sutter a land grant in the Sacramento Valley totaling 11
leagues, or about 38 square miles.[12] Sutter received an additional grant of 22
leagues on February 5, 1845, from another governor, Manuel Micheltorena, as
a reward for military service. Micheltorena also commissioned him a captain
in the Mexican Army. Both land grants would later be challenged in American
courts, but that would be years in the future.

Sutter became a Mexican citizen in 1840. More importantly to Sutter,
Governor Alvarado appointed him Mexico's official representative in the
Sacramento Valley with the title of Representante del Gobierno en las
Fronteras del Norte y Encargado de la Justicia, responsible for enforcing "all
the laws of the country." It gave Sutter, at age 37, the power and authority to
which he had long aspired—"the whole country stood in awe of me."[13]

Sutter's manner of dress was distinctive, to say the least, for someone living
in the rugged California interior. A visitor to Sutter's Fort found him "dressed in
frock coat, pantaloons, and cap of blue, carrying a gold-headed Malacca [cane]

in hand." In such attire, the visitor said, "you would rather suppose him pre-pared for a saunter on the boulevards."[14]

For much of the 1840s, Sutter ruled over 225 square miles from his headquar-ters at Sutter's Fort. The expansive fort was built over four years using laborers from the dominant tribes in the region, notably the Nisenan, also known as the Southern Maidu, and the Miwok. He at one time employed as many as six hun-dred Nisenan, who planted and harvested his crops and tended his large herd of cattle. They also served as soldiers in his "army." Sutter insisted he treated his workers well, although the evidence suggests otherwise.[15]

The fort's outer walls were built of adobe brick nearly 3 feet thick and cov-ered with white stucco, enclosing a 5-acre site in which Sutter had laid out a self-contained town, with administrative offices, living quarters, an armory, blanket factory, barrel maker, workshops, large kitchen, and, eventually, a small hotel. Sutter had purchased two brass cannons in Hawaii and placed them atop two-level bastions at the southeast and northwest corners, with prison cells below.[16] The cannons proved useful for intimidating troublesome tribes—Sutter called them "great reputation builders."

The only remaining building of the original fort is the two-story building that once housed Sutter's office and living quarters. The office and the adjacent doctor's office are on the second floor, opening onto a large room, probably used for meetings and dining. The building was centrally located within the fort's walls and is the first thing a visitor sees today when entering through the rebuilt front gate from Sacramento's L Street. The other structures were arrayed around the inside of the walls. The fort, which had fallen into serious disrepair, was reconstructed as a community project in 1893 and is maintained as Sutter's Fort State Historic Park. Downtown Sacramento has grown up around it.

One of Sutter's most fateful and foolish acquisitions was his purchase in 1841 of Fort Ross, the Russian fur-trading settlement established in 1812 at Bodega Bay on the California coast. He committed to pay the Russian American Fur Company $32,000 for land, buildings, crops, and livestock, including 1,700 cattle, 900 horses, and 900 sheep. Also in the deal was a 20-ton schooner. Sutter evidently was not interested in the large chapel bell, cast in St. Petersburg, which rang out hourly and was left at Fort Ross.[17]

Sutter considered Fort Ross a great bargain. But the Russians set rigid con-ditions—payment was to be made in wheat and other produce over a four-year period. Sutter put up New Helvetia and his other holdings as security, but when his fields produced far less than what was needed to make the scheduled payments, it didn't take long for him to fall seriously in arrears.[18]

A skilled New Jersey–born carpenter, 33-year-old James Marshall, changed everything, not just for Sutter but for California as well. When Marshall appeared at Sutter's Fort in 1845, after some time in Oregon, Sutter hired him to build his long-desired sawmill on the South Fork of the American River at Coloma, 50 miles to the northeast. While inspecting a mill race on January 24, 1848, Marshall spotted "shining yellow metal at the bottom of the race."[19] After testing the metal, Sutter and Marshall knew they had discovered gold.

Sutter helped to spread the word before he had done much about it. He naively asked his construction workers to keep the discovery secret for six weeks until the mill was finished. The workers turned out to be more interested in gold than the mill—many were former members of the Mormon Battalion, which fought in the war with Mexico—and they deserted Sutter almost overnight. "Everybody left from the clerk to the cook," he later complained.[20]

One might have thought Sutter would come away from the discovery a rich man: debts paid, set for life. But while the discovery of gold at his mill, and the other discoveries that soon followed, lured tens of thousands of gold seekers, and propelled California into explosive growth and a path toward statehood, it proved a disaster for Sutter. He failed to capitalize on the opportunity to sell supplies to the newcomers, allowing others to get ahead of him. He lost $25,000 on the unfinished mill alone.[21]

August Sutter arrived at the fort in the summer of 1848 amid his father's financial crisis. Father and son hadn't seen each other in fifteen years, since the elder Sutter left—or abandoned—his wife and children in Switzerland. August was just 21.

Writing years later, August recalled that while stopping over in San Francisco, he "heard some very strange and contradictory rumors" about his father. "Some said he was the richest man on earth and did not know himself his [own] wealth; others on the contrary told me in confidence that my father on account of his dreadfully loose and careless way of doing every business transaction was on the brink of ruin . . . surrounded by a parcel of rogues and immoral men."[22]

August was soon to learn that his father was $19,000 in debt to the Russians for Fort Ross and hadn't made a payment in three years. The Russians had initiated legal proceedings, threatening New Helvetia with foreclosure. They didn't want Fort Ross returned, but they wanted their money.

By one estimate, Sutter's combined debts totaled $80,000.[23] His inability to focus on his financial difficulties was compromised by bouts of drunkenness. Historians have had little sympathy for Sutter's plight. Bancroft, in his *History of California*, wrote that Sutter "would perhaps have bought anything at any price if it could be obtained on credit."[24] Moreover, the Sutter holdings hadn't been maintained. Sutter's Fort was falling apart, described in 1849 as "a decaying adobe structure surrounded by mounds of whiskey, champagne and beer bottles left by the miners who congregated there."[25] Sutter was then making his home at Hock Farm, 20 miles to the north on the Feather River, where he maintained a large herd of cattle.

The Sutters—father and son—devised a strategy to keep New Helvetia out of the hands of the Russians. Sutter transferred title to his properties to his son for $50,000, although no money changed hands. The assets included the 11 leagues from the Mexican grant in the Sacramento Valley, the Fort Ross properties amounting to another 6 leagues, the sawmill, a square mile of land at Coloma, and a lot in San Francisco. Other property yielded to August included 1,500 horses, 50 mules, 600 cattle, 20 saddles and bridles, and Sutter's schooner, named the *Sacramento*.[26] The maneuver was of dubious legality—August said years later he knew it was "an illegal act"—but it bought the Sutters time. It also created a golden opportunity—pun intended—for Burnett.[27]

August had possession of his debt-strapped father's extensive properties, but he lacked the experience to manage them. August needed legal advice and offered the newly arrived Burnett a position as his attorney and agent, for which he would be handsomely compensated. He also had a major project in mind. Gold miners were descending on the region by the thousands. They needed tools, food, and supplies of all kinds, along with housing for those occasions when high water and winter cold shut down mining activity for weeks, even months, at a time.

Encouraged by a scheming newcomer from New York, Samuel Brannan, August developed plans for a new inland port city called Sacramento at the confluence of the Sacramento and American Rivers, immediately south of the fort. The elder Sutter, however, had already developed competing plans for a town called Sutterville, 3 miles farther south. Sacramento had the advantage of being better situated for a port, but it was prone to flooding; Sutterville was on higher ground.

August offered Burnett one-fourth of the gross proceeds to sell land in Sacramento.[28] We can't know what conversations might have preceded this attractive offer. But they might well have been one-sided in Burnett's favor. The inexperienced young Sutter was barely out of his teens and newly arrived from Switzerland, while the experienced Burnett was, when he wanted to be, the consummate glib-tongued hustler.

August instructed Burnett to sell land for Sacramento "at such prices as he . . . may think right." According to Burnett, "I was to attend to all of his law business of every kind, sell the lots in Sacramento City, and collect the purchase money."

The agreement dated December 30, 1848, brought August and Burnett together in a joint venture that succeeded in establishing the new Sacramento City—whose explosive growth over the next few years surely exceeded the expectations of either man. Of the two, however, only Burnett would come away with any lasting benefit.

"They don't much like him at the [California State] Indian Museum," said Kyle Floyd, working for the Friends of Sutter's Fort bookstore and souvenir shop in the fort complex. Floyd, a student at Sacramento State College, didn't recognize Burnett's name until reminded he was the state's first governor and once lived at the fort. He recalled with disgust hearing that Burnett as governor had once forecast "a war of extermination" against California's Native American population.

Chapter 13
Sutter
"THEY . . . ATE MY GOOD INDIANS!"

While working his Yuba River claim, Burnett had sometimes stayed at the nearby ranch of Michael Nye, whom he'd known in Missouri. Nye's wife, Harriet, was a survivor of the 1846–47 Donner Party tragedy. Burnett also met two other Donner Party survivors, William M. Foster and Foster's wife, Sarah, who was Harriet Nye's sister. All had tragic stories to tell, which they shared with Burnett.

William Foster had accidentally shot and killed Harriet's first husband, William Pike, weeks before the Donner Party became stranded. The shooting occurred along the Truckee River when Foster's six-shooter discharged, striking Pike in the back; he died within the hour.[1] Harriet was just eighteen. Following their rescue months later from Donner Pass, she went to live with the Fosters until she met Nye, an 1841 immigrant.[2]

The Fosters' only child had died at Donner Pass, where Harriet lost one of her two children. Harriet had been witness to unspeakable events. "For hour after hour, I would listen in silence to her sad narrative," Burnett recalled.[3] He later met and became friends with another Donner survivor, William H. Eddy, who lost his wife and three children. Burnett and Eddy also discussed the tragedy, although Burnett didn't mention whether the unpleasant subject of Eddy's cannibalism came up—Eddy was among those who survived by eating the remains of others.[4] "It was a terrible struggle for existence," Burnett said.[5]

The Donner Party had organized as thirty-two California-bound emigrants, most from Illinois, under the leadership of brothers George and Jacob Donner, farmers from Springfield, and also Irish-born James F. Reed. The party of nine wagons left Springfield in May for Independence, Missouri, where they joined a larger group of settlers with sixty-seven wagons, led by William H. Russell.[6] The size of wagon trains was constantly in flux, with wagons leaving and joining.

After crossing the Continental Divide, the Donner-Reeds took their wagons on the new and untried Hastings Cutoff toward California. As happened on many wagon trains, other wagons dispersed in different directions. Wagons led by former Missouri governor Lilburn Boggs set out on the established California Trail. Some of this group left Boggs in Nevada to turn onto the Applegate Trail, also new and untried, into southern Oregon. Still others proceeded down the Columbia River route to Oregon City. Peter Burnett's brothers and their families were in this group.[7]

A dozen wagons joined the Donner-Reeds on the Hastings Cutoff, raising the number to eighty-seven emigrants in twenty-three wagons. Other wagons, including forty wagons of an entirely different wagon train, the Harlan-Young Company, named for George Harlan and Samuel Young, went ahead on the cutoff. William Russell and a few companions left their wagons and traveled the cutoff on mules.

The cutoff was a project of Lansford W. Hastings, a promoter and land speculator from Ohio, who assured the emigrants his cutoff would save them 200 miles by passing south of Fort Hall through present-day Utah. Both the Donner-Reeds, on the cutoff, and the Boggs Party, on the California Trail, aimed toward the same Truckee Pass crossing through the Sierra Nevada into California. The since-renamed Donner Pass has a peak elevation of 7,095 feet and was accessible by wagons, so long as the emigrants beat the winter snows.

Hastings had traveled with the 1842 Elijah White Party to Oregon, where he was employed by John McLoughlin as land agent for Oregon City.[8] He left Oregon after a year and rode overland to California and Sutter's Fort in 1843, signing on to the ambitions of John Sutter and Samuel Brannan. His plan for a cutoff across Utah was one piece of a strategy by the three men to make money from the anticipated arrival of thousands of new settlers. Sutter made Hastings his land agent, responsible for sales in Sutterville. Hastings and John Bidwell, also working for Sutter, laid out the town.[9] Sutter gave Hastings a half square mile of riverfront land, which could have made Hastings a rich man if Sutterville succeeded—it didn't.[10]

Hastings had returned east in 1844 to promote emigration to California by writing a misleading and inaccurate manual, *Emigrants' Guide to Oregon and California*, which became the travel atlas for many emigrants, including the Donner Party.[11] The widely read guide was short on directions but long on promise for California, while dismissing prospects in Oregon.

Among Hastings's wild claims was that the Sierra Nevada posed little difficulty for wagons. "Wagons can be taken as readily from Fort Hall to the bay of St. Francisco, as they can, from the States to Fort Hall." Conversely, he said, travel to Oregon was far more difficult with scant reward at the end. "From Fort Hall to the Pacific, by the Oregon route, a distance of about eight hundred miles, there is but one continued succession of high mountains, stupendous cliffs, and deep, frightful caverns, with an occasional limited valley."[12] Hastings returned to California in 1845.

To lure emigrants to his cutoff, the 27-year-old Hastings rode on horseback in May 1846 to Fort Bridger, a small fur-trading post on Wyoming's Green River, to intercept the wagon trains. He more or less followed in reverse the trail he would propose, following the California Trail for part of the journey before turning southeast across the Great Salt Desert of the future Utah and then north through the Wasatch Mountains to Fort Bridger. The cutoff didn't win a vote of confidence from James Clyman, the well-known trapper and frontiersman who rode with Hastings. Clyman described the salt desert as "a boundless salt plain without vegitaton . . . and covered in many places three inches deep with pure white salt." There were long stretches of 20 miles or more without water. "My belief is that it [is] verry little nearer and not so good a road as that by Fort Hall," Clyman said.[13]

From Fort Bridger, Hastings rode east along the Oregon Trail, "stopping to sing the praises of his new cutoff to each company of wagons he encountered." He encouraged those who would follow him, including the Donner-Reeds, to gather at Fort Bridger.[14] But when the Donner-Reeds reached Fort Bridger, they discovered that Hastings had departed eleven days earlier with the Harlan-Young wagons. He left instructions for the Donner-Reeds and other late arrivers to follow.

While most in the Donner group were eager to take the cutoff, one who was highly skeptical about following such vague directions was Tamsen Donner, George Donner's wife. "She was gloomy, sad, and dispirited . . . that her husband and others could think for a moment of leaving the old road and confide in the statement of a man of whom they knew nothing, but who was probably some selfish adventurer."[15] Tamsen Donner's reservations would prove well founded, tragically so.

Heinrich Lienhard, a Swiss-born emigrant who was also lured to take the cutoff, later called it not a shortcut, but the "Hastings Longtripp." Lienhard said it took nearly a week longer to reach California than those on the established trail.[16] Lienhard was one of the so-called "five German boys" who traveled separately and, like so many others, later went to work for Sutter.[17]

The cutoff led southwest from Fort Bridger through the rugged Wasatch Mountains to the Salt Lake Valley, passed south of the Great Salt Lake, and continued across the 80-mile-wide salt desert into Nevada to connect with the California Trail and the rest of the journey to Truckee Pass. The distance from Fort Bridger to the Great Salt Lake was 118 miles, with another 500 miles to the California Trail. In a letter sent July 31, the day the party left Fort Bridger, an enthusiastic Reed said the cutoff was 400 miles shorter than the Fort Hall route, a greater savings in distance than even Hastings claimed.[18] Reed's goal was to reach Sutter's Fort in seven weeks.[19]

As promised, Hastings left notes along the way with directions for the Donner-Reeds. But one note found "sticking to the top of sagebrush" near the entrance to Weber Canyon, the expected route, signaled a fateful detour.[20] The canyon led steeply downward through the Wasatch Mountains into the Salt Lake Valley. Hastings urged the Donner-Reeds to find a different route into the valley. A 5-mile section of Weber Canyon was said to be especially perilous, described by Lienhard as "a deep cleft through which the water roared and foamed over the rocks." He would later tell how the five German boys had taken their four wagons through one at a time.

> In places we unhitched from the wagon all the oxen except the wheel-yoke, then we strained at both hind wheels, one drove, and the rest steadied the wagon; we then slid rapidly down into the foaming water, hitched the loose oxen again to the wagon and took it directly down the foaming riverbed, full of great boulders, on account of which the wagon quickly lurched from one side to the other; now we had to turn the wheels by the spokes, then again hold back with all the strength we had, lest it sweep upon a low lying rock and smash itself to pieces. In going back for each wagon we had to be very careful lest we lose our footing on the slippery rocks under the water and ourselves be swept down the rapid, foaming torrent.[21]

Hastings recommended another route through the mountains, which was also difficult and cost the Donner-Reeds a great deal of time. Wielding axes and shovels, the emigrants built their own wagon road down steep and forested hillsides, finally emerging into the Salt Lake Valley on August 22. It took eighteen days to travel 30 miles.[22]

It seems reasonable to speculate that Hastings, discovering that Weber Canyon would not do for a major emigration, was using the Donner-Reeds to explore an easier route. Indeed, the road that the Donner Party did locate, and labored to build, was used during the major Mormon emigration in 1850.[23] According to the late historian J. Roderick Korn, the Mormons were grateful to discover that "the Donners had found the best, if not the only route for crossing the Wasatch along the general line they adopted."[24]

The long delay in the mountains was compounded by impossibly slow going in the mudlike consistency of the salt desert south of the Great Salt Lake. Wagon wheels shrunk and lost their rims in the dry climate; wagons were abandoned, cattle and oxen dead of thirst or stolen or killed by harassing Paiute tribesmen. Reed alone lost nine yoke of oxen.[25]

The Donner-Reed wagons finally intersected the California Trail about 7 miles southwest of today's Elko, Nevada. The Harlan-Young wagons reached the same point eighteen days earlier, time enough to cross Truckee Pass ahead of the winter blizzards. Lienhard, with the five German boys, also beat the snow, crossing on October 4.[26] Lilburn Boggs, on the established trail, crossed even earlier. Boggs wrote later that the most difficult challenge occurred after reaching the Truckee Pass summit. He said it took twelve to fifteen days to cross more than 100 miles of "prodigious steep and rocky mountains" before reaching the nearest settlement, known as Johnson's Ranch.[27]

Having endured lengthy delays, some of their own doing, most of the Donner-Reed wagons finally reached Truckee Lake—now Donner Lake—at the foot of Truckee Pass—now Donner Pass—on October 30.[28] They decided to rest a day before trying to cross, a costly delay. Their first attempt on October 31 failed. Ten feet of snow already blocked the pass, and more was coming. Winter was upon them.[29]

Realizing their plight, and perilously low on food, the party sent two men, Charles Stanton and William McCutcheon, on horseback across the mountains to Sutter's Fort for help. James Reed had already gone ahead, no longer traveling with the party. He had been expelled after fatally stabbing another emigrant, John Snyder, during a fight along the Humboldt River on October 5.[30] Reed's wife, Margaret, and their five children stayed with the Donners and would become stranded with the rest.

John Sutter, who for all his faults seldom, if ever, failed to respond to a cry for help from struggling emigrants, sent a rescue party that included Stanton and two of Sutter's Native American cowhands, Lewis and Salvadore, along with seven provision-laden mules.[31] When they reached the stranded emigrants, the rescue party found them already near starvation. Sutter's men remained with the party, a decision that would cost them their lives in a most unkind manner.

The emigrants built three cabins near the lake to await a thaw they hoped would come soon, but wouldn't for months. But George and Jacob Donner, who had fallen behind when one of their wagons overturned, were alerted by a rider to the heavy snow ahead, and stopped 8 miles from Truckee Lake at Alder Creek Canyon, still deceptively free of snow.[32]

George and Jacob built what was described as "a crude shelter" for each of their families. But they picked a location in a clearing rather than near trees, not anticipating the blizzards that would keep them stranded for months. They would be forced to expend scarce energy trudging through deep snows to find fuel.[33] By the end of November, snow at Alder Creek exceeded 6 feet, a depth confirmed by the height of the stumps of trees cut for firewood.[34]

Food soon ran out for all the emigrants. Livestock that would have provided life-saving meat were buried in deep snow, virtually impossible to find.[35] By the time the ordeal ended in late spring, thirty-nine of the emigrants were dead, some in their cabins, others dying in desperate attempts to cross the mountains on foot. Forty-seven would be rescued.[36] Nearly all of the survivors stayed alive by eating the flesh of those who perished. Eddy ate his first "cannibal meal" on December 29.[37]

One group of sixteen—eleven men and five women—tried to cross the pass in mid-December, struggling through snow up to 15 feet deep. Known as the "snowshoe party"—although they would soon eat their snowshoe strings—it was led by the two Sutter cowhands, Lewis and Salvadore. The group became lost in the snow and wandered helplessly for days.

For thirty years following the tragedy, a book written by J. Quinn Thornton was considered the most definitive account of events, although even Thornton readily acknowledged he didn't know the whole story. Thornton had started from Missouri in the same 1846 wagon train as the Donner-Reeds but continued to

Oregon, surviving his own perilous experience on the Applegate Trail. He succeeded Burnett as Oregon's supreme judge.

Thornton included the Donner-Reed tragedy in his two-volume history
Oregon and California in 1848. His edited account, with corrections and information from other sources, is included in *Unfortunate Emigrants*, a comprehensive account of the tragedy by Kristin Johnson, published in 1996. Much
of Thornton's information evidently came from Reed and from Eddy, who may
well have given a self-serving version of events.[38] With this caveat in mind, here
is some of what Thornton wrote about the snowshoe party:

> The morning of Jan. 8th they . . . found the tracks of Lewis and
> Salvadore for the first time since Mr. Eddy informed them of their
> danger. Foster immediately said that he would follow them and kill
> them if he came up with them. They had not proceeded more than
> two miles when they came upon the Indians, lying upon the ground
> in a totally helpless condition. They had been without food for eight
> or nine days, and had been four days without fire. They could not
> probably have lived more than two or three hours; nevertheless, Eddy
> remonstrated against their being killed. Foster affirmed that he was
> compelled to do it. Eddy refused to see the deed consummated, and
> went on about two hundred yards, and halted. Lewis was told that he
> must die; and was shot through the head. Salvadore was dispatched in
> the same manner immediately after. Mr. Eddy did not see who fired the
> gun. The flesh was then cut from their bones and dried.[39]

A survivor among the women, Mary Ann Graves, wrote to the father of Jay
Fosdick, one of the men who perished, that toward the end of the ordeal she
and the others were "subsisting on human flesh," including the "Two Indians
[who] were killed, whose flesh lasted until we got out of the snow and came
where Indians lived."[40]

Aided by natives, the survivors arrived at Sutter's Fort about January 19, a
month after starting out from Truckee Lake. All five women survived, but only
two of the men, Eddy and Foster. Sutter, who had sent Lewis and Salvadore
to help the Donner-Reed party and later welcomed the survivors to his fort,
lamented in later years, "They killed and ate first the mules, then the horses, and
finally they killed and ate my good Indians."[41]

Burnett wasn't entirely surprised to learn from Eddy and Foster that "all the women escaped, while eight of the ten men perished"—or fourteen of sixteen men, according to Thornton. When Burnett asked why all the women survived, "They said that at the start, the men may have performed a little more labor than the women, but taken altogether, the women performed more than the men," even carrying a rifle the men were too weak to carry.[42]

Burnett said the survival of the women underscored his belief that "Women seem to be more hopeful than men in cases of extreme distress, and their organization seems to be superior to that of men." Possibly speaking from his own experience of watching his wife tend to their six children, he added, "A mother will sit up with a sick child much longer than the father could possibly do."[43]

Among those who perished during the winter-long ordeal were the Donner brothers and their wives, George and Tamsen, ages 62 and 44, respectively, and Jacob and Elizabeth, ages 65 and 45. Jacob was among those whose remains became sustenance for others, including his children. Again, allowing for possible exaggeration, Thornton described the macabre scene that confronted a rescue party when it reached the Donners' Alder Creek camp on or about March 1, five months after the emigrants became stranded. Thornton presumably obtained this portion of his account from James Reed, who was among the rescuers.

> When Mr. Reed arrived there he found Messrs. [Charles] Cady and
> [Charles] Stone, who had been sent in advance with provisions to this
> camp. They informed him that when they arrived at the camp, [John]
> Baptiste had just left the camp of the widow of the late Jacob Donner
> with the leg and thigh of Jacob Donner, for which he had been sent
> by George Donner, the brother of the deceased. That was given, but
> the boy was informed that no more could be given, Jacob Donner's
> body being the last they had. They had consumed four bodies, and
> the children were sitting on a log, with their faces stained with blood
> ... Mrs. Jacob Donner was in a helpless condition, without anything
> whatever to eat except the body of her husband, and she declared that
> she would die before she would eat of this.[44]

Tamsen Donner had been strong enough to be saved by an earlier rescue party but refused to leave her husband, who was too weak to travel. According to Eddy, Tamsen was the only one of the group who refused to eat human flesh.

While she and her husband perished, all five of their daughters, ages 3 to 13, were rescued. Two of Jacob and Elizabeth's five children survived.[45] In a sad postscript to the tragedy, three of the Donner daughters were later seen begging near Sutter's Fort, allegedly crying, "We are the children of Mr. and Mrs. George Donner. And our parents are dead."[46]

Many of the survivors would resume normal lives—to the degree any normality was possible after the horror they had been through. Foster owned a store and mining claim; Eddy went to work for Sutter. Reed, who was forced to leave the party prior to its becoming stranded, became a successful businessman in San Jose. As for Hastings, he maintained his close ties to Sutter and was later elected a delegate to California's 1849 Constitutional Convention. He managed to avoid blame during his lifetime for misleading the emigrants.

Chapter 14
Samuel Brannan
THE MIDAS TOUCH

Samuel Brannan shares in the same emigration story as Peter Burnett and John Sutter, all restless men seeking fame and fortune in a remote and rugged region about which they knew next to nothing. The lives of all three would intersect, and all three would advance the interests of California, each in his own way.

Of the three, Brannan alone initially ventured west for religion, although he would soon be consumed with making money. And he made money better than most. Only his vices stood in his way.

Brannan arrived in California in 1846 aboard the three-masted trading ship *Brooklyn*, bringing 230 Mormons from the northeastern United States. The Maine-born Brannan led a mission for the Church of Jesus Christ of Latter-Day Saints (LDS) to establish a homeland in sparsely settled California, where Mormons might live free of the prejudice and conflict they had encountered elsewhere.

As it turned out, there would never be a Mormon homeland in California, but it was not for lack of effort by Brannan, who was not one to accept failure graciously. Described as "fiery, coarse-grained, and erratic," Brannan had a rocky relationship with his church. He had already been excommunicated once and would be excommunicated again, eventually to be known as "Mormonism's most notorious apostate."[1] But in 1846, at age 27, this son of an Irish immigrant was riding high in the church hierarchy, as the presiding elder for East Coast Mormons. Brannan, "the young lion of Mormonism," as a newspaper once called him, had little formal education but a great deal of street smarts.[2] He had every reason to believe an earlier breach in his relationship with Mormon leader Brigham Young had been healed.[3]

Acting on behalf of the church, Brannan chartered the *Brooklyn* for $1,200 a month or, according to one account, purchased it for $16,000. Passengers paid their own way: $75 for an adult. Brigham Young had advanced Brannan as much as $50,000 to cover costs.[4] He loaded the ship with enough tools and equipment to support a self-sustaining community. Included were two sawmills, a gristmill, and a printing press for a church newspaper—Brannan had published a profitable church weekly in New York, the *New York Messenger*.

When the ship sailed into San Francisco Bay on July 31, 1846, following a seven-month voyage from New York, Brannan was surprised to discover an American warship, the USS *Portsmouth*, at anchor. He had expected to find Mexico still in nominal control, and easily persuaded to make a substantial land grant for a Mormon colony. But the war with Mexico erupted while the *Brooklyn* was still at sea. Captain John B. Montgomery, commander of the *Portsmouth*, had seized Yerba Buena two weeks earlier without serious resistance. The American occupation dashed Brannan's hopes that the Mormons might establish an independent government suitable to themselves.

On February 4, 1846, the same day the *Brooklyn* weighed anchor in New York, another group of 1,600 or so Mormons departed overland in wagons from Nauvoo, Illinois, where church members had been in bitter and often violent conflict with the non-Mormon population. Brannan expected—in truth, he was led to expect—that the Mormons emigrating by land and sea would reunite in California in 1846. "We will meet you there," Brigham Young wrote on September 15, 1845.[5] But the overland emigrants settled temporarily along the Missouri River in Nebraska to wait out the winter of 1846–47. The site, part of today's Omaha, is remembered in Mormon history as the Winter Quarters.

Brannan expected the overland emigrants to continue to California in the spring. To prepare for their arrival, he set about to develop a settlement called New Hope on the Stanislaus Rivers near its junction with the San Joaquin River, about 80 miles south of Sutter's Fort. He put twenty Mormon settlers to work, clearing land and building houses and a gristmill. They also planted 300 acres of wheat. In January 1847, however, New Hope was washed away by flood waters.[6]

Brannan next signed on to John Sutter's planned development at Sutterville. Lansford Hastings's half square mile of riverfront land was envisioned as a Mormon settlement.[7]

Hastings had confidently predicted thousands of mostly Mormon emi-grants would arrive in 1846.[8] In a letter to Thomas O. Larkin, the US consul at Monterey, Hastings wrote with wild optimism, "The emigration of this year to this country and Oregon will not consist of less than twenty thousand human souls, a large majority of whom, are destined to this country."[9] It's not difficult to imagine Brannan salivating at the prospect of being the one to put down the first roots for a new Mormon homeland—not to mention the money to be made.

But such a large emigration was a pipe dream. The numbers of emigrants on the Oregon and California trails in 1846 was estimated at 2,700, of which 1,500 went to California and 1,200 to Oregon. It was a considerable number, but nothing like Hastings predicted. Also, unbeknownst to Hastings and Brannan, the church leadership, known as the Quorum of the Twelve Apostles, was hav-ing second thoughts about California. The Mormons remained ensconced at Winter Quarters until 1848, when they moved into the Salt Lake Valley.

The leadership may have decided on the Salt Lake Valley as early as the pre-vious August, although Brigham Young didn't communicate this to Brannan.[10] When the Mormons failed to show up, Brannan rode on horseback to Young's temporary camp near Fort Laramie to inquire about the delay. Young appar-ently told Brannan they lacked the money to continue to the West Coast at that time, holding out hope they might someday continue the journey. Over time, however, it became evident they would not come. Young would eventually sug-gest the Mormons already in California might want to join him in the future Utah, which many did.

Although Brannan retained his status as president of the LDS Church in California, he complained in a letter to his brother and sister, Alexander and Mary Ann Badlam, that church leaders might have wanted him dead. "They have forsaken me. . . . I am unable to see what I was sent here for unless it was to get me out of the way supposing it being a Spanish country I would be killed."[11]

It was during this period that Brannan, under his authority as leader of the California church, collected tithes from Mormon miners. There were suspi-cions he siphoned a significant share of the tithes for his own use. During a July 1848 tour of the gold fields at the so-named Mormon Island, where many Mormons mined, the then-military governor, General Richard Barnes Mason, was asked by one disgruntled Mormon why Brannan had any right to collect the tithes. Mason reportedly quipped in response: "Brannan has a perfect right to collect the tax, if you Mormons are fools enough to pay it."[12]

Brannan pivoted away from the church for good in 1848 and turned toward making money. He delivered his final sermon, a farewell, in San Francisco on April 30, 1848.[13] His timing was propitious. At virtually the same time he severed his relationship with the church, gold was discovered. He took full advantage.

Brannan was to become the first millionaire in the American West.[14] He achieved his wealth by hook and crook—a lot of crook—ably assisted by Burnett and the Sutters. Burnett, in turn, benefited from favors he extended to Brannan. But no such luck for the Sutters, who surely wished Brannan had stayed in New York.

Brannan opened his first store at Sutter's Fort to supply the newly arriving miners with tools, clothing, and other needs. With business booming, he relocated in 1848 to the future Sacramento, the first fixed structure in that planned new city. He offered miners a place to safely store their gold—for a fee, of course—an important service, as there were no nearby banks.[15] Operating under the name Smith, Brannan & Co., he conducted what Sutter later described as "an immense business," catering to the miners' needs.[16] He told his brother and sister he cleared more than $100,000 in the first year.[17] He opened two other stores at Coloma and Mormon Island. He was already well on his way to becoming a rich man. His wife, Ann, whom he married in 1844, joined in the money-making, boasting she made $500 sewing cheap clothing for miners.[18]

Over the next two decades, Brannan seemed involved in virtually every opportunity California offered to make money. According to one account of his life, "Like Midas, he could touch nothing that did not turn to gold in his hands."[19] Speculation in real estate accounted for much of his wealth. He acquired important properties in both Sacramento and San Francisco. In San Francisco, he built Armory Hall on Montgomery Street and the Express Building, also known as the Brannan Building, at the corner of Montgomery and California Streets.[20] Brannan also was the largest property owner in Sacramento, much of it purchased through Burnett, with other property given him by young Sutter in what amounted to a virtual blackmail.

Brannan used the printing press he brought around Cape Horn to establish San Francisco's first newspaper, the *California Star*.[21] Although he didn't seem to aspire to political office, he was elected in 1849 and 1850 to the San Francisco Town Council, called the Ayuntamiento, a position that served to greatly enhance his wealth and would also bring Burnett further into his orbit.

But although Brannan achieved financial success, he acquired a reputation as a drinker and womanizer that stuck to him like tar for the rest of his life.[22]

An article in the *Salt Lake Daily Tribune* on March 24, 1877, called Brannan "a sly old boy [who] lusted after the fair maidens, matrons and even the widows of Zion." It reported that the church never received an accounting of the $50,000 that Brigham Young had given him to establish the California settlement. Rather, according to the newspaper, Brannan had invested the money in "corner lots and outside lands" for his own benefit. It added: "More than twenty years ago, he was a full-fledged, orthodox saint, enjoying the full confidence of Brother Brigham . . . but he fell from grace and never returned."[23]

Brannan was "disfellowshipped" from the church on September 1, 1851, for a "general course of unchristianlike conduct, neglect of duty, and combining with lawless assemblies to commit murder and other crimes."[24] The accusation of murder stemmed from Brannan's role in hanging a suspected arsonist, John Jenkins, in Portsmouth Square on the early morning of June 9, 1851.[25]

Brannan was only one of many who seized the opportunity to make money from the influx of miners—figuratively transferring gold from the miners' pockets into theirs. Brannan did it better than anyone else, but Burnett also benefited. The opportunity should have been Sutter's to exploit. Already deeply in debt, however, Sutter was unable to any longer obtain credit to buy goods to sell, leaving the field wide open to Brannan and others.

Chapter 15
Spoils of an Unwanted War

John Sutter played both sides in the struggle for California, at first lining up with Mexico and later trying to attach himself to American forces. But his Mexican citizenship and military rank made him suspect. The problems Sutter created for himself would eventually ensnare Burnett, but those problems were years away. For Sutter, they were now.

Sutter had proudly received a commission in the Mexican Army in 1844 as a reward from Governor Manuel Micheltorena for providing four hundred men, including his Native American army, to confront a rebellion by Californios. These were California-born Mexicans who chafed under the leadership of the government in Mexico City. Their revolt preceded by two years the US war with Mexico.

The Californios prevailed, forcing Micheltorena to capitulate. There was little fighting, many desertions from Sutter's force, and Sutter himself was briefly taken prisoner near Los Angeles. After his release, Sutter retained his authority over the Sacramento Valley, in large part because there was no one else to represent the interests of the new government, led by Governor Pio Pico.[1]

Sutter sought to ingratiate himself with the Californio government by warning in April 1846 that many American emigrants were headed toward California. He urged the military commander, Jose Castro, to post "a considerable garrison at this point [the fort] before the emigrants from the United States enter the country."[2] His unspoken hope was that the Mexican government might purchase the deteriorating fort to help relieve him of his debts.

Castro, however, was no friend of Sutter's. He had unquestionably heard that Sutter, while leading his military force during the revolt, threatened to hang Castro, one of the revolt's leaders. Sutter, in turn, would later accuse Castro of plotting to kill him.[3] According to his biographer, Sutter "understood that he was unlikely to have a bright future in Mexican California, at least if Castro had anything to say about it."[4]

As the clouds of war with the United States gathered, Sutter's situation became progressively more perilous. John Fremont, still engaged in his California expeditions, pushed Sutter aside and took command of Sutter's Fort to house Mexican officers captured during yet another rebellion, the so-called Bear Flag revolt, led by American settlers in June 1846. Sutter had opposed the revolt and wrote later that "The Bear Flag was raised at Sonoma by a band of robbers under Fremont's command."[5]

The revolt involved a rag-tag force of thirty-two American settlers, led by Robert Semple, cofounder of the *Californian* newspaper. The largely bloodless rebellion resulted in a brief period of independence for Northern California. Among those taken into custody was General Mariano Vallejo, the commander of the Sonoma garrison, who invited the rebels into his walled compound to accept his surrender, but kept them waiting while he donned his uniform. His sister Rosalia Leese Vallejo voiced disgust at the rebels' appearance. She called them "rough looking desperadoes . . . several had no shirts [and] shoes were only to be seen on the feet of fifteen or twenty among the whole lot." Vallejo was hauled off to Sutter's Fort with other prisoners.[6]

By this time, Sutter had burned too many bridges. While Castro viewed him with suspicion, there was no love lost either with Fremont, the result of several misunderstandings and perceived insults. Their relationship had started well enough at their first meeting in March 1844, during the second of Fremont's four government-sanctioned expeditions. Sutter graciously received Fremont at the fort and granted his request to purchase mules, horses, and other supplies for the three dozen men in his exploring party. But when Fremont sought to banish three of his men for stealing sugar, Sutter—in his role as a Mexican official—insisted on conducting an ad hoc trial, after which he acquitted all three of Fremont's men. Adding insult to injury, Sutter hired the men to work for him. Fremont was said to be greatly annoyed.[7]

The Bear Flag Republic lasted less than a month, from June 14 to July 9, 1846, when the US military occupied Sonoma during the conquest of Mexico, and Navy Lieutenant Joseph Revere ordered the American flag raised over both the Sonoma Barracks and Sutter's Fort. There had been no actual fighting around the fort during the Bear Flag revolt, and for that matter there would be little actual conflict there during the war with Mexico.

Sutter resigned his rank in the Mexican Army and switched his allegiance to the Americans by the time the war broke out. But it did him no good, except possibly to avoid arrest. According to one account, Sutter left a meeting with Fremont in tears after Fremont lectured him to the effect that "he was a Mexican, and that if he did not like what he [Fremont] was doing he would set him across the San Joaquin River and he could go and join the Mexicans."[8]

President Polk hadn't wanted war with Mexico, but he wanted Mexican territory even more than he didn't want war. One of his goals as president was to acquire California—pay for it, if he had to, or find another way.

The annexation of Texas in 1845, which won its independence from Mexico in 1836, created the opportunity. Polk was willing to pay Mexico a substantial sum for the region that included California. "He supposed it might be had for fifteen or twenty million, but he was ready to pay forty million for it, if it could not be had for less," according to an account of a cabinet meeting on September 16, 1845. "In these views the Cabinet agreed with the President unanimously."[9] But rapid-fire developments prevented the offer from being communicated to Mexico.

Mexico, angered over Texas, was not in a mood to negotiate and broke off diplomatic relations. At the next cabinet meeting on September 17, Polk was told Mexican President Jose Joaquin de Herrera was in "a war spirit."[10] Disagreement also emerged over Texas's southern boundary, whether it was the Nueces River—Mexico's position—or the Rio Grande, 160 miles farther south—the American claim.

A standoff ensued, with the armies of both nations lined up on opposite sides of the Rio Grande. Scarcely a hundred yards separated an American force of 3,500, under the command of General Zachary Taylor and several thousand Mexican soldiers, led by General Francisco Mejia. The Mexican forces were well fortified in the small town of Matamoros. The situation was ripe for conflict.[11]

Mexico drew first blood on April 26, 1846. General Taylor had sent a unit of 63 dragoons to investigate a Mexican force of 1,600 that had crossed the Rio Grande into the disputed border area. Mexicans pounced, overwhelming the outnumbered dragoons, killing eleven and taking the rest prisoner.

Retaliation was not long in coming. General Taylor attacked with his full force on May 8, forcing the Mexicans back across the Rio Grande. The Mexicans lost an estimated 1,200 killed and wounded. Jackson's rout of the

Mexicans effectively ended any threat of a Mexican invasion, and the war was fought almost entirely on Mexican soil.[12] The war was far short of a cakewalk, however. Taylor's forces suffered 394 dead, including 14 officers, on September 20 during one of several battles to capture Monterrey.

Senator John J. Crittenden of Kentucky was among critics who accused Polk of provoking the conflict by sending General Taylor's army to the Rio Grande in the first place. Crittenden said it was impossible not to anticipate "that the angry armies of two angry and quarreling nations should day after day face each other with cannons pointed at each other, and only a fordable river between them, and conflict not result."[13] Nevertheless, both the House and Senate gave the conflict overwhelming support, and war was declared May 13.

The war reached its inevitable outcome on September 12, 1847, when General Winfield Scott invaded Mexico City and seized Chapultepec Castle. In the process, he inflicted staggering casualties on the army of General Antonio Lopez de Santa Anna—seven thousand dead or wounded, and four thousand taken prisoner.

The Treaty of Guadalupe Hidalgo, named for a town near Mexico City, was signed on February 2, 1848. The United States gained an enormous territory encompassing all of today's California, Arizona, Utah, Nevada, half of New Mexico, and parts of Wyoming and Colorado. In exchange, the United States paid Mexico $15 million—far less than the $40 million Polk once was willing to pay—plus absorbing an estimated $2 million in debts Mexico owed to American citizens.

California's place in the United States was secure. Manifest Destiny was achieved.

Chapter 16
Selling Sacramento

From the outset, there was risk in the Sacramento land sales—for the Sutters, for Burnett, for Brannan, and for everyone who purchased their properties. But the risk wouldn't materialize until later.

The arrangement between Burnett and August Sutter, reached on December 30, 1848, brought them together in a joint venture that would chiefly benefit Burnett and Samuel Brannan, and would establish Sacramento City, the future state capital. August's goal was not to make money for himself—and he didn't—but to use the profits from the land sales to pay his father's debts and save New Helvetia.

The poorly defined land grant Sutter had obtained from Governor Alvarado in 1841 was understood to extend 60 miles along the east side of the Sacramento River and to include both sides of the American River where it merged with the Sacramento, and both sides of the Feather River. Within this area are today's cities of Marysville, Yuba City, and Sacramento.[1]

For Sacramento, August picked a site immediately south of Sutter's Fort, extending south from the mouth of the American River for 1,000 yards along the east bank of the Sacramento River and 300 yards back from the river bank.[2] It included the embarcadero, the wharf built earlier by Sutter to accommodate shipping.

Among those encouraging the Sacramento project was Brannan, then making a handsome profit selling mining supplies out of his store at Sutter's Fort. But he needed more space. With thousands of gold seekers in the region, and more arriving every day, there had been general agreement on the need for a town to accommodate the stores, warehouses, boarding houses, and other buildings attendant to mining activity, as well as convenient access to shipping. Sacramento met that test. But the elder Sutter hadn't been consulted, an omission that would cause August no end of grief in the months

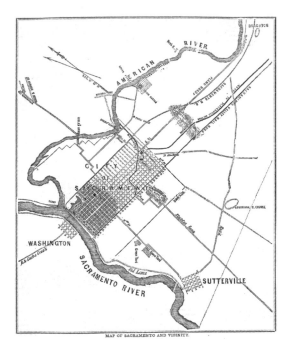

MAP OF SACRAMENTO AND VICINITY.

Map of Sacramento City in 1855. Peter Burnett became wealthy selling the first lots for the new city in 1849 as property agent for John Sutter Jr. His properties sustained significant damage from floods and fires that devastated Sacramento in the early 1850s. Courtesy of the California History Room, California State Library, Sacramento.

ahead. Sutter doggedly and angrily clung to the idea of Sutterville, although it would never develop into more than a small town.

Brannan took advantage of both Sutters, playing them against one another to acquire major holdings of land in Sacramento at virtually no cost. Lansford Hastings created the opportunity for what can only be described as Brannan's blackmail of young Sutter. To keep his own fading hopes alive of profiting from Sutterville land sales, Hastings approached Brannan and some other prospective Sacramento merchants in the spring of 1849, offering them eighty free town lots if they would locate in Sutterville rather than Sacramento, where Brannan already had his new store and warehouse.[3]

Others getting offers were the owners of Hensley, Reading and Co., a mercantile store, and Priest, Lee and Co., a dealer in mining equipment. Both businesses operated out of Sutter's Fort and planned to expand into Sacramento.

Brannan took Hastings's offer to August, demanding the same amount of free land in Sacramento to dissuade him from moving his store. Fearing a fatal setback to his ambitions for Sacramento, August gave Brannan and the others what they wanted. As it happened, Burnett wasn't around to give advice to his young client; he was in San Francisco on business.[4] Brannan and the other merchants came away with five hundred town lots, amounting to about 80 percent of all the lots in Sacramento, for which they paid nothing.[5] Brannan and yet another group of investors would further finagle young Sutter out of the remainder of his Sacramento properties in another questionable transaction the following year.

Until August's giveaway to the Brannan group, Burnett had commanded complete authority over land sales. With August's approval, he priced the most desirable lots near the Sacramento River at $500, half that for lots outside the planned business center. To discourage speculators, they agreed to limit the maximum number of lots for a single buyer to four.[6] The gift to Brannan, however, blew open those limits. Land prices soared, far beyond the prices set by Burnett. Some prime lots, those controlled by Brannan and his cohorts, were said to command prices in the thousands.

Nobody could fault Burnett's ability as a salesman. He was good at it. He kept a ledger of sales during the first six months of 1849, which totaled $38,020. There were additional sales not recorded in the ledger, as Burnett separately listed total sales of $99,850. He claimed $24,987 as his one-quarter share, or "my part of sales." By the summer of 1849, after just six months, Sacramento boasted three hundred canvas structures.

Among the initial purchasers in January 1849 was Brannan, who paid $250 for a lot, probably the lot on which he built his new store.[7] Brannan would also soon open the two-story City Hotel on the waterfront at the corner of Front and I Streets—accommodations were a pricey $5 per night.[8]

The largest purchaser cited in the ledger was Hensley, Reading and Co., which acquired forty-two lots valued at $27,500—these appear to be the lots that August gave away, for which Burnett nevertheless claimed his quarter share. One of the Hensley partners was Pierson Reading, a former Sutter employee who had his own Mexican land grant on which extensive gold deposits were found. Burnett's friends and acquaintances also purchased lots, among them his brother-in-law John Rogers, Morton McCarver, and William Carpenter, the doctor with whom Burnett shared living quarters at Sutter's Fort.[9]

The months-long competition of Sacramento versus Sutterville soured relations between father and son. The elder Sutter couldn't, or wouldn't, appreciate what August was doing for him. He felt betrayed. He didn't care for Burnett, either. But he had been trapped by winter snows at his mill at Coloma, apparently with no inkling of what his son was up to. He complained in later years that Sacramento was planned, promoted, and developed behind his back by Brannan—whom he chiefly blamed—and also by Burnett, with August's complicity. "This would never have happened if I had not been snowbound at Coloma."[10]

One fallout from Burnett's Sacramento land dealings was a breach in his relationship with Morton McCarver, his partner in Oregon. McCarver had arrived in the gold fields months ahead of Burnett and took out a claim along the Feather River. Like Burnett, however, he found the work too tedious, and sought better prospects at Sutter's Fort, where he met the Sutters.

A biography of McCarver written by his son-in-law, journalist Thomas W. Prosch, claimed McCarver helped August lay out the town site for Sacramento, in expectation he would also handle property sales.[11] But when the later-arriving Burnett got the job, McCarver felt Burnett had undercut him. Burnett "secured to himself the business that had been promised to McCarver," Prosch wrote. McCarver recognized that Burnett, a lawyer, had an advantage, although McCarver "was astounded at what he regarded as the duplicity and treachery of his former friend." According to Prosch, McCarver "never forgave Burnett and took care thereafter to have nothing to do with him."[12]

Better-than-expected profits from the sale of Sacramento lots enabled Burnett and August to pay off the elder Sutter's debts, including the $19,788 owed to the Russians for Fort Ross. Burnett personally settled the debt, handing the Russians $800 in gold, plus personal notes totaling $13,648.

Not long before his death, Burnett wrote to young Sutter on January 24, 1894, wondering why the payment of the notes to the Russians had been credited to him. Although it's not entirely clear what Burnett had in mind, he seemed to suggest one of three outcomes: that he might not have been reimbursed, that the debt wasn't fully paid, or that August was owed the money by his father. While it's difficult to conceive Burnett would have let such a costly oversight go by at the time, he put the issue squarely in August's court. "If you should think that there remains anything yet to be equitably done by either of us, be so kind as to state it, and your statement will receive careful and kind attention." He concluded the stiffly worded letter—all his surviving letters are stiffly worded, except for correspondence with his family—by saying he expected "an early reply." It's not clear he ever got one.[13] Burnett died seventeen months later.

Among the elder Sutter's other long-standing debts, Burnett paid $3,000 to William French, the Honolulu merchant who had helped bankroll Sutter at New

Helvetia. Another debt of $2,000 was paid to the Hudson's Bay Company—Chief Factor James Douglas apparently collected in person. An additional $15,000 went to Brannan for unpaid bills, the amount repaid in Sacramento lots. This transaction was not listed in the ledger, so it may have occurred after August returned the business to the father. One of the last debts Burnett paid was $10,000 to Don Antonio Suñol for a thousand head of cattle that the elder Sutter purchased soon after arriving in California.

Even Sutter's Swiss debts were paid.[14] But although the father was debt-free for the first time in his adult life, Burnett and August received little thanks. August wrote in 1855 that Burnett "was in the eyes of my father, before they had ever had an interview, a hypocrite, a Jesuit [i.e., Catholic], a designing swindler . . . My father unhappily never changed his prejudicial opinion." August was convinced that had Burnett been allowed to continue managing the Sutter properties, "my father would be now one of the richest men in California."[15]

At Sutter's insistence, August returned the remaining Sacramento properties to his father on June 15, 1849. Sutter promptly fired Burnett, who had "made a fortune much too quickly to suit me."[16] But Sutter failed to promptly notify Burnett that he had been fired, and Burnett continued selling Sacramento lots under his charge from August. Burnett took the position that his authority to sell lots couldn't be rescinded on the father's say-so alone.[17]

Before yielding his authority to the elder Sutter, Burnett insisted on being compensated for unsold lots. To rid himself of Burnett, Sutter turned over 82 centrally located city blocks, and 109 lots elsewhere in the city, a windfall for Burnett.[18] Maybe this is why Burnett later described their parting as "amicable."[19] The lots proved a lucrative source of income for Burnett for years to come. He sold 35 lots in 1850, while he was governor, 6 in 1851, and 14 in 1852. His relatives also sold properties.[20]

Burnett would brag of an event that further enhanced his wealth following his settlement with Sutter. Two men, he said, offered to buy an undivided half of his Sacramento property for $50,000 in gold dust. He accepted the offer with the caveat that he would retain ownership of a few choice lots within the purchase area. Burnett said the buyers celebrated as if they had taken advantage of him. But Burnett brought them back to earth, observing: "Gentlemen, I am glad to hear that I am a much richer man than I supposed I was. If these gentlemen can make a fortune out of the undivided half they have purchased, what do you think I can make out of my half, and the fifty thousand dollars to begin with."[21] The buyers are identified in county records as Victor John Fourgeaud and Frank Ward, who purchased 801 individual lots, all separately listed in a deed dated September 3, 1849.[22]

The elder Sutter, although debt-free and back in possession of his property, would soon resume his careless ways, borrowing on excessive terms at gold-inflated prices with commitments to repay, as it turned out, after the price of gold declined. He was again using property as collateral for loans, and sometimes it wasn't even his property. In his biography of Sutter, historian Alfred L. Hurtado wrote that, "The gold rush giveth, and the gold rush taketh away." He said Sutter must have been "one of the poorest businessmen in the history of capitalism."[23]

Prior to the properties being returned to the elder Sutter, August had sold decaying Sutter's Fort for $40,000. This after his father refused an offer six months earlier from the Mexican military commander, Jose Castro, to buy the fort for $100,000. Some of the buildings at Sutter's Fort—a dominant fixture in the Sacramento Valley for a decade—were unceremoniously dismantled to salvage their lumber. In what might have seemed to Sutter like a symbolic twist of a knife, the lumber was used for buildings in Sacramento, including Brannan's new store.

Within the following year, August would once again assume responsibility for the properties, or what was left of them. But Burnett would no longer be involved. In November 1849, he was elected the first governor of California.

Burnett came away from his dealings with the Sutters having acquired the fortune he had so long sought. The value of his remaining Sacramento properties was estimated at $343,711 in 1851, excluding the properties he'd previously sold at a considerable profit.[24] California and the Sutters had been good to Burnett. But he would soon be challenged to protect his wealth.

"In conjunction with Samuel Brannan, Burnett was in a lot of ways one of the founders of Sacramento City," said William Burg, a Sacramento historian and author. Burg, who grew up in Sacramento, said Burnett, Brannan, and even young Sutter, "kind of get written out of the story," in part because of a "mythology" that "John Sutter built the town." The mythology overlooks that the elder Sutter opposed his son's Sacramento project and favored Sutterville instead. "You really don't hear much about Sutter Jr."[25]

Chapter 17
Matching Wits with the General

Peter Burnett had more in mind on those first trips to San Francisco than selling lots in Sacramento. He was in the early stages of a political campaign, even though there was as yet no office for which to campaign. But the possibility of high office beckoned.

Only a few days after arriving at Sutter's Fort, Burnett said, "the question arose as to some governmental organization." He didn't say who posed the question, but given his past adeptness at filling a political void, he almost certainly helped pose it.[1]

Californians, especially the Americans, were growing increasingly impatient at the region's undefined status. California had been administered by military governors since being seized from Mexico in 1846. Even after Mexico formally conceded California to the United States in 1848, Congress dithered on status, leaving the government in the hands of the military. California had the following seven military governors from July 7, 1846, to December 20, 1849.[2]

1. July 7–29, 1846: Commodore John Drake Sloat. Sloat occupied Monterey on July 7 and initiated the military conquest. American control was then largely limited to Northern California.
2. July 29, 1846, to January 19, 1847: Commodore Robert Field Stockton. Stockton conquered Southern California and issued a declaration on August 23 from Los Angeles that California henceforth belonged to the United States.
3. January 19 to March 1, 1847: Lieutenant Colonel John Charles Fremont. Fremont the pathfinder captured Santa Barbara and accepted the surrender of the Mexican/Californio military commander General Andres Pico in Los Angeles on January 13, 1847.[3]

4. March 1 to May 31, 1847: General Stephen Watts Kearny. Kearny led a 300-man force into California that was badly mauled by General Pico at the Battle of San Pascual, near San Diego, on December 6, 1846. Reinforcements sent by Stockton helped turn the tide of battle. Kearny had earlier organized a force of 2,500 that seized New Mexico.

5. May 31, 1847, to February 28, 1849: Colonel Richard Barnes Mason. During Mason's term, gold was discovered at Sutter's Mill. Mason reported the discovery to President Polk in a report that contributed to the gold rush.

6. February 28 to April 12, 1849: General Persifor Frazer Smith. Smith was commander of the Tenth Military Department for California and the Eleventh Military Department for the Oregon Territory. While Smith is included on some lists of governors, he evidently considered Mason to still be governor, although Mason had requested in February to be relieved.[4]

7. April 13 to December 20, 1849: Brevet Brigadier General Bennet C. Riley. The last of the military governors, Riley faced the difficult challenge of transitioning California from military oversight to elected civilian government.[5] He managed the change brilliantly while under considerable political pressure, including from Burnett.

Transitions from one governor to the next were not without controversy. Colonel Philip St. George Cook, who led several hundred members of the Mormon Battalion into California, wrote an amusing commentary on the fractured and confusing authority that prevailed in March 1847. "General Kearny is supreme somewhere up the coast; Colonel Fremont supreme at Pueblo de los Angeles; Commodore Stockton is commander-in-chief at San Diego; Commodore [William Bradford] Shubrick the same at Monterey, and I at San Luis Rey; and we are all supremely poor; the government having no money and no credit; and we hold the territory because Mexico is poorest of all."[6]

The most turbulent of the transitions was from Fremont to Kearny, with Fremont's time in office lasting just fifty days. He had been appointed by Stockton, with whom he had close ties. But General Kearny, who outranked Fremont, demanded Fremont turn the office over to him. Fremont refused, but Kearny had the support of President Polk and prevailed.[7]

Brevet Brigadier General Bennet Riley, the last of the American military governors who administered California after it fell to the United States during the war with Mexico. Riley is credited with paving the difficult transition to civilian rule in 1849. He was succeeded by Peter Burnett, California's first elected governor. Courtesy of the California History Room, California State Library, Sacramento.

Not only was Fremont replaced as governor but he was also recalled to Washington to face court-martial on charges of mutiny, for refusing a lawful command from a superior officer (Kearny), and for conduct prejudicial to military discipline. Fremont was represented at the trial by Missouri senator Benton, whose effervescent and talented daughter Jessie was Fremont's wife. Despite Benton's spirited defense during a trial that lasted twelve weeks—and became a public sensation—Fremont was convicted on all counts on January 31, 1848, and dishonorably discharged from the army.[8] Within weeks, however, President Polk commuted the popular Fremont's sentence.

Polk could afford to be in a forgiving mood. With the victory over Mexico, he had achieved his goal of acquiring California and New Mexico and received Mexico's acquiescence to the annexation of Texas. Polk recognized that Fremont was regarded by many as a national hero and offered to reinstate him into the army. Fremont, claiming to be grievously insulted, declined.

On assuming office as the last military governor, General Riley had to walk a fine line between the government in Washington and discontented Californians. At age sixty-one, Riley was regarded as humorless and profane but also as a strong and effective leader who served with distinction during the war with Mexico. He commanded the Second Brigade, a force of 850.

But even Riley could not control men lured by gold. His men deserted in droves, leaving him with too few men to support his authority in the face of political turmoil. "He could not put a sentinel outside the gate for fifteen minutes, but he would be gone musket and all," wrote Elisha Crosby, a delegate to California's 1849 Constitutional Convention and a future state legislator.[9]

Senator Benton had stirred the political cauldron the previous August by prematurely announcing an end to the military government. Benton told Californians in a letter on August 27, 1848, that the treaty with Mexico had made them all citizens and that the military government was at an end. Moreover, he said "the edicts promulgated by your temporary governors Kearny and Mason . . . are null and void, and were so from the beginning." He called the two military governors "each an ignoramus."[10]

As it appeared Congress would delay in approving territorial status, however, Benton said, "I recommend you to meet in convention—provide for a cheap and simple government—and take care of yourselves until Congress can provide for you." The major hindrance to territorial status or statehood was slavery. Slave-state senators sought to preserve a balance in the US Senate between free and slave states as a check against antislavery legislation. "I know of nothing that you can do at this time that can influence the decision of that question here," said Benton. "When you become a state, the entire and absolute decision of it will be in your own hands."[11]

At the time of Riley's arrival, Burnett was already moving to fill what he perceived as a political vacuum. On January 6, 1849, scarcely two months after first setting foot in California, Burnett was elected president of a public gathering in Sacramento, held to make plans for an undefined government. He was becoming, in the words of one historian, the "chief political theorist and propagandist for the settlers."[12]

Burnett presided over a second public meeting two days later, which issued a resolution declaring "the inhabitants of California should form a Provisional Government to enact laws, and appoint officers . . . until such time as Congress shall see fit to extend the laws of the United States over this territory." The resolution called for delegates from throughout California to convene in San Jose on March 5 to draft a governmental structure to submit to voters. Anticipating that slavery would be an issue, the Sacramento delegates would be "instructed to oppose slavery in every shape and form in the Territory of California."

Burnett was instructed—volunteered, perhaps—to appoint a committee to communicate with other districts. In a letter to the new San Francisco newspaper, the *Daily Alta California*, Burnett complained of Congress's "unaccountable inactivity" in failing to give California territorial status.[13]

The Sacramento meetings followed similar meetings in San Jose on December 11, 1848, and San Francisco on December 21. According to the *Alta*, the consensus favored "immediate action for the establishment of a provisional government."[14]

When President Polk signed the legislation approving territorial status for Oregon, he said he hadn't objected because the Oregon Territory was north of the theoretical line dividing the slave and nonslave territory established by the Missouri Compromise in 1820. But Polk said if Oregon had "embraced territories south of that compromise, the question presented for my consideration would have been of a far different character, and my action upon it must have corresponded with my convictions." It was a qualification that would clearly apply to California and the other lands acquired from Mexico.[15] Polk was himself a slave owner with as many as two dozen slaves.[16]

Secretary of State James Buchanan, a future US president, assured Californians in an open letter on October 7, 1848, that Polk regretted congressional inaction on territorial status, and voiced confidence the lawmakers would "at an early period of the next session provide for them a territorial government suited to their wants." In the meantime, Buchanan said the president wanted Californians to live "peaceably and quietly" under a temporary military government.[17] Buchanan agreed with Senator Benton that the military government no longer had a legal reason to exist. But he insisted that a de facto civilian government was already emerging, which President Polk believed had the "presumed consent of the people."

But the ambiguity of such a government was unacceptable to Burnett and many others; it left California under military jurisdiction, subject to difficult-to-understand Mexican laws. While Buchanan's letter was dated October 7, 1848, it wasn't widely known in California until printed in the *Alta* the following March.

Burnett went to San Francisco for the first time on March 23, 1849, to promote Sacramento properties to the newcomers arriving by ship. San Francisco's name had been changed from Yerba Buena in 1847. Burnett described San Francisco

as a simple village of a thousand inhabitants, overwhelmingly young men—
"It was difficult to find a man with grey hair." Burnett set up shop on a corner
of Kearney Street in front of Naglee's Bank, opposite Portsmouth Square, the
city's center.[18] From this vantage point, he greeted those arriving on ships "full
of gold seekers."

From but a few hundred in 1847, San Francisco's population exploded
to as many as 100,000 within two years. Ulysses S. Grant was impressed
by the city's energy when he stopped over in August 1852 en route to the
Vancouver Barracks in the Pacific Northwest. In a letter to his wife, Julia, he
called the city "the wonder of the world." But he was saddened to learn of
the many broken men who failed in the mines. "Some realized more than
their most sanguine expectations; but for one such there were hundreds disappointed, many of whom now fill unknown graves; others died wrecks of
their former selves, and many, without a vicious instinct, became criminals
and outcasts."[19]

Burnett reconstituted his Oregon role as a one-man chamber of commerce,
now selling the attractions of California. "I had been in the mines myself," he
said, "and had 'seen the elephant' and could give them any information they
desired."[20] He already knew the miners from Oregon and Missouri; now he
was getting to know those from elsewhere, expanding his circle of influence.[21]
Not surprisingly, Burnett was also sizing up the local government. "I had not
been in San Francisco more than ten days before I became fully aware of the
unsatisfactory condition of the government of this district."[22]

Burnett met with General Persifor F. Smith, the temporary governor, to
discuss California's status, and came away pessimistic that Congress would
allow the people to decide the status issue for themselves. Burnett wrote a
long and indignant letter to the *Alta* under the headline "The Rights of the
People," intended to rally Californians to take charge of their own destiny.
The letter was spread across two full columns on the front page of the April
26 issue, with a jump to a half column inside.

As with other letters Burnett would write over the next few months, it was
ponderous and full of hyperbole. "Have the people of California any rights?"
Burnett wrote. "Have they not certain rights, founded, based and implanted
in man's very nature—that belong to them as men, as human beings—rights
that derive no force from human legislation, but trace their origin up through
nature to nature's God?"[23] The letter was intended to arouse the public. It also
brought Burnett to the attention of California newspaper readers.

In his letter, Burnett rejected the notion that President Polk or members of his administration could impose a civil government without congressional approval. He mocked the idea that Californians had given such a government their "presumed consent," asking, "What is the difference between no consent, and 'presumed consent'? . . . Can the President, or any man living, presume away the liberties of a people? Never! If we have no power to dissent we have no power to consent."[24]

Plans for a convention to consider a provisional government had been postponed several times in anticipation that Congress would grant territorial status during its winter session in 1849. But Congress adjourned in late March, again without taking action.

Nevertheless, the imbroglio over status was coming to an end. General Riley issued a proclamation on June 3 calling for a constitutional convention in Monterey on September 1 to draft a territorial or "a state constitution." If voters approved, it would be submitted to Congress. Riley's proclamation provided for elections on August 1 to choose thirty-seven convention delegates, along with four Superior Court judges, justices of the peace, mayors, and town councils. He said he would "appoint" those receiving the most votes.[25]

In the meantime, Riley said his government "must be recognized." It "is the course advised by the President and by the secretaries of state and war of the United States and is calculated to avoid the innumerable evils, which must necessarily result from any attempt at illegal local legislation."[26] His comment was aimed at San Francisco, which had established its own governing body in March 1849 called the Legislative Assembly. Riley challenged the assembly's authority to do anything with respect to California's future: "The body of men styling themselves the legislative assembly of San Francisco has usurped powers which are vested only in the Congress of the United States."[27]

Burnett had been elected to the Legislative Assembly, a position that gave him status to speak as a public official.[28] He chaired the assembly's legislative committee, which recommended that the previously postponed convention be rescheduled for San Jose in August. "We have the question to settle for ourselves, and the sooner we do it, the better," Burnett said.[29] He claimed the committee's recommendation, approved by the full assembly and printed in the *Alta* on June 14, 1849, "was written by me."

With typical rhetorical flourish, Burnett also criticized the federal government's collection of customs duties in California. "For the first time in the

history of the 'model Republic' and perhaps in that of any civilized government in the world, the Congress of the United States . . . have assumed the
right not only to tax us without representation, but to tax us without giving
us any government at all."[30]

As there appeared to be general agreement on a constitutional convention, there was no longer any reason for Burnett to continue to challenge
Riley. But Burnett persisted. He wrote his own account of what had transpired in a letter to Oregon's congressional delegate, Samuel Thurston, on
August 7, 1850. He insisted that, independent of Riley, he had successfully
lobbied the Legislative Assembly to draft an address proposing the convention. One can almost envision Burnett thrusting out his chest as he penned
his letter: "I believe I have a right to claim the responsibility of making the
first public movement toward the formation of a state government. I know I
did not follow General Riley or anyone else."[31]

It is absurd that Burnett would try to claim all the credit. But, as always,
Burnett's ego was front and center in his political calculations. He said he
and others agreed to Riley's plan "in part for the purpose of harmony." It's
noteworthy that Burnett's braggadocio about being "first" has received virtually no validation from California historians, no doubt because many people
besides Burnett were strategizing for self-government. Historian Kevin Starr
gave credit to General Riley for directing the outcome with his June 3 proclamation calling for elections and a constitutional convention. "It was a breath-
taking proclamation, one that forever secured Riley's place as a founder of the
state," Starr wrote.[32] He made no mention of Burnett's role.

There were more letters, more arguments, more sniping back and forth,
and a major rally in Portsmouth Square on June 12 at which Burnett and
the newly arrived William McKendree Gwin—soon to be a US senator—
declared that California's future was not for Riley to decide. Burnett's address
was notable for being "too long."[33] But within a relatively short period of time,
both sides had dragged themselves kicking and screaming to the resolution
they wanted: a constitutional convention. It was scheduled for Monterey on
September 1.

Burnett could not resist a parting shot at Riley. The Legislative Assembly
issued a statement on June 21—written by Burnett—in which it accepted
Riley's plans, including the August 1 election, while "not recognizing the least
power, as matter of right, in Brevet Brigadier General Riley, to 'appoint' a time
and place for the election of delegates and the assembling of the convention."

While Burnett saw Riley as an adversary in California's status debates, they were in fact old friends. Or so Burnett would claim in later years: "I knew that old and tried soldier in Missouri, years before either of us came to California, and had always entertained for him the greatest respect." Burnett claimed that in September, while the convention was meeting in Monterey, Riley confessed to him that Burnett may have been right all along about Californians having the right to make their own decision on self-government. Yet Riley's orders from Washington were otherwise. Burnett accepted Riley's explanation, as "it would have been idle to contest the determination of that honest and brave old man."[34] We have only Burnett's recollection of the discussion, as there is no record of this meeting among the few Bennet Riley papers at the Bancroft Library in Berkeley, California.

Burnett was elected on August 1 as one of four Superior Tribunal judges and was formally appointed by Riley. Burnett said he received 1,298 votes to the runner-up's 212 votes—the *Alta* reported the vote as 1,374 for Burnett and 448 for runner-up Kimball H. Dimmick. Burnett said his election occurred "without my knowledge" while he was on a trip to Sacramento. Nevertheless, he was pleased to accept, apparently overlooking that he'd previously challenged Riley's authority to hold elections or appoint public officials. Indeed, he included the text of Riley's appointment in his *Recollections*: "Know all men by these presents, that I, Bennet Riley, Brevet Brigadier General U.S. Army, and Governor of California, by virtue of authority in me vested, do hereby appoint and commission Peter H. Burnett Judge or Minister of the Superior Tribunal of California, to date from the 1st day of August, 1849."[35]

Burnett said the other judges elected him chief justice. But there wasn't much to do. "The business before the court was very small."[36] Burnett had higher aspirations anyway. He wanted to be governor.

Burnett's family had joined him in San Francisco in mid-May after having been separated since Burnett left Oregon six months earlier. They moved in August to San Jose. Burnett's 8-year-old daughter Sallie had fallen ill with what was diagnosed as consumption, or tuberculosis. The humid San Francisco climate had worsened her condition, and her physician held out little hope for recovery. But the drier climate of San Jose, plus a change in treatment, led to Sallie's improvement and eventual recovery.[37] Nevertheless, the tuberculosis lingered. Sallie died May 4, 1861. She was nineteen.

Burnett didn't remain with his family for long. He learned that August Sutter had returned the remaining unsold Sacramento properties to his father. Burnett rushed to Sacramento and during the next six weeks hammered out the agreement with the elder Sutter that worked to Burnett's benefit.

Chapter 18
Slavery and the Border

Delegates to California's constitutional convention arrived in Monterey during a drenching rain and windstorm that turned surrounding roads into nearly impassable mud. They met in Colton Hall, a new two-story structure of white stone, built by convict labor as a schoolhouse and assembly hall, said to be the most impressive building on the West Coast at the time.[1]

Among the forty-eight delegates was the politically ambitious William McKendree Gwin, newly arrived from Mississippi, who was destined to play a major role in shaping the new constitution. Gwin had been one of the wealthiest men in Mississippi with several plantations, as many as two hundred slaves, and a 2,000-acre estate at Vicksburg.[2]

Gwin's background as a Southern plantation owner made him suspect to the antislavery majority, who denied his bid for convention chairman. Instead, the convention chose Robert Semple, the newspaper editor and leader of the Bear Flag revolt. Gwin was named chairman of the committee to draft the constitution.

Other delegates of note included Lansford Hastings, who led the Donner Party to tragedy in 1846; Henry W. Halleck, secretary of state in General Riley's military government; Morton McCarver; and the elder John Sutter. Regarded as something of an "ornamental appendage" to the convention, Sutter was accorded the honor of being one of three delegates to lead the delegates into the hall for the convention opening.[3]

There were thirteen Californio delegates, whose chief interest seemed to be preserving their Mexican land grants. Among them was Pablo de la Guerra, known as the "King of Santa Barbara" owing to his family's long dominance in the region. Although de la Guerra had resisted the American conquest, he would later be elected a state senator. Most of the Californio delegates required an interpreter.[4]

Colton Hall in Monterey, site of California's 1849 constitutional convention. Said to be the most impressive building on the West Coast in its day, it is today maintained as the Colton Hall Museum. Courtesy of the California History Room, California State Library, Sacramento.

Twenty-two delegates were from Northern states, fifteen from slave states, and seven California-born non-Mexican whites. Three delegates, Sutter among them, were foreign born.

The convention faced the unique challenge of bypassing territorial status and moving directly to statehood. "Never in the history of the world did a similar convention come together," wrote Bancroft. "They were there to form a state out of unorganized territory; out of territory only lately wrested from a subjugated people."[5]

Slavery was a contentious issue, and the delegates moved quickly to put it to one side. They unanimously declared slavery would be unlawful in California: "Neither slavery nor involuntary servitude unless for the punishment of crimes, shall ever be tolerated in this state." Given Gwin's pro-Southern sentiments, he surprised, even shocked, other delegates by supporting the prohibition of slavery. "He forthrightly stated that geography itself had decided against slavery in California," wrote one historian. "Gwin not only voted for the ban, but also brought with him all the southern delegates, including a few like him who actually still owned slaves in their home states."[6]

But Gwin seemed to be looking beyond the vote against slavery, which was certain to pass whether he opposed it or not. Moreover, that issue would surface again in a different debate. Gwin had his eye on a seat in the US Senate, a prize that had eluded him in Mississippi. He didn't want a losing argument over slavery to stand in his way.

The delegates also rejected a proposal by McCarver to enact an exclusion law prohibiting African Americans—free or slave—from coming to California. McCarver had voted with Burnett in enacting a similar prohibition in Oregon. Although some delegates spoke in favor of banning blacks, the majority believed it would be improper to write an exclusion clause into the constitution. They also rejected an alternative proposed by McCarver to require a future legislature to adopt an exclusion law.[7]

Like McCarver, many delegates opposed both slavery and allowing African Americans to live among them. As in Oregon, some used the economic argument that blacks would work for less, thereby depriving white workers of jobs. There was also plenty of blatant racism. Delegate John McDougal, a future governor who emigrated from Ohio, warned that without an exclusion law, "We will have herds of slaves thrown upon us, people totally incapable of self-government." He predicted they would prove "a curse to California as long as she exists."[8] Chairman Semple argued that without a law to exclude blacks, thousands of slaves would be brought to California to work in the gold fields in exchange for their freedom. Semple, from Kentucky, warned: "The whole country would be filled with emancipated slaves—the lower species of the population—prepared to do nothing but steal, or live upon our means as paupers."[9]

Not everyone endorsed such racism. William E. Shannon, from New York, scoffed at Semple's argument. He told the delegates, "Knowing that many men of color there [in New York] are most respectable citizens, that they are men of wealth, intelligence, and business capacity; men of acknowledged mental ability; men who have, to some extent at least, considerable influence in their different communities, and who have all the rights and privileges of citizens of that State—I cannot agree to exclude them here from the rights which they possess there."[10]

The most contentious debate, with slavery at its core, occurred in the final week, during deliberations over the location of California's eastern boundary. Several options were discussed. One was to fix the line at the Sierra Nevada. Another was an expanded boundary to include all the territory ceded to the United States by Mexico. A third option was to let Congress decide.

A leading proponent for the expanded boundary was Gwin, who argued that Congress could decide later whether to carve California into two or more states—he suggested there could be as many as six. Other delegates suspected Gwin of maneuvering to open part of a divided California to slavery.

Hastings predicted Southern senators would deny California statehood if it proposed an expanded boundary within which slavery was prohibited. "I know the South will insist that we have no right, as a State here, to present our claims to Congress for a State Government extending over a country as large in extent as all the Northern States. . . . Will the South permit it? No, sir!"[11]

McCarver warned that if California proposed an expanded boundary, Congress might decide to establish two Pacific states, one free and one slave. "There is certainly too much territory for one. The whole question as to slavery in one of these States is therefore to be brought up again." He urged the convention to "clearly and definitely settle the question of slavery for that portion of California that we expect shall remain permanently the State of California."[12] Delegate Elisha Crosby wrote years later that "the only argument for dividing the state into north and south was found in the slavery question, the north to be free and the south slave."[13]

McDougal saw a ploy by proslavery mining interests and others to delay statehood and allow time for slaves to be brought to California. "Gentlemen have risen on this floor and stated that they had received letters from the South; and that they knew of many others, who want to bring their slaves here," he said. "The people may change their notions about slavery after they get hold of the territory, they may assemble in Convention and adopt slavery."

Halleck, originally from New York, took a different view of an expanded boundary, which he favored. He said if the convention prohibited slavery throughout the entire region, it would close "forever this agitating question of slavery in all the territory this side of the Rocky mountains." He argued that California was much larger than the area defined by the Sierra Nevada. "It is not for a mere corner or piece of this territory for which we are now organizing a government . . . but for California, as she was ceded to us by Mexico, and as she is recognized and marked out in the official acts of the Government of the United States."[14]

Winfield S. Sherwood, a former member of New York's Legislative Assembly, said the overwhelming opposition to slavery in California would stand, no matter where the boundaries were drawn: "The people of Mexico have said by their action that they do not want slavery; we have said by our action that we do not."[15]

The delegates voted on October 8 to approve an expanded boundary by a narrow margin of twenty-four to twenty-two. The outcome precipitated an explosion of protest from some delegates and came close to derailing the convention. An incensed McCarver demanded immediate adjournment, declaring, "We have done enough of mischief." Jacob R. Snyder, from Pennsylvania, cried out, "Your Constitution is gone! Your Constitution is gone!" J. D. Hoppe, from Maryland, warned that emigrants "will never sanction the Constitution if you include the Mormons [in present-day Utah]."[16]

Because of the close vote on such an important issue for the future of the state, the delegates reconsidered and voted two days later, on October 10, to approve a boundary along the lines of the Sierra Nevada. The vote was thirty-two in favor to seven against. To restore comity, nearly all of those who had voted for the expanded boundary switched their votes in favor of the Sierra Nevada line.[17] At one point, McCarver walked out in protest after being declared out of order when he tried to speak. This prompted McDougal to sarcastically remark that McCarver had been upset ever since "the sad fate of his free negro project," referring to his failed attempt to write an exclusion clause into the constitution.[18]

Another decision bearing on race that met with virtually no opposition was to restrict the right to vote to white male Americans as well as to Mexicans predominantly of European descent who chose to become US citizens. People of color, including African Americans and Native Americans, were excluded. The delegates also picked San Jose for the state capital.

The state constitution was approved and signed October 13, 1849. John Sutter was given the honor of delivering the signed copy to the governor's official residence in Monterey, where an emotional Riley accepted it with "tears in his eyes."[19]

It seems odd that Burnett didn't weigh in publicly on such a critical issue as California's boundary, or, if he did, that there's no record of it. He was already in Monterey attending a September session of the Superior Tribunal and remained there during the first two weeks of the convention before returning to San Jose. But perhaps he didn't have an opinion to express, underscoring a criticism aimed at him months later that he suffered from "unaccountable apathy" as governor.[20]

Prior to the convention, Burnett's campaign for governor had been conducted out of sight. But in mid-September, with the convention "leaving no reasonable doubt" it would write a constitution, he decided it was the opportune time to announce for governor.[21]

Burnett had already plowed fertile ground for his candidacy. He had worked with the miners and knew many of those from Oregon and Missouri; he had greeted and offered advice to miners and others arriving in San Francisco by ship; he had assumed leadership at public meetings; he served in the San Francisco assembly; and he had written long and indignant letters on California's political plight that appeared with regularity in newspapers, including the most important, the *Alta*.

Although California wasn't yet a state, an election for state officers was scheduled for November 13. Leaving little to chance, Burnett, now 42, embarked on a rigorous campaign tour that took him from Sacramento, to the gold fields at Mormon Island, Coloma, and Placerville, back to Sacramento, then to San Jose, and finally to San Francisco, where he closed his campaign with a rally at Portsmouth Square.

During the Portsmouth Square rally, Burnett demonstrated his political acumen by taking advantage of what could have been a tragic accident. He said he was standing on a platform 6 feet above the ground with other dignitaries seated behind him when part of the platform collapsed: "In the midst of my address, the platform gave way and fell to the ground, except a small portion where I was standing. I paused only for a moment, and then went on with my speech, remarking that though others might fall, I would be sure to stand."[22] He didn't mention whether anyone was hurt.

Burnett received 6,783 votes for governor, more than double those of the second-place candidate, Winfield Sherwood, who received 3,220 votes. Sutter was third with 2,201, followed by John W. Geary, soon to be the first mayor of San Francisco, with 1,358, and William Steuart with 619.[23] The constitution was also approved.

Once again, Burnett's ability to make a favorable first impression was of huge benefit. A historian of the period, Frederic Hall—who evidently knew Burnett—wrote that although he was not widely known, "the few who chanced to meet him were favorably impressed, and their opinion was widely circulated."[24] According to Hall, Burnett may have been helped by the popularity of his daughters Martha and Romietta, both "affable, pretty and interesting." There were few women in California, he wrote, and "men stood on tip-toe to get a sight of a female."[25]

The only real surprise in the election was how few people voted, just one-sixth of California's eligible voters. The low turnout was blamed on a combination of the unusually inclement weather, poor election preparations, and widespread disinterest. California's nonnative population was estimated at the time at 107,000, of whom 76,000 were Americans, 18,000 were foreigners, and 13,000 were California born.[26]

The first governor's "mansion" was a modest one-story home in San Jose on the east side of Second Street, near San Carlos Street. Frederick Hall wrote of the house in 1870 that it "presents anything but the appearance of an executive mansion." Burnett moved his family in December 1850 into a much more suitable two-story, twelve-room house in nearby Alviso.[27]

Burnett now had the office he sought and the prestige that came with it. In fairness, there was probably no one else as well qualified, at least on paper. The question still to be answered was whether he was up to the huge responsibilities that awaited him.

Chapter 19
Stumbling Out of the Gate

Burnett's inauguration was awkward, to say the least. Originally scheduled for the morning of November 19 in San Jose, it was postponed until that afternoon because of miscommunication between the assembly and senate over the appointed time. But when both houses of the legislature convened that afternoon, Burnett wasn't there.

Edward Gilbert, editor of the *Alta* and soon to be one of California first two congressmen, went in search of Burnett. He found him at home "suffering slightly from indisposition,"[1] suggesting a mild cold or other illness. On the other hand, General Riley, the outgoing military governor, did show up, even though he was suffering from a "severe cold." The inauguration was rescheduled for the following day.

The new inauguration day was a miserable day. Rain had fallen steadily for twenty-four hours. Roads were nearly impassable. Streams overflowed. Homes and docks were flooded. The inauguration was held in the newly constructed state capitol on Market Street, a two-story building, 60 feet by 40 feet, with a piazza in front. Members of the assembly occupied the entire second floor, where the inauguration was held. The senate chambers were on the ground floor.[2]

This time, Burnett appeared and took the oath of office for a two-year term from Kimball Dimmick, who succeeded Burnett as chief justice of the California Superior Tribunal. General Riley, however, missed the inauguration, although through no fault of his own. The legislature had failed to notify him of the new date. Gilbert, reporting the events in his newspaper, said the leadership should be ashamed. "After obliging the old hero [Riley] to make a journey of a hundred miles [from Monterey] at this most inclement season, they forgot to give him the notice.... Shame upon such thoughtlessness!"[3]

Burnett followed the oath with his inaugural address. Speaking with uncharacteristic humility, he told the combined chamber that being "chosen chief magistrate of California at this period of her history, when the eyes of the whole world are turned toward her, is a high and distinguished honor." He predicted "a proud and happy destiny" for California and pledged to do all in his power to discharge "the weighty and responsible duties" of his office.

In his newspaper column, Gilbert praised Burnett's everyman entrance into the legislative chambers to deliver his inaugural address, and for the address itself. "He came alone and unattended—no pomp, no ceremony—no venal guards, no useless parade of armed men"—the latter undoubtedly a contrast to the entrances of Mexican and military governors. Gilbert found the governor's address "a document every way worthy of its author, and breathing that patriotic desire for the good of the state."

Burnett quoted his full inaugural address in his autobiography, but made no mention of his far more important "First Annual Message" to the legislature, in which he outlined his legislative priorities. The omission probably stemmed from the poor reception it received.

Burnett did not deliver his message in person; it was read aloud by the respective clerks of the assembly and senate. Burnett's written address began with rhetorical flourish. He told the lawmakers, "You compose the first legislature of the first free American state organized upon the distant shores of the Pacific. How rapid, astonishing and unexampled have been the changes in California."[4] Burnett's list of legislative priorities started with a "first question," that the legislators must decide whether they had the authority to enact legislation, or should wait for Congress to approve statehood. It was a curious question, even nonsensical, as that decision had already effectively been made.

But what drew an outcry from many legislators was Burnett's recommendation that they enact an exclusion law banning African Americans, which Burnett called an issue of "the first importance." That he proposed such a law was not in itself surprising, as he had successfully promoted such a law in Oregon. But it is astonishing that he made it a top priority. He used the same racist arguments he had used in Oregon: African Americans would take jobs from whites, and they would be a discontented element in society because they were second-class citizens, deprived of the same rights as the white population. To this he added a prediction that manumitted slaves from the South would be "brought to California in great numbers."

The same arguments had been hammered home ad nauseam by Morton McCarver and others in Monterey. Why Burnett thought he could win approval for an exclusion law so soon after it was rejected at the convention is puzzling. But he mocked anyone who opposed such a law as succumbing to "weak and sickly sympathy." He insisted that banning African Americans would produce the greatest good for the greatest number: "We have certainly the right to prevent any class of population from settling in our state that we may deem injurious to our own society. . . . They [blacks] are not now here and the object is to keep them out." Burnett also raised eyebrows with his recommendation that the legislature enact a law denying access to courts for people who failed to pay their taxes, another law he successfully helped enact in Oregon.

As much as the *Alta* had praised Burnett's inaugural address, it condemned his legislative message the following day. Gilbert, or another editor, fired the first salvo in a long, unsigned front-page editorial, saying the message fell short of what should be expected from the "reputation of Governor Burnett, as a gentleman of acquirements and merits." The editorial added, "We had expected an abler, a more definite and comprehensive document. . . . It is far below what we had a right to expect."

The newspaper denounced Burnett's call for an exclusion law. Such a law would be "a blot unworthy of a people, who had repudiated forever slavery from their shores." As for whether African Americans would be second-class citizens, the newspaper declared: "We are not to consider whether their position will be disagreeable to them, but merely our right to exclude them from California. In our minds, we have no such right."[5] The newspaper said that Burnett appeared to be trying to rally the old "Oregon lobby"—singling out McCarver for special mention—to support an exclusion law.

The *Alta* also ridiculed Burnett's "first question" that the lawmakers must decide whether to proceed with enacting legislation or wait for statehood. It thought this silly and accused Burnett of being "too timid" by failing to exert leadership on the issue of self-government, which Californians had already heartily endorsed. It also denounced as "unjust and tyrannical" Burnett's recommendation to deny access to California courts for people who failed to pay their taxes. Such a measure, it said, "should never be entertained for one single instant." It also faulted Burnett for what he didn't address, notably public education and mining regulations.

The governor's recommendation to bar African Americans was defeated in the senate, which indefinitely tabled the measure by a vote of eight to five after it passed in the assembly by a vote of eighteen to seven. The legislature did vote to prohibit African Americans from testifying in court against whites, which was denounced by the early California historian Theodore Hittell. "The infamy of this provision disgraced the statute book for thirteen years and constituted the one dark spot in an otherwise exceedingly brilliant record" of the first legislature, he wrote.[6]

There would be no honeymoon period for Burnett. The *Alta* had for months obliged him by opening its news columns to his pronouncements. But the region's leading newspaper was now setting a negative tone for his administration. Other newspapers followed suit. Although Burnett must have been stung by the *Alta's* severe critique, he did not respond, unusual silence for someone with such thin skin and given to penning inordinately long commentaries about events of the day.

Burnett's message to the legislature exposed what historian Hubert Bancroft called "a lack of forcefulness." While Burnett seldom made enemies, "He was a little too slow in action and too wordy in speech for quick-witted men of deeds; a little too conservative for the men of 1851."[7]

Among his legislative proposals, Burnett had urged adoption of a code of laws that combined features of both common and civil law, which puzzled some legislators. Following considerable debate, they settled on a code of laws based on English common law. Hittell, in his 1898 *History of California*, wrote that had Burnett's recommendation been followed, it would have made "the law of California probably one of the most difficult, confused and complicated in the world."

To the relief of the American population, the legislature repealed the Mexican-era laws. It also provided for an official translator, as legislation and official correspondence needed to be available in Spanish as well as English. The translator faced an unenviable task, as Burnett's first legislative address ran to eleven pages in the senate journal. The practice of translating documents and debates into Spanish ended in 1879.

Following Burnett's address, the legislature elected California's first two US senators, John Fremont and William Gwin. Fremont, an abolitionist, was elected on the first ballot. Gwin, the Mississippi slaveholder, was elected on the third. Fremont drew the straw for the short term. They had to wait for statehood, however, before they could take their seats.

Elisha Crosby wrote that the election of the popular Fremont was intended partly as a rebuke to Washington for removing Fremont as military governor in 1847. Gwin, on the other hand, was elected because California needed to send "an extreme southern man" to Congress to satisfy Southern senators and facilitate California's acceptance as a state. Gwin didn't disappoint. "No northern man, no friend of the north, who was known to be strongly against slavery, ever received anything at his hands," Crosby wrote. "Everything he did was in favor of southern interests."[8]

According to Crosby, Gwin promised Southern senators that in exchange for admitting California into the Union, he would encourage Southerners to emigrate to California with the goal of "making the southern part of it, slave."[9] Others disagree this was Gwin's strategy. Hallie Mae McPherson, in a doctoral thesis for the University of California in 1931, said such a motive was "unfounded" and cited as evidence Gwin's statement to the Constitutional Convention that the climate of California was unsuited for slavery.[10]

There was no single misstep that spelled failure for Burnett's brief time as governor. Rather, he was doomed by a pattern of indecision and perceived incompetence. Crosby, who chaired the Senate Judiciary Committee in both the first and second California legislatures, found Burnett to be a gentlemanly fellow, but also that he was "timid in all that he did." Added Crosby, "He had not the backbone; the Gen'l Jacksonism in his composition to maintain the position to which he had been elected."[11]

As governor, Burnett vetoed some legislation. His first veto, of a bill to contract out the services of a printer, was upheld. The assembly bowed to his wishes to make the printer a state position. It also supported his recommendation on February 2 to reject an application from a proposed state of Deseret—a portion of which would become the future state of Utah—to temporarily combine with California.[12]

The circumstances of the Deseret application were unusual, to say the least. Two delegates from the would-be state arrived in January to inform the governor that the population of the Salt Lake Valley—mostly Mormon—had organized a proposed state, but the population was too small to qualify for admission into the union. They said this deficiency would be rectified when additional Mormons arrived. In the meantime, they proposed to Burnett that California hold a new constitutional convention to create a West California and an East California, with the eastern portion embracing all the lands acquired from Mexico east of the Sierras, which could someday become a separate state. There was little, if anything, in the proposal to appeal to California. Burnett recommended against it, and the senate indefinitely tabled the idea.[13]

Burnett's vetoes were often poorly received. Examples were his vetoes of bills to incorporate Los Angeles and Sacramento as cities. The governor objected to the Los Angeles bill on grounds it gave unlimited taxing authority to the local government. His veto message on February 8, 1850, ran to six pages and detailed recommendations for a comprehensive bill setting incorporation standards for proposed cities.[14] All eleven senators voted to override. But the assembly failed to muster the necessary two-thirds majority, so Burnett's veto was narrowly upheld. Both houses did override Burnett's veto of the bill to incorporate Sacramento. The legislature yielded to his request for enactment of a comprehensive bill. The Act to Provide for the Incorporation of Cities was signed by the governor March 18, the same day the legislature completed action to incorporate Sacramento and San Jose.[15] Los Angeles was approved April 4.

A prime example of Burnett's indecisiveness involved a controversy over the sale of hundreds of prime lots, called water lots, in the tidelands fronting San Francisco. There were fortunes to be made from these lots, and big money interests—Samuel Brannan at their fore—were buying them on the cheap in insider deals. Brannan had turned his attention from Sacramento to San Francisco, where there was more money to be made. According to one historian, "the notorious water lots became one of the greatest California real-estate investments of all time."[16]

At issue were some 434 lots along the waterfront that the city, short on land, could use to extend streets and wharves into San Francisco Bay. Former military governor General Kearny allocated the water lots to the city in March 1847, to include all the area "between the points known as the 'Rincon' and 'Fort Montgomery.'" Kearny stipulated the lots be sold to the highest bidder, with "proceeds from the said sale to be for the benefit of the town of San Francisco."[17]

Hemmed in by its many hills, San Francisco had limited land suitable for commercial development. Existing streets were described as "channels of mud" in which merchants placed empty cigar boxes for stepping stones.[18] The water lots helped ease the land shortage. Once they were filled with dirt and rock, and with the addition of pilings, they became foundations for streets, buildings, and wharves. Developing the lots cost millions but paid off in a "large return to the projectors [sic], mostly private firms," wrote Bancroft in his California history.[19]

Although the lots initially were a city responsibility, controversy over conduct of the sales, and by whom, soon fell into the governor's lap. Everyone involved was fighting to hold on to a piece of a lucrative pie. San Francisco's alcalde, Thaddeus M. Leavenworth, proposed an 800-foot Central Wharf along Commercial Street for steamers and oceangoing ships after two smaller wharves between Clay and Broadway, built in 1848, had already proved their worth.[20] The city's Legislative Assembly, on which Burnett had briefly served, authorized the incorporation of the Central Wharf Joint Stock Company on May 3, 1849, to build and operate the wharf.[21] Completed later that year, the immediate success of the wharf—at 400 feet initially—ignited a speculative rush by rivals to obtain water lots along virtually the entire waterfront.

By the fall of 1850, 6,000 feet of pier space extended into the bay, looking much like "the fingers of two large hands," according to one description. Owners imposed tolls ranging from $100 to $200 per day for vessels using the wharves, depending on a ship's size. Fees were also imposed on passengers and cargo, and on the wagons and drays used in loading and unloading. The wharves were a gold mine for the owners and investors—actually, better than a gold mine.[22]

In the meantime, a new, more formal organization, the Ayuntamiento, or town council, succeeded the Legislative Assembly as the city's governing body—local governments were still organized under outdated Mexican laws. Brannan was among the original twelve elected members of the Ayuntamiento, which moved quickly to assert its authority over the water lots. Among the first water lot–related issues was a prior sale by the alcalde, Leavenworth, on May 3, 1849, before the council took office. The council opposed the sale after the fact. There can be little doubt it was motivated by the financial interests of its members.

The council voted August 17 to prohibit the alcalde from making further sales or grants without its approval.[23] In the meantime, Leavenworth had been succeeded by John Geary, soon to be elected under American law as San Francisco's first mayor.[24] The council declared on December 24, 1849, that Leavenworth had exceeded his authority by failing to give the required three-month notice of the sale. It annulled the sale and voted to hold Leavenworth responsible for any losses to the city.[25] It also approved a proposal for the

Central Wharf Joint Stock Company to develop another wharf between Clay and Sacramento Streets.

At Brannan's urging, the council moved swiftly to consolidate its authority over sales. Typically, the lots were of two sizes: 50 and 100 square varas—a vara was a Spanish unit of measurement of slightly less than a yard. Prices varied, depending on location, but a suggested price might be $200 for a 50-vara lot and $500 for a 100-vara lot.[26]

Brannan proposed on October 3 to sell all remaining lots from the Kearny allocation, including those auctioned by Leavenworth, which "are illegal and remain the property of the town." On November 3, he directed the city surveyor to divide unsurveyed land into more lots to be auctioned by the alcalde. He also wanted an immediate survey of remaining water properties granted to the city by Kearney to a depth of 12 feet "at low tide," with those lots readied for the next sale. The council resolved to sell all the lots over the next four months, ending on March 15, 1850.[27]

Behind the scenes, maneuvering was evident but unexplained. The council on November 19 authorized the alcalde, Geary, to conduct the sale, but withdrew his authority on November 24 without giving a reason.[28]

One reason for the council's rapid-fire sales may have been the imminent incorporation of San Francisco as a city on April 15, 1850, with Geary as mayor. The governing body of newly elected alderman might not look favorably on the council's process for handling water lot sales, especially as Brannan and other members of the council were purchasing lots in legally dubious transactions.

Justice of the Peace G. Q. Colton touched off the crisis that put the issue on the governor's desk in early 1850. Acting on the authority of the town prefect, Horace Hawes, Colton auctioned 434 lots on January 4, 1850. They included many of the same lots targeted for sale by the council. Hawes said he directed Colton to circumvent the council because he believed the council members were unlawfully selling the land to themselves. Moreover, he said, the prices were too low, depriving the city of needed revenue. As prefect—another position of the Mexican government—Hawes was a nonvoting member of the council, or ayuntamiento, with oversight responsibility for expenditures and the execution and enforcement of laws. He reported directly to the governor.

The council responded with a court injunction barring Colton from conducting his auction. Hawes annulled the injunction and the auction went ahead, however, collecting $635,000 for the city treasury.[29] The council alleged

Hawes exceeded his authority and petitioned Governor Burnett on February 5 to suspend both Hawes and Colton.[30]

Burnett suspended Colton but for the time being sided with Hawes, who alleged to the governor that the council was acting improperly by resisting Hawes's request for records of past sales, particularly the prices. Burnett directed Hawes on February 8 to suspend all future sales. "I . . . do order and declare that no further grants or sales of any municipal lots belonging to the city of San Francisco shall hereafter be made by any justice of the peace of said district until the further order of the executive." He agreed with Hawes that previous sales had apparently been at below value. "If said lands were sold to the highest bidder, a much larger amount of municipal funds could be raised."[31]

To support his accusation of improper behavior, Hawes cited the large number of water lots held by Brannan and other council members. According to Hawes, Brannan had purchased thirty lots outright, with an interest in twenty-seven more. He said Brannan acquired ten lots on November 19, 1849, seven lots on November 28, 1849, and thirteen lots on January 3, 1850. An additional fourteen lots were jointly purchased with fellow council member and business partner T. W. Osborne on January 3.[32]

Hawes alleged the council's purchases violated a Mexican law prohibiting government officials from purchasing properties for which they were responsible: "A man cannot be the seller and buyer of property at the same time."[33] Amid the turmoil, Brannan resigned from the council on February 25. But by then he owned the lots that would augment his already considerable wealth.[34]

Hawes said Brannan had attended an unannounced council meeting the night of February 28—after he resigned—at which time the council approved spending $200,000 for a wharf at the foot of California Street, and an additional $100,000 for related work on Market Street. Hawes alleged Brannan and Osborn would "be benefited" by the appropriation.[35] Still siding with Hawes, Burnett issued an order February 15 "setting aside all purchases made by any member of the Ayuntamiento."[36]

Not surprisingly, the council turned on the governor. It adopted a resolution on March 2 declaring, "We consider the interference of the governor . . . to be a high-handed act of usurpation on his part and one in which neither the law nor the opinion of the public sustains him." The resolution alleged Hawes had also purchased lots from the Colton sales, and cited a questionable payment to Hawes of $2,500 in legal fees. The council asked for Hawes's suspension.[37]

Burnett was not deterred. He directed Attorney General E. J. C. Kewen to consider a legal "proceeding" to prohibit the council from selling additional lots. He also asked Kewen to consider the legality of "setting aside all"—he underlined "all"—the lots purchased by council members both before and after his February 15 order. He claimed that under still-applicable Mexican law, the governor had the final say over the sale of public lands.[38]

Burnett's orders and directives represented probably the most forceful action of his entire term as governor. But on March 25, he backed down. He suspended Hawes. He also set aside the Colton land sales, with the excuse that there were insufficient funds to complete the planned projects. He reversed his earlier order and authorized the council to conduct its own auction, which it did on April 20.[39] Most likely, there had been considerable behind-the-scenes pressure on Burnett by the council and its supporters, many of whom he knew. The attorney general may also have advised him that he might be exceeding his authority by trying to annul the council's sales, as the water lots remained a city responsibility.

Now it was Hawes's turn to react with outrage. He refused to vacate his office. He considered Burnett's attempt to suspend him to be "null and void." Moreover, he sent a formal request to the California assembly on April 2 to impeach the governor, alleging he was "guilty of a plain and gross violation of the Constitution and laws of the state of California."[40] Assemblyman John Bigler, a future governor, moved on April 4 that the impeachment request be tabled, and no further action was taken.[41] But a request for Burnett's impeachment just four months after taking office must have been an embarrassment.

Burnett's indecisiveness in first siding with Hawes against the council, and then with the council against Hawes, did not augur well for his standing with the public or the legislature. Yet his suspension of Hawes was popular with editors of the *Alta*, seen as "always loyal to Brannan," one of its founders.[42] The *Alta* directed its ire at Hawes: "His course was so intolerable as to awake the inference of the Executive [Burnett] who very properly put a check to the further acts of the Prefect by suspending him from office."[43]

As for Hawes's assertion that Burnett exceeded his authority, the newspaper said: "Under the Mexican code Governor Burnett has acted up to the strict letter of the law and surely the Prefect cannot reasonably find fault with that under which he has professed to act so rigidly."[44] Burnett's long history with Brannan can't be discounted as a factor in the governor's decision to suspend

Hawes. That Brannan suffered no adverse consequences from his own questionable machinations over the water lots doesn't come as much of a surprise. Brannan, wrote one historian, was "a law unto himself."[45]

Chapter 20
Squatters Everywhere

The *Alta* was less kind to Governor Burnett regarding his handling of a major controversy in which he had an obvious conflict of interest, the so called squatter movement of 1849–50. The movement challenged Spanish and Mexican land grants issued before the United States acquired California. It escalated into bloody conflict. Among the challenged grants were John Sutter's Sacramento land grants.

Squatters were typically new settlers or miners from the nearby gold fields who brazenly moved onto unoccupied properties included in the original grants. The squatters' attitude toward the land grants might be summarized in two words: "So what?"

Prior to 1846, more than eight hundred grants were extended by Spanish and Mexican officials to favored recipients. The combined grants totaled as much as 14 million acres of California's best land. Most of it—including the bulk of John Sutter's extensive land grants—was still unoccupied and undeveloped at the time of the American conquest.[1] Newcomers claimed that the unoccupied land belonged to the United States as one of the spoils of war. These lands should be up for grabs, just as undeveloped land had been up for grabs in Oregon, where settlers had only to push the American Indian tribes aside.

A special US land commission would eventually uphold the validity of 553 of the California grants—75 percent of the total—embracing nearly 9 million acres. But rulings were years away; the last appeal wouldn't be decided until the 1870s.[2] Elisha Crosby wrote that the lengthy process, where cases could be appealed all the way to the US Supreme Court, was unfair to land owners because of the cost—many owners had only a lot or two. "There was not one in fifty . . . who could stand any such expenses and the result has been the transfer of these claims to speculators and men of wealth who took them up for little or nothing."[3]

The vast holdings of John Sutter, who claimed much of the most productive land in the Sacramento Valley, courtesy of the Alvarado grant in 1841 and the Micheltorena grant in 1845, were the prime targets of squatter activity. "The squatters are loose in my fields; all is squatted over," Sutter complained in 1853.[4] Also challenged was Burnett's right to sell the Sacramento lots for young Sutter, and the right of others to purchase them. Burnett's ownership of the lots acquired from the elder Sutter in his employment-ending settlement in 1849 was likewise at issue.

Bayard Taylor, an author and poet reporting for the *New York Tribune,* wrote in his 1850 book *El Dorado* of the squatters' passions at a meeting he attended in Sacramento: "They were all located on the vacant lots, which had been surveyed by the original owners of the town and were by them sold to others. The emigrants, who supposed that the land belonged of right to the United States, boldly declared their intention of retaining possession of it. Each man voted himself a lot, defying the threats and remonstrances of the rightful owners."[5]

By June 1850, more than two thousand squatters were claiming vacant land in Sacramento and the surrounding area, staking out lots and erecting fences, cabins, and tents. The stage was set for a struggle between the haves and the have-nots.

The nominal leader of the squatters was Charles Robinson, originally from Massachusetts and a future governor of Kansas. Leading the property owners was Samuel Brannan, who organized them into a "Law and Order Association." To Brannan, the squatters were "crime-hardened conspirators against life and property."[6]

Among measures enacted by the first legislature was a squatter-related bill called the Unlawful Entry and Forcible Detainer Act, or forcible entry law, that benefited speculative landowners, such as Brannan, Sutter, and Burnett. The bill, which would prove useful for ejecting squatters, was signed by Burnett on April 22, 1850, the last day of the legislative session. It provided penalties for persons forcing their way onto land of a previous occupant—the presumed owner—but without any requirement for the occupant to have a legal title. All titles were then in question. Lower courts generally sided with the property owners, upholding the legality of the Mexican grants.

Everything became subject to interpretation. The squatters interpreted the boundary of Sutter's Alvarado grant as stopping short of Sacramento and produced maps they claimed backed them up. This interpretation, if upheld—it was not—would have meant that the original Sacramento lands did not legally belong to Sutter, and Burnett therefore had no right to sell them. Squatters became progressively more agitated as courts ruled against them.

A ruling on a property belonging to Burnett's brother-in-law John Rogers provided the spark that ignited violence. A squatter named John Madden had moved onto one of two lots Rogers had purchased from Burnett for $700 in early 1849. Madden was accused of violating the forcible entry law. Judge Edward J. Willis of the Sacramento County Court ruled in Rogers's favor on August 8, 1850. Attorneys for Madden considered appealing to the California Supreme Court on grounds that Rogers failed to show a legal title. But Judge Willis said he knew of no law authorizing an appeal, a comment interpreted, rightly or wrongly, as meaning the squatters could not appeal.[7] Angry squatters threatened to take matters into their own hands.

Charles Robinson, who published a short-lived squatter newspaper, the *Settlers' and Miners' Tribune,* issued a "manifesto" refusing to recognize the authority of the legislature and other officials, and claiming the right to resist if authorities interfered with squatter actions. Robinson took the position that because California wasn't yet a state, legislative actions such as the forcible entry act were purely advisory and lacked the force of law.[8] Squatters continued to hold the occupied properties.

The hot-headed Brannan responded to the manifesto by leading a mob that destroyed the foundations of a home being built by Robinson. In a show of force, Brannan wrapped "a piece of manila rope around his waist, in which two revolvers were stuck." He also directed a rider on horseback to hitch a rope to his saddle to pull down the walls of another structure.[9] Tensions mounted. The conflict could only get worse, and it soon did.

On August 14, Sheriff Joseph McKinney expelled squatters from a house on Second Street. The squatters returned with reinforcements and retook the house, led by their designated military leader, a sword-waving firebrand named Joseph Maloney, directing the action from horseback. Fueled by their initial success, armed squatters marched through Sacramento's streets, a crowd of adversaries not far behind. The squatters first sought, but failed, to free two fol-lowers who were jailed offshore in the city's prison ship, the *La Grange.*

At the corner of Fourth and J Streets, Sheriff McKinney and Mayor Hardin Bigelow—the mayor was also on horseback—ordered the squatters to lay down their arms and submit to arrest. The squatters refused and shooting erupted from both groups. Three bullets hit the mayor, who fell from his horse, gravely wounded. County Assessor J. M. Woodland was shot dead. On the squatter side, the sword-waving Maloney was killed, and Robinson was badly wounded.[10]

The casualties were four dead and five wounded. Among the wounded, albeit not seriously, was Roger's daughter, Burnett's niece. Robinson would recover from his wounds, as would Mayor Bigelow, although he would die not long after from cholera. The popular Robinson was charged with murder. But the charge was dropped after he was elected—while still in jail—to the 1851 California Assembly.[11]

Governor Burnett on August 15 ordered Brigadier General Albert Winn, commander of the California militia's Second Brigade, to suppress the "riotous and unlawful assembly" in Sacramento. He urged Winn "to order out the whole of your command . . . and give all the aid in your power to the civil authorities in suppressing violence and enforcing the laws." Burnett signed the order as governor and "commander-in-chief."[12]

To say General Winn's own interests were at stake would be an understatement. He had only recently been employed as Sutter's agent to sell land along the Sacramento and Feather Rivers. He was also president of Sacramento's first city council and owned some of the disputed properties. Winn's commission to the rank of brigadier general came courtesy of Burnett in April of 1850.

The Sacramento riot wasn't the end of it. Shooting broke out two days later when Sheriff McKinney led a posse that tried to arrest a group of suspected squatters holed up in a saloon called Allen's, run by members of the Allen family, 6 miles from Sacramento. In the confrontation that followed, McKinney was shot dead, as were two of the suspected squatters. There were injured on both sides. Four of the surviving suspects were arrested after General Winn arrived with reinforcements.[13]

The Sacramento squatters had lost on multiple counts—lost their leadership, lost in the courts, and, following the violence, lost much of the public's support. Their movement would later win the sympathy of historian Bancroft. While he couldn't endorse the squatters' tactics, he did not consider them entirely in the wrong: "there was good ground—in the belief of the squatters that the Alvarado grant did not extend to Sacramento, and in the fact that the Micheltorena grant was actually invalid—for the feeling of the squatters that Sutter was playing into the hands of a set of soulless speculators, who used the pretence of a grant for securing paper titles to the best portions of California."[14] Did Bancroft consider Burnett one of the "soulless speculators"? He didn't say.

The *Alta* faulted Burnett for a failure of leadership during the disturbances. With the mayor critically wounded and the police chief dead, there had been no one in authority in Sacramento to take charge of a turbulent scene. The newspaper wrote on August 25, "the city is not yet under martial law. Governor Burnett has not been posted, and so, of course, has promulgated no advice, nor doctrines—declared nobody guilty of 'attempting a felony.' "[15]

While Burnett had little to say about his personal involvement with squatters, a letter written by his private secretary, Caius Tacitus Ryland, made clear the governor was fully occupied in trying to expel them from his Sacramento properties.[16] Ryland, soon to also be Burnett's son-in-law, apologized on behalf of the governor to the former US consul, Thomas Larkin, for failing to promptly thank him for a gift of historical documents. The governor, he explained, was busy dealing with the squatter challenges to his Sacramento properties, which he had been unable to address during the legislative session. Since adjournment, Ryland said Burnett was now "doubly busy" with both his official duties and business interests, notably the squatters.[17]

Ryland told Larkin that the squatters targeted Burnett because of his involvement with the Sutters. "The squatters, in hope of busting up the title of Captain Sutter for his Sacramento or New Helvetia grant, have squatted on the governor's property on account of which he has been for nearly two months trying to get them off and has not yet affected his object," Ryland wrote. "He is now absent [from San Jose] attending court at Sacramento City and I think he will hoist [*sic*] the squatters this term."[18]

Burnett limited his comments about the squatters to a passive observation in his *Recollections* that "it was dangerous for a man of property to be absent from the State even for a few months, as others were almost certain to administer upon his estate in his absence." Even if a property were left in care of an agent, Burnett added, "one would be very likely to find upon his return that his agent had sold his property and absconded with the proceeds."[19]

Chapter 21
Racing toward Statehood

While Governor Burnett was being faulted for timidity and indecisiveness, the California legislature of sixteen senators and thirty-six assemblymen accomplished a great deal, acting pretty much on its own. During their four-month session, the lawmakers established twenty-seven counties, incorporated cities, set up a court system to replace the Mexican courts, enacted a code of laws both civil and criminal, and initiated projects to build roads and hospitals, drain swamps, and regulate the all-important gold mines. Historian Judson A. Grenier considered it "the most creative and probably the most competent" of all of California's early legislatures.[1]

The lawmakers' major failing was not providing sufficient revenue to run the state. They levied a property tax of 50¢ for every $100 of property value, plus a poll tax of $5 for white males, and a controversial—and largely ignored—foreign miners' fee of $20 a month. They also approved a revenue-raising bond issue of $300,000 at 3 percent monthly interest. But the lawmakers simultaneously appropriated $750,000 for state expenses—money the treasury didn't have. The consequence was "a financial straight-jacket that crippled the government's ability to function" for years to come.[2]

The legislature didn't receive much credit from the press and public for its accomplishments, in part because of behaviors that caused it to be known disparagingly as the "legislature of a thousand drinks." Grenier offered this description of the sometimes chaotic atmosphere in the legislative chambers: "While debating, members could be found whittling, smoking, and toying with guns. . . . As the time of adjournment drew near each day, the genial chair of the Senate Committee on Finance, Thomas Jefferson Green, would proclaim, 'Well boys, let us go take a thousand drinks.' The invitation would be accepted by most."[3]

Burnett could hardly be blamed for the legislature's financial failings. But he could hardly receive credit for its accomplishments, either. He refused to take stands on major issues. Moreover, he depended on other state officials to administer the state government. He was, said Grenier, "politically ambitious, but reserved and aloof," preferring to have "played the role of judge rather than innovator."[4]

One problem that wouldn't go away was attacks by tribes on emigrants and miners. Burnett received frequent requests to dispatch militias to punish the tribes. But he concluded it was both useless and expensive to call out the militia to deal with each and every attack, and he believed local sheriffs could best respond. While his reasoning had merit, it hardly endeared him to the victims of the attacks.

On the few occasions when Burnett did step in, the response often bordered on ineptness and accomplished little. In fairness, however, information about attacks was frequently incomplete and inaccurate, and took days or even weeks to reach the governor's desk.

In one cautious response in March 1850, Burnett notified the unnamed commander of American military forces at Sonoma—probably General Persifor Smith—of "very serious disturbances" around Sonoma. He said he had directed the local justice of the peace to investigate "and if murder was committed, to issue a warrant for the arrest" of those responsible. If arrest proved impossible, however, Burnett instructed the commander to deal with the situation. "It may be attacks of the Indians will have to be repelled." He ended his letter with the semi-apologetic acknowledgment that "I know nothing of military affairs and I must trust all to your discretion."[5] It's not clear anything came of this.

On another occasion, he ordered a response because he believed emigrants were threatened. Burnett wrote to Major General J. H. Bean of the Fourth Division of the California militia on June 1, 1850, directing him to respond to attacks in April by Quechan, or Yuma, tribesmen at a ferry crossing on the Colorado River near its confluence with the Gila River. He told Bean he had instructed the sheriffs of San Diego and Los Angeles to gather sixty men in Los Angeles and proceed under Bean's command to "punish the Indians."

In a follow-up on June 4, he said additional information suggested Bean would need one hundred men. In yet a third letter on September 4, he complained he had not received any report about the mission. However, he heard elsewhere that the "Indians were not as hostile as expected" and "the expedition had failed from the impossibility of procuring the requisite number of men." One has to wonder whether his orders were taken seriously.[6]

What Burnett failed to mention in the third letter—and possibly didn't know—was that the clash at the ferry had been misrepresented. According to one account, the conflict was initiated by a gang of outlaws led by a known scalp hunter, John Joel Glanton from Texas, who was believed to have killed both Native Americans and emigrants. Glanton wanted to stop the Quechans from operating a ferry at the junction of the Colorado and Gila Rivers in competition with a ferry operated by A. L. Lincoln, with whom Glanton had made himself a partner. The Quechuans' ferry had been a money-making enterprise for the tribe, and Glanton sent his men to destroy the ferry to end the competition. Several Quechuans were killed. The Quechans retaliated by attacking the Lincoln ferry, killing nine workers, including Lincoln and Glanton. Four workers escaped. Their anger unleashed, the Quechans killed other whites at the ferry landing, and an appeal went out to the governor to send the militia. A series of inconclusive skirmishes ensued before the militia force withdrew.[7]

Burnett again sent out a militia in response to attacks on settlers and miners in El Dorado County by a band of Nisenans. The possibly exaggerated attacks occurred in an area around a ranch named for William Johnson, an English-born sailor from Boston who arrived in California in 1842. The ranch, located on the Bear River about 35 miles north of Sacramento, in Yuba County, was the first white settlement emigrants saw after crossing over Truckee Pass. A Sacramento newspaper warned its readers in 1851, "It is not safe for a party to go five miles beyond Johnson's Ranch on the emigrant road, so great is the probability of their being attacked by the savages in that vicinity."[8]

The El Dorado conflict may have been started by whites to provoke a native response and in turn bring the militia to punish the tribes. It was not an unusual strategy for whites who wanted natives out of the way, or who anticipated making money from selling food and other supplies to the militiamen. An early county history reported that "some Indians" had been killed near the Johnson Ranch, citing "rumors . . . that it had been done [by whites] with a view to stir up the Indians to commit some outrage or depredation in retaliation, and then have the strongest measures taken against them." The account went on to say that "the scheme worked well enough, the Indians . . . killed several miners, whereupon the settlers and miners complained in a petition to the county and State, asking for relief from the ravages of the Indians."[9]

The militia launched two campaigns. The first, lasting four weeks around Johnson's Ranch, was unsuccessful in capturing or subduing the Nisenan attackers.[10] Both sides sustained casualties, although apparently not so many as claimed in the militia's subsequent report. One of Johnson's relatives, a miner, was reportedly wounded in the leg by an arrow.[11]

In a letter to the governor dated May 16, 1850, Major General Thomas Jefferson Green of the First Division of the California Militia—the senator who led the "thousand drinks" brigade in the legislature—reported hearing that fifteen American Indians and eight whites were killed in a clash along Deer Creek, a tributary of the Sacramento. Green told the governor that a volunteer militia was in pursuit of a Native American force that may be led by "white men and some Chileans." He urged Burnett to call up additional militia and consider asking assistance from the army if the tribes continued their attacks.[12]

Green followed with a second letter to Burnett on May 25, saying the militia had encountered the attackers, killing five and capturing six. On reaching Deer Creek, they found the Nisenan villages deserted. The militia followed the natives' trail to Bear River, a tributary of the Feather River, where a "Col. [Samuel] Holt was murdered and burnt in his mill" in an earlier attack.[13] In that incident, Holt and his brother, George, were attacked May 3 at a sawmill they operated on the Bear River. George escaped, although wounded, but Samuel was shot dead with arrows, his body left in the mill, which was set on fire.[14]

Green boasted that he had personally led the charge to dislodge as many as three hundred tribesmen from a nearby hill and drive them toward other militiamen lying in wait. In the battle that followed, he said an unspecified number of natives were killed and eight captured, while the militia's losses were just four wounded.[15] According to the early county history, however, the battle may never have happened and "was only manufactured to stimulate the townspeople." A subsequent search of the alleged battlefield turned up no evidence of conflict, suggesting the battle was "a hoax."[16]

Whatever the truth of the encounter, Major Green reported to the governor that, following the success of his campaign, he sent a note to several chiefs proposing a truce, which he wrongly called a treaty. He claimed to have met with the chiefs May 20, at which time they agreed to halt their attacks. Green suggested he was holding captured Native American women and children as hostages. He enclosed the text of an ultimatum addressed to chiefs identified only as "Weima, Buckler, Poollal, and others."

> Your people have been murdering ours, robbing their wagons and
> burning houses. We have made war upon you, killed your men and

taken prisoners your women and children. We send you this plain talk
by one of your grandmothers.

When you cease to rob and murder our people, we will cease to
make war upon you and then you can come in and get your women
and children who will be taken care of in the meantime. If you wish
peace come down to Johnson's old Rancho on Bear River and report
yourselves to Capt. Charles Hoyt, who will protect you until your
great Father shall speak.[17]

Some military leaders, Green among them, voiced sympathy for the tribes,
with emigrants and miners invading their lands and treating them unfairly.
Green said among natives' grievances was poor compensation for work in the
gold mines. "These Indians can be made very useful to the miners, if they have
even a small portion of justice extended to them," Green told the governor.
"Heretofore, a few persons have monopolized much of their labor, by giving
them a calico shirt per week, and the most indifferent food. This is not only
wrong but highly disgraceful, when they would be content with the pay of one
fourth of the wages of the white man."[18]

Burnett must have been pleased. Here was a report of a successful mission
when others had failed. But his reply to Green on June 3 lacked the enthusiasm
and effusive congratulations Green might have expected.

Your communication of the 16th, as well as your last report,
communicating the result of the expedition against the Indians, have
been received, but by some accident the letter has been mislaid.
Your course in reference to this expedition is entirely satisfactory
and is fully approved. Although as Executive of the State I have no
power to make treaties with any of the Indian Tribes, still I hope the
arrangements you have made will provide beneficial and preserve
peaceful relations between the whites and Indians until some more
permanent line of policy shall be adopted by the United States.[19]

Green had arranged a meeting with other chiefs who desired peace, but
the chiefs failed to show. General Thomas Eastland, who succeeded Green,
wrote Burnett on June 15 that he regretted the meeting hadn't happened
because it might have prevented "a continuation of the disturbances occurring

so frequently, causing the indiscriminate and wholesale murder of both white men and Indians."[20]

There were new hostilities—two miners were found dead in the vicinity. While Eastland assumed they had been killed by American Indians, he said the tribes had good cause to be outraged at whites: "While no one will attempt to justify the Indians in such barbarous deeds, it may well be asked if they may not frequently be perpetrated in retaliation for similar ones committed (mostly, no doubt, by lawless white men) upon their people? It is a well-known fact that among our white population there are men who boast of the number of Indians they have killed and that not one shall escape them."[21]

Burnett again called out the militia after reports the Nisenan had emerged from mountain hideouts and returned to harassing whites. In a dispatch on October 25, 1850, he directed Sheriff William Rogers of El Dorado County to organize two hundred men to "punish the Indians engaged in the late attacks . . . along the emigrant trail leading from Salt Lake to California," specifically around Ringgold Creek, east of Johnson's Ranch. He urged the sheriff to offer "any assistance in his power to protect the emigrants and all others traveling the route."[22] Evidently, not a great deal was accomplished, as the attackers again retreated into the mountains and avoided combat.

The *Alta* was unforgiving, calling the Ringgold Creek mission "a farce" that cost the state many thousands of dollars. "We fully believe there has been no necessity for warfare . . . the recent ridiculous attempt to get up an Indian war in El Dorado County had its origin in a desire on the part of a few provision dealers to supply troops with their 'grub.'" It said the waste of "all this expenditure of patriotism and military ardor" was underscored by the inability of the troops to find the alleged attackers. The newspaper lamented that white mistreatment of the tribes had driven them to acts of desperation. It said this didn't have to be. "Oppression, abuse and hunger have driven these miserable beings to acts of robbery and murder, we doubt not, but it does not necessarily follow that they are alone to blame. It is our settled opinion, founded upon experience and other sources of information, that there have been no necessities for Indian wars in this state and that a just and honorable course by the whites would have ensured lasting and unbroken peace between the two races."[23]

Dispatching the militia to confront attacks, or suspected attacks, was indeed expensive. Arming, equipping, and provisioning the militia for the Gila expedition to the Colorado River cost $76,588, while the bill for the El

Dorado mission amounted to $72,611, a combined $150,000 at a time when the state was already struggling to pay its bills.[24]

Many crimes against Native American tribes in California received little public attention, if they weren't ignored entirely, as was the case throughout the continent. For example, no mention was made in Burnett's autobiography, or in his surviving correspondence, of the so-named Bloody Island Massacre on May 15, 1850. Even today, the details of this massacre remain sketchy. But what is known is that the First Dragoons Regiment of the US Calvary massacred dozens, possibly hundreds, of members of the Pomo tribe, including women and children, at their island village at Clear Lake in Lake County. Among survivors was a 6-year-old named Ni'ka, or Lucy Moore, who, the story goes, survived by submerging herself in the lake and breathing through a tule reed. The attack was said to be a reprisal for the killing of two white settlers, Charles Stone and Andrew Kelsey, who had effectively enslaved and severely abused Pomo workers.[25]

The late California historian Kevin Starr wrote that an estimated population of 150,000 Native Americans living in California in 1845 had been reduced to fewer than 30,000 by 1870, more than half of the decline due to disease, and the rest from murders and massacres.[26]

Without question, the major event in California during the Burnett administration was its admission into the United States as the thirty-first state on September 9, 1850. Burnett's tireless advocacy of self-government helped bring this about, although General Riley and many others played roles equally as important, if not more so.

The stumbling block in Congress, of course, had been slavery. Southern senators objected that admitting California would upset the balance of power in the Congress between slave and free states, then equally divided at fifteen states apiece. "Whenever the word 'California' was pronounced," wrote Bancroft, "close after, came the word 'slavery.'"[27] The result had been a stalemate.

After months of debate, agreement was reached on statehood as part of the Compromise of 1850, proposed by the aging Senator Henry Clay of Kentucky. The compromise was a package of eight separate bills. The most important of these for California was the statehood bill, which won Senate approval by a vote of thirty-four to eighteen on August 13, 1850. Other measures included territorial status for Utah and New Mexico; abolishment of the slave trade in the nation's capital—but not slavery—and, in a major gain for slave states, a tough new Fugitive Slave Act. The act required authorities in nonslave states to return fugitive slaves to their owners and imposed costly penalties for anyone assisting a slave or failing to cooperate in enforcing the act.

Senator Stephen Douglas of Illinois helped cobble together the majorities for the eight bills, each voted on separately. Northern and Southern senators voted their interests. Of the sixty senators, only four voted for all the measures, and, of the Deep South senators, only Sam Houston of the newly admitted Texas voted for California statehood.[28]

As it turned out, there was little for Southern senators to fear from California. The antislavery Fremont was officially a US senator for just twenty-one days—he couldn't be seated until California was admitted into statehood. He failed to win reelection in 1851 from a deadlocked California Senate— his supporters gave up after 141 ballots. His former seat in the US Senate remained vacant for a year with only Gwin, who sided with Southern interests, representing California. The seat would finally be filled in 1852 by John Weller, a Northerner with Southern sympathies and a supporter of Gwin. "In North-South struggles, Weller and Gwin might as well have been representing Mississippi," wrote historian Leonard L. Richards.[29]

The South's quarrel with Northern states did not extend to California or Oregon. Senator John H. Hammond of South Carolina said as much during an acrimonious debate over whether to accept Kansas as a state under its 1857 proslavery Lecompton Constitution. In his so-called "Cotton Is King" speech on March 4, 1858, Hammond denounced the antislavery activities of Northern states but added: "I do not speak of California and Oregon; there is no antagonism between the South and those countries [*sic*], and never will be."[30] The Lecompton Constitution, previously adopted at a stacked Kansas convention of proslavery advocates, failed to pass, although not without a great deal of acrimony that further aggravated the developing crisis between North and South.

Two years later, as if underscoring Hammond's point of "no antagonism," the California and Oregon delegations joined Southern delegates in walking out of the 1860 Democratic National Convention rather than accept Senator Douglas as the party's nominee for president. The dissident delegations instead nominated proslavery John Breckinridge of Kentucky for president and Joseph Lane of Oregon for vice president. With Douglas and Breckinridge splitting the Democratic vote, Republican Abraham Lincoln was elected president. He narrowly carried both California and Oregon.

The mail steamer SS *Oregon,* its guns booming and flying red-white-and-blue bunting, brought the news of statehood to Californians on October 18, 1850, setting off weeks of celebration. Governor Burnett eagerly joined in. Although he wasn't one to engage in demonstrative behavior, on this occasion he cut loose. Burnett had just arrived from Sacramento when the Oregon steamed into San Francisco Bay with the news. After joining a large and joyous celebration in Portsmouth Square that evening, Burnett left by stagecoach for San Jose the next day, racing another stage to be first to deliver the news.[31]

Burnett sat beside the driver he remembered as Crandall, probably Jared Crandall, one of the owners of the Hall & Crandall stage line. Racing neck and neck with their rivals, they covered the 50 miles to San Jose at breakneck speed, winning by the proverbial nose. Waving his hat over his head, Burnett said they shouted to cheering people as they passed, "California is admitted into the Union!" Recalled Burnett: "I never witnessed a scene more exciting, and never felt more enthusiastic."[32]

It proved the high point of Burnett's time as governor and probably of his entire political career. Nine weeks later, he would resign.

Chapter 22
A Governor Resigns, but Why?

Peter Burnett devotes two full pages in his autobiography to the predations of the California squirrel—"one of the greatest obstacles agriculture has had to meet in California." Dirty gray in color, they were twice as large as their Mississippi Valley cousins, and "so numerous as to destroy whole fields of growing grain."[1]

The space Burnett gives to "these little pests" exceeds the space allotted to his last months in office and his controversial final address to the legislature. Avoided almost entirely were any thoughts on his resignation on January 9, 1851. Perhaps it was just too painful, or perhaps he no longer cared.

Burnett did include his two-paragraph resignation message to the legislature in his *Recollections*. It is remarkably brief for someone given to excessive verbosity. But in these two paragraphs he gives more poignant expression to his affection for his adopted state than in his letters and speeches, which often ran for dozens of pages and thousands of words.

> Circumstances entirely unexpected and unforeseen by me and over which I could have no control, render it indispensable that I should devote all my time and attention to my private affairs. I therefore tender to both Houses of the Legislature my resignation as Governor of the State.
>
> I leave the high office to which I was called by the voluntary voice of my countrymen with but one regret—that my feeble abilities have allowed me to accomplish so little for the state. In the humble sphere of a private citizen, I shall still cherish for her that ardent attachment she so justly merits. Within her serene and sunny limits I intend to spend the remainder of my days, many or few; and should an unfortunate crisis ever arise when such a sacrifice might be available

and necessary for her safety, my limited fortune and fame, and my life, will be at her disposal.[2]

Citing private affairs as the reason for his resignation seems a stretch, especially as Burnett offered no clue, then or later, to a specific issue of sufficient gravity to justify it. Problems with his finances, blamed for previous resignations, were surely not the reason, nor were the squatter challenges in Sacramento. As governor, he drew an annual salary of $10,000, hardly a paltry sum for the time. The reason for his resignation was most likely found in his declining popularity and the insulting reception from lawmakers to his second annual address on January 7. But by this time, he had made so many missteps that perhaps nothing he could say or do would salvage his political standing with the legislature and California voters.

And he didn't seem to much care. He wrote his brother George in Oregon on September 2, 1850, that he looked forward to the end of his term. He apologized for not writing sooner, explaining "the cares of office are too great." He wished to return to his personal business, which he'd been forced to neglect as governor. "The work for me is tiring and it is hard for me to keep along," he wrote. "My mind is too much occupied. I shall be glad when my time is out. I hope I shall never be in such another predicament."[3]

The well-off Burnett said in the same letter that he admired a comment from George, that he was satisfied with his modest living as a farmer. Burnett second-guessed his own desire for wealth. "I have fancied myself to be rich, and the balance of my life, I have known myself to be poor, and I hardly know now which is the happier condition of the two, but if there was any difference it was in favor of the poverty."

Among Burnett's more curious missteps was his announcement on November 4, 1850, that Thanksgiving would be observed in California on Saturday, November 30, rather than on a Thursday. He offered no explanation other than the timing was "in accordance with his own feelings."[4] He faced immediate ridicule. The *California Daily Courier* said Burnett must never have set foot in New England, or "he would know that it is just as impossible to have Thanksgiving on any other day, save Thursday, as it is for the Fourth of July to come on the Eighth of January." One wag predicted "the day when such a governor goes out of office will more generally be observed as a day of Thanksgiving."[5] The *Alta*, with its typical sarcasm when writing about the governor, said, "We should almost as soon think it possible to have a Thanksgiving dinner without pumpkin pie as to appoint the festival for Saturday."[6]

We can't know how many Californians bowed to the governor's edict to observe Thanksgiving on a Saturday, but Burnett and the "Sons of New England" most certainly did. They observed the day at a gala banquet in Sacramento's Columbia Hotel, making one wonder whether Burnett changed the date for the convenience of this particular celebration. Guests dined on salmon, mutton, roast beef, veal, pork, venison, and of course turkey, along with mock turtle soup and a variety of sauces, salads, and desserts. To wash it all down, they drank champagne, Madeira wine, brandy, sherry and hot punch.[7]

Burnett must have been in his glory. The *Sacramento Transcript* reported he was toasted as the first governor of California, to which he responded with "short and very appropriate" remarks while standing in front of two celebratory banners, one of gold-fringed blue satin and a second emblazoned with "California" in large letters. A band played the "Governor's March." Burnett next offered a toast of his own. When the different states were recognized during yet more toasts, Burnett rose a third time as the representative of Tennessee, his birthplace. The elder John Sutter also attended and was toasted for his "service to America."

The praise lauded on Burnett at the banquet could not save him from what followed. His second annual address to the Legislature on January 7 dug his political grave deeper. It was faulted on many counts, not the least of which was its length—nearly twelve thousand words, which filled twenty-seven pages in the legislative journal, an unseemly length even for Burnett.[8] The *Transcript* ran the address in sections over three days.[9] The *Alta* printed "this immense document" in a special section. Other newspapers serialized it, if they ran it at all.

Members of the assembly treated the address with disdain. They allowed the clerk to read only a few paragraphs before endorsing a motion by John Cook of San Diego that further reading "be dispensed with."[10]

Burnett received a slightly better reception in the state senate. David Broderick said it would be "discourteous" to not read the governor's address in its entirety. But Broderick, who was soon to be elected senate president, suspended the rule that members could not "read any newspaper, converse, or walk across the room" during the reading.[11]

If there was a theme to Burnett's rambling address, it was his negative out-look for California. He began by citing problems facing the state, including its abysmal financial situation. "Our cities have been visited by fire, pestilence and flood, and our whole state has passed through a severe monetary crisis, producing extensive failures and great pecuniary embarrassment," unable to pay its bills.[12] Burnett nevertheless acknowledged that he had resisted pres-sure to call a special session of the legislature to deal with the financial crisis, saying, in effect, it wasn't crisis enough. He was concerned the legislature would want to borrow more money to cover ordinary expenses, thereby plunging California further into debt, and imposing an unfair burden on future taxpayers.[13]

On another subject of pressing importance to many Californians, Burnett acknowledged rejecting most of the "repeated calls" to dispatch the militia to punish Native Americans for attacks on whites. He was aware that "hostilities more or less formidable have occurred at intervals and many valuable lives have been lost." But attacks were so numerous that he "determined in my own mind to leave the people of each neighborhood to protect themselves, believ-ing they would be able to do so."[14]

He also no doubt infuriated some lawmakers by blaming injustices by set-tlers against the native tribes as the underlying reason they attacked whites. "We have suddenly spread ourselves over the country in every direction and appropriated whatever portion of it we pleased to ourselves, without their con-sent and without compensation."[15] He would be applauded today for speaking the truth, but in the conflict zones of the 1850s, it was not a message many wanted to hear.

Burnett also predicted "a war of extermination will continue to be waged between the races until the Indian race becomes extinct." He didn't see any other way. "While we cannot anticipate this result but with painful regret, the inevitable destiny of the race is beyond the power or wisdom of man to avert."

Oddly, he complained to the legislators that the military leader, Major Bean, had failed to respond or even acknowledge his orders during the Gila expedi-tion. Burnett said he learned elsewhere that Bean received his orders but failed to reply. That Burnett would use his legislative address to complain about the insub-ordination of a senior officer seems an unusual admission of ineffectiveness.[16]

Burnett could not let go of his obsession with blacks, once again urging "the necessity and propriety of excluding free persons of color from the State." Because African Americans were denied many of the rights of citizens, and lived in conditions of servitude, according to Burnett, they lacked the ability to contribute meaningfully to the development of the state. "They have no ideas and no recollections of a separate national existence—no alliance with great names of families—no page of history upon which they recorded the glorious deeds of the past—no present privileges—and no hope for the future. To expect any race of men thus situated to make any sensible improvement as a class, is the wildest dream of the imagination, and utterly incompatible with all our sober experience."[17]

If Burnett believed this tripe, he didn't bother to explain what might have brought these conditions about. There was no mention of Africans being torn from their families and kidnapped from their native lands, no reference to their enslavement, and no mention they were denied education and all manner of humane treatment.

Moreover, just as Burnett argued that a war of extermination with Native Americans was inevitable, he predicted armed conflict with African Americans if they were allowed into the state. "When those who come after us shall witness a war in California between the two races, and all the disgrace and disasters following in its train, they will have as much cause to reproach us for not taking timely steps [to exclude African Americans], when they were practicable."

Burnett revealed a lack of humanity, as well as common sense, on another subject. He called for the temporary imposition of the death penalty for persons convicted of robbery and major property crimes. To Burnett, the expense of holding criminals was "exceedingly oppressive" for local governments. Executions would save money—and thus "For grand larceny and robbery I would suggest the punishment of death." He said the death sentence should be temporary until the state constructed a penitentiary and there were adequate county jails. Temporary, of course, would not spare the lives of those already executed. The legislature imposed no such penalty.[18]

One could sum up his address this way: a war to the death with native tribes . . . a war with African Americans . . . the death penalty for theft . . . officers who didn't obey his orders. It's of little wonder that Burnett chose to gloss over his address when he wrote his autobiography in the 1870s, instead writing about squirrels.

There was much more. Burnett concluded by talking of the "many difficulties of governing the state." Perhaps attempting to explain away his failings as governor, he said: "To start a new system under ordinary circumstances is no easy task, but no new state has ever been encompassed with so many embarrassments as California."[19] He gave no hint he would resign two days later.

Criticism of the address was unbridled, ranging from tepid to condemnatory. But few, if any, eviscerated Burnett with as much apparent relish as the editors of the *Daily Alta California* on January 8. They first offered a preview of what they would say in subsequent editions. "We have not yet digested this endless communication, and shall not today attempt a criticism except to say that His Excellency evidently wrote against time, and as time kept running, he kept writing. He has been as silent and unheard as a dormouse all the year, but has 'spread himself' at last."[20]

A more fulsome and blistering critique of Burnett's "not very well written document" appeared on January 11, following his resignation, although the critique was apparently written beforehand. The *Alta* denounced his renewed call for legislation banning African Americans. "We utterly disagree with the well-known principles of the governor, now reiterated, for the exclusion of all colored persons from the state and will not acknowledge the soundness of his arguments on this point or admit the question of slavery will ever be agitated within our borders."

While the newspaper supported Burnett's call for better law enforcement, it would "utterly oppose" the governor's recommendation for capital punishment in cases of robbery and grand larceny. "We trust that our statute books will never be disgraced by so odious a blot as that recommended . . . shame that such an argument should ever be used by the executive of the state." The editors did agree with Burnett's refusal to call a special session of the legislature to deal with the state's financial difficulties.[21]

It isn't surprising that the newspaper greeted Burnett's resignation on January 9 with "the most unqualified satisfaction." It added sarcastically, "We believe it will be a popular measure throughout the state, the most popular act" of Burnett's brief term in office. "It is not to be denied that the people were most shamefully deceived and egregiously disappointed in their selection for the head of the state government." In the *Alta*'s view, Burnett was elected because of his reputation as "a man of talent and ability," but those qualifications failed to translate into effectiveness. The voters "expected much from his acknowledged ability, and as we said before have been utterly disappointed."

The newspaper reported that Burnett suffered from "an almost unaccountable apathy," evidently content with the simple task of signing bills and dealing with trivial matters. "We are unaware of any instance where, when it would have been of essential service, he exercised his right to veto obnoxious measures . . . The power existed, but the will was wanting."[22] Even when Burnett did act, it was considered too little, too late—or too unwise.

The newspaper dismissed Burnett's excuse that he resigned to attend to pressing personal affairs. Rather, it said, Burnett may finally have realized it was improper for the people to "pay him a very large salary simply to mind his own business."[23] A year later, the same newspaper wondered whether Burnett wanted the governor's chair simply for the "gratification of being known as the first governor of California—the empty honor of a title."[24]

A less harsh commentary appeared in the *San Francisco Herald*, which believed Burnett would leave office with his integrity intact. "In a time of almost universal depravity, he has been thoroughly honest and, not withstanding a great many temptations, he has maintained a character of uprightness." But the newspaper's editorial pinpointed a shortcoming that plagued Burnett throughout his career: a failure to build alliances with colleagues who could help steer him from some of his ill-conceived notions. "He has made many enemies and few friends," it said. "He was swayed by bad advisers and has suffered himself to be the dupe of men of more cunning and less honest than himself."[25]

To the *Herald*, Burnett's address contained "many recommendations which we hope the Legislature may turn a deaf ear to." But the one "great piece of injustice" it singled out was not Burnett's recommendation to ban African Americans. Rather, it was his decision to replace the state printer, H. H. Robison.[26]

Not all newspapers were critical. The January 11 issue of the *Sacramento Transcript* indicated that Burnett deserved respect as California's first governor. "Long may he live, to watch the progress of the state that has given immortality to his name, by choosing him as her first chief magistrate." The newspaper hoped Burnett would make his home in Sacramento, where he had "hosts of friends."[27] The *Sacramento City Directory* for 1851 mentioned in a laudatory biographical sketch of Burnett—one that Burnett himself may have written or edited—that he resigned as governor "for reasons that are not perfectly clear."[28]

To one recent writer of California history, Arthur Quinn, it seemed Burnett's "only legislative objective" as governor was to exclude African Americans, similar to what he'd achieved in Oregon. "Of his contributions to Oregon, he, as a former slave owner, seemed to be particularly proud of his role in excluding free blacks."[29]

The legislature accepted Burnett's resignation at a joint session by a vote of thirty-four to seven. David Broderick was the only senator to object, joined by six assemblymen. Broderick argued that Burnett had made a contract with the people when he was elected governor and was obligated to carry it out.[30]

Broderick and Burnett had no love for one another. Broderick had derailed Burnett's exclusion law in the Senate after it passed the assembly. He maneuvered to bottle the bill up in committee so it never came to a vote.[31] Broderick also tried unsuccessfully to block a California version of the Fugitive Slave Act. Nevertheless, Burnett endorsed the abolitionist Broderick for the US Senate in 1857 over William McKendree Gwin. "I think he is not to be relied on," he wrote an acquaintance in Grass Valley, California. "As for Broderick, I think he is frank, independent, and straight forward."[32] He may have remembered Broderick's vote against his resignation, and his support for a full reading of his address.

Burnett's prejudice against African Americans had its parallel in his attitude toward Chinese. Allowing Chinese into the country, he wrote in his autobiography, risked subjecting the western United States to Chinese domination "to the ultimate exclusion of the white man."[33]

Burnett finished *Recollections* before Congress enacted the Chinese Exclusion Act in 1882, which prohibited additional Chinese laborers from entering the United States. But there is little doubt he would have been among its most ardent supporters. "I have long been opposed to the residence of the Chinese among us, except for purposes of trade," he wrote. And in a reversal of his argument that African Americans would be unable to contribute to California's prosperity, he said the Chinese might contribute too much. Were they to enjoy the same rights and privileges as white Americans, they "would own all the property on this coast" because of "their greater numbers and superior economy."

Burnett knew that tens of thousands of Chinese had already been in the country for decades, providing much-needed labor.[34] As many as eleven thousand Chinese had helped build the Central Pacific Railroad, the western leg of the first transcontinental railroad, completed in 1869, and other railroads throughout the West. Thousands also came to mine gold, often working claims abandoned by whites, but with far more success. They cleared land, drained swamps, and worked in fish canneries. Generally speaking, they were more reliable than white laborers and worked for less pay, which made them attractive to employers.

Although decrying the violence aimed at Chinese immigrants, Burnett suggested the harassment and assaults, arson attacks, and evictions from their homes were the fault of the Chinese themselves.[35] To him, the temptation to harass the Chinese was too much for many young people to resist. "The worst effect of the presence of the Chinese among us is the fact that it is making tyrants and lawless ruffians of our boys," he said.[36]

Burnett claimed his feelings about the Chinese were based on "practical statesmanship"—whatever that meant—rather than prejudice. "I am not conscious of prejudices against any race of men," he said in a statement that today boggles the mind.[37]

In a day of fast-moving events on January 9, after accepting Burnett's resignation, the legislature endorsed Lieutenant Governor McDougal as his successor, and elected David Broderick to replace McDougal as senate president. McDougal promptly took the oath as governor from Henry A. Lyons of the California Supreme Court. Burnett was invited but, not surprisingly, stayed away.[38]

If the lawmakers were looking for a successor who demonstrated ability to govern, McDougal didn't set the bar especially high in his remarks to the legislature. According to the *Sacramento Transcript*, the new governor "expressed distrust of his ability to discharge the duties of his highly responsible office."[39] McDougal proved not to be an improvement. Elisha Crosby said McDougal "drank too freely" and was generally ineffective.[40] He served just long enough to complete Burnett's two-year term. His successor was John Bigler, the first governor to complete a full term.

As for Burnett, although the *Transcript* said he was leaving office with "enough of the good things of the world" to comfortably retire, a sedate future wasn't yet in Burnett's plans.[41] He had a joyous family event in which to look forward: the marriage of his daughter Martha to his close aide Ryland on January 23. A family history called the wedding a "fandango" of a celebration, held at the Burnett home in Alviso.[42] In a letter to his brother George, Burnett called Ryland "a superior young man and all that I could ask him to be." He wrote in the same letter that his eldest son, Dwight, and his wife, Mary, who had wed the previous January, were living "very happily" at their home, also in Alviso.[43]

Chapter 23
Rescue at Sea

Looking back on his time as governor, Burnett found no fault in his leadership. But perhaps unintentionally, he underscored a major weakness of his abbreviated term in office. He bragged in his *Recollections* he had neither sought nor taken advice from others.

The person he listened to most, he said, was himself. "He who relies on himself," he wrote, "knows the man he trusts. . . . Self-reliance is the only sure path to success in life."[1] He went on to say, "I do not follow the opinions of others, unless they agree with my own. . . . My business is my affair and not theirs."[2]

The downside to this approach to governing was that there were no trusted advisers to help him avoid some of his more egregious blunders and impolitic statements. While Burnett frequently mentioned "friends," he offered little evidence that they were more than acquaintances.

Burnett's comments on self-reliance were written much later in life. In the months following his resignation, however, he appeared to fall into a depression to the point that he predicted he might soon die. It wasn't just his failure as governor that set him back; he and Harriet were both in poor health. He also had learned his brother-in-law John Rogers had died in Sacramento.

"This world has now for me no great charms; none that I cling to with any anxiety," he wrote on December 26, 1851, to his sister Elizabeth, extending his condolences on the death of her husband. "One by one, our friends are dropping off, and soon it will come to our turn to go." Referring to a recent episode of bleeding by Harriet, Burnett said, "Her health has much declined of late and she cannot reasonably expect to live long. My own constitution has felt the shock of the hardships I have endured and the natural advance of years. We are in the paths that lead to the grave."[3]

Peter Burnett's desk and portrait in the Burnett room at the Roberto Adobe and Suñol House Museum in San Jose. The dress in the corner may have been worn by Harriet at the inaugural ball when Burnett was elected governor. Courtesy of Judge Paul Bernal, museum chair and official historian of the City of San Jose.

But the path still had a long way to go. Burnett, age 44, would live nearly another forty-four years, until 1895; Harriet would live twenty-four more years, to 1879, and would be well enough for a long sea voyage to China and back.

While Burnett's official correspondence portrays him as stiff, aloof and officious, his personal correspondence with family members reveals a more sympathetic and caring side. In a letter to George on July 27, 1862, Burnett wrote of his grief over serious health issues affecting his children. Harriet had just returned from eight months in China, where she had taken John and Armstead in the hopes of improving Armstead's health. Sallie had died a year earlier of tuberculosis, and Armstead was suffering from what was probably also tuberculosis.[4]

The family sought treatment for Armstead in China. "The trip improved him, but he is not well," Burnett wrote. "He is able to walk about and to go out in good weather, but his cough is distressing. . . . I fear he must go as Sallie did." Moreover, Burnett's son John was having eyesight problems. Nothing had caused so much grief, Burnett said, as "the sickness of my children." Armstead did not recover. He died later that year at age 22.[5] Burnett complained of his own health issues: his hands shook—from palsy perhaps?—and he endured frequent recurrences of the fever he had suffered as a young man in Tennessee.

Letters that Burnett wrote to George were kept by Burnett's great-grand-daughter Elizabeth Arques Motheral of San Francisco who upon her death in 1988 left them to her daughter Emily Arques Douville of Antioch, California. "She saved them," said Douville. "She was very interested in Peter Burnett and that was a big thing for her to be related to him."[6]

In his *Recollections*, Burnett wrote of another death that affected him deeply. A young judge, James F. Jones, died of tuberculosis on December 15, 1851, less than a year after taking office as the first US District Court judge for the Southern District of California. Jones, from Kentucky, was just 27 years old and had served as a delegate to California's constitutional convention. Burnett and Jones frequently discussed legal and other issues while Burnett was governor. He admired Jones for maintaining "a great reserve, never obtruding his private affairs upon the public." In this, they were apparently kindred souls. It would be in death that Jones exerted his greatest influence over Burnett's later life.[7]

Burnett returned to law after his resignation as governor. He joined a San Jose law firm with his former aide and son-in-law, Ryland, and William T. Wallace, a future chief justice of the California Supreme Court from 1872 to 1879. Wallace married Burnett's daughter Romietta on March 30, 1853.[8] Burnett also formed a partnership in Sacramento with the law firm of Burnett, Edwards and Gass, with offices on J Street, between 4th and 5th Streets.

On occasion, Burnett did favors for friends. A former acquaintance, James S. Thomas from Platte City, Missouri, appeared unexpectedly at Burnett's Sacramento office seeking help. Burnett had known Thomas as a competent but struggling attorney in Missouri. Thomas was still struggling; his only possessions were the wagon and mules with which he'd traveled to California. Burnett arranged for Thomas to be nominated for magistrate judge and campaigned on his behalf. Thomas won.[9]

Burnett spent much of his post-governor period focused on his Sacramento properties, which had been damaged by flooding during the winter of 1849-50 and would be further devastated by a fire that destroyed much of the city in 1852. It was fortuitous for Burnett that he had already taken his profits from selling the Sutter lots.

Sacramento experienced explosive growth virtually from the first day Burnett began selling city lots; miners by the thousands flocked to the region from throughout North America and abroad. By October 1849, the city boasted a population of 2,000, with forty-five wooden buildings and three hundred tent homes. In the following two months, the population doubled to 3,500, and in 1850, the US Census recorded a population of 9,087. Two years later, it was 12,418.[10]

The floods of 1849–50 dealt a severe blow to the young city. Heavy rain over many days, followed by a violent storm on January 8, 1850, sent the Sacramento and American Rivers out of their banks, spilling "great walls of water" into populated areas with virtually no warning.[11] The *Placer Times* reported on January 19 that the entire city, up to a mile back from the embarcadero, was under water: "The damage to merchandise and to buildings and the losses sustained by persons engaged in trade is very great." Few houses escaped damage, many knocked off their foundations.[12]

There were stories of lives lost—"some were drowned in their beds," according to one report, although there was no official count—and "great numbers" of livestock drowned, their decaying bodies left in the streets.[13] The local hospital was evacuated and the patients moved to Samuel Brannan's old store at Sutter's Fort.

The elder Sutter may have felt some degree of "I-told-you-so" satisfaction, as he had warned of low-lying Sacramento's vulnerability to flooding. After the flood waters receded, Sacramento built levies to protect the city from future flooding, but the levies were breached time and again, in March 1852 and during the winters of 1852–53 and 1861–62. The city bounced back each time.

A fire that broke out November 2, 1852, in a millinery shop on the north side of J Street was as devastating as the floods, if not more so. Gale-force winds picked up the flames and carried them from building to building— there were accounts of burning boards catapulting through the air like sticks. The fire nearly destroyed the entire downtown core in a single night. Damages were put at $6 million.[14]

Burnett rushed to Sacramento to assess the damage to his properties. He found the commercial district "one waste of dark desolation—the streets could scarcely be distinguished from the blocks." He estimated his own losses at $25,000. But whether it was fire or flood, Burnett praised the people for their perseverance in rebuilding the city after each disaster—"All honor to that noble people."[15]

Peter Burnett's house, which he built in Alviso in 1850 and lived in with his family during his final year as governor. In 1854, he had it moved piece by piece 8 miles to 441 North First Street in San Jose. Later used by the California Printing Company, the house was demolished in 1955. Courtesy of the San Jose Public Library.

Burnett moved to Sacramento to help with the rebuilding. He was elected to the city council—another entry on his already lengthy resume. He remained in Sacramento for the next eighteen months, returning to Alviso in March 1854. He had been involved in several schemes in Sacramento, including an unsuccessful project to develop a railroad from Sacramento to Grass Valley, a distance of about 60 miles. He wrote his friend Jonas Winchester on March 21, 1854, that the project had "never jelled." He also told Winchester of his plans to return to Alviso, where he would "live as a quiet recluse, far from the disturbing cares of earth."[16]

Back in Alviso, he proceeded to dismantle his two-story home and move it piece by piece 8 miles to San Jose at 441 North First Street. He gave no reason for moving his house, but it may have been because low-lying Alviso was flood prone. Moving the house also proved a better bet financially than selling it, because the real estate market had collapsed, and he could get nowhere near the $10,000 he paid to build it.[17] The house was demolished in 1955.

Burnett announced to his brother in June 1854 that he had closed his Sacramento office and was retiring from law. "I have now retired, hopefully forever, from the law." He said he wished to devote his time to studying his religion.[18] But the quiet life he envisioned didn't stay quiet.

In September 1856, Burnett and Ryland went to the East Coast in a trip that almost ended in disaster. After a voyage from San Francisco to Panama on the steamship SS *John L. Stephens,* they made a land crossing to Colon, where they transferred to the steamship SS *George Law* for the rest of the trip to New York. The *George Law* was a side-wheeler built in 1852 for the gold rush, ferrying California-bound prospectors from New York to Panama and returning with gold from the mines. The captain was a well-known navy officer, William Lewis Herndon. Burnett and Ryland were among a thousand or so passengers. The ship also carried a substantial quantity of gold.

The voyage from Panama to New York typically took nine days, with a refueling stop in Cuba. On this voyage, however, Captain Herndon was warned of an outbreak of yellow fever in Cuba and detoured to Key West to take on more coal. But the evening after departing Key West, the fully loaded 2,100-ton vessel ran aground on a coral reef 5 miles off Florida's east coast. High tide came and went with no success in freeing the ship, which was pounded relentlessly by large waves. A storm approached. It was a disaster in the making.

Writing about the incident years later, Burnett described the passengers as being aware of their peril: "I never saw a more solemn assemblage of people."[19] The captain ordered much of the coal thrown overboard, followed by whatever else passengers could find to lighten the ship. But the ship remained stuck. When a Spanish clipper ship came near, Herndon arranged to transfer some of the passengers. Burnett and Ryland were just about to board a launch for the rescue ship when the *George Law* began to move. Crewmen had thrown a heavy anchor forward onto the reef, and—with the lightened load, another high tide, and crewmen grasping the anchor line—the ship scraped free. Although sustaining some damage, the steamship was sufficiently seaworthy to safely resume the voyage.

In one of those self-aggrandizing comments Burnett was prone to make, he claimed that once the ship was floating free, Captain Herndon threw his arms around him, weeping. "'Governor, my heart was almost broken.'" Burnett praised Herndon for saving the ship and for his dedication to the safety of the passengers, adding, "I remember him with feelings of the most tender regard."[20]

A year later, on September 12, 1857, the *George Law,* renamed the *Central America,* went down in a hurricane off Cape Hatteras. It carried 600 passengers and 15 tons of gold bullion. About 152 passengers were rescued, but the

remaining passengers were lost.[21] Captain Herndon was last seen standing at
the railing outside the wheelhouse in full uniform as water engulfed the ship.
He was said to have handed his watch to one of the rescued passengers to give
to his wife.[22]

From New York, Burnett continued on to Platte County in Missouri, where
"he visited scenes and friends of my early days."[23] He would make two other
trips to the East Coast, at least one of which was to meet with his publishers.

Burnett became seasick on that first voyage, and the illness evolved into
a serious attack of neuralgia, a painful nervous disorder. Burnett said he was
"sick two-thirds of the time" for the next five years.[24]

Chapter 24
On the Court with Archy Lee

Peter Burnett added yet another distinguished position to his resume when Governor J. Neely Johnson appointed him associate justice on the California Supreme Court on January 13, 1857, filling a vacancy created by the resignation of Judge Solomon Heydenfeldt.

Burnett's unpopularity as governor was apparently forgotten by voters, because he was easily elected to the unexpired term in October, receiving 54,991 votes, more than twice the vote for any of five other candidates.[1]

Once again, Burnett had landed on his feet. But once again, he couldn't keep his balance. And once again he was undone by his prejudice toward African Americans, reflected in a controversial 1858 ruling in the case of Archy Lee, a Mississippi slave.

As for any positive memories from his nearly two years on the court, Burnett apparently had none, at least none worth mentioning in his *Recollections*. He noted both the date of his appointment and the date his term ended in October 1858. Nothing more. It could not have been Burnett was tired of writing. He still had much to say about other subjects, just not about his experience on the court. Others, however, would have much to say.

Burnett's appointment was initially welcomed with an effusive endorsement by the *Sacramento Union*, which praised him as "a pure man, a good man . . . a man of sterling sense [and] sound judgment." It said his appointment was "one of the cases where the office literally sought the man."[2] But it didn't take long for the newspaper's praise to turn to regret.

The case that undermined Burnett's judicial reputation was, predictably, a slave case, *Ex Parte Archy*. Historian Stacey L. Smith called the decision in this case "the dying gasp of slaveholder rights in California."[3]

It centered on Archy Lee, a 19-year-old slave brought to California from Mississippi in 1857 by his owner, Charles Stovall. Although California entered the Union as a free state, it still harbored a great deal of proslavery sentiment, notably among miners and immigrants from Southern states. Suggestions that California might someday be divided into a free north and a slave south had never quite gone away. Proslavery sentiment had helped push a fugitive slave act for California through the legislature on April 15, 1852. One of the advocates of the California measure was state senator James Estell, who emigrated from Missouri in 1849 with a dozen slaves to work on his farm in Salamo County.

The California act supplemented the federal Fugitive Slave Act, which gave slaveholders the right to claim runaway slaves who escaped across state lines, but did not apply to slaves who escaped after being voluntarily taken by owners to free states. Even so, the California legislature decided that owners of slaves who escaped prior to statehood could continue to claim escapees as slaves. Any slave who escaped after statehood presumably could not be claimed.[4] Senator David Broderick led attempts to defeat the bill through parliamentary maneuvering, but ultimately it passed the senate by a vote of fourteen to nine.[5]

The California Supreme Court upheld the act in a controversial 1852 ruling that the historian Smith called "one of the most deeply pro-slavery decisions ever rendered in a free state."[6] The two presiding judges in the case were from slave states, Chief Justice Hugh Murray from Missouri and Alexander Anderson from Tennessee. The act, which took effect April 15, 1852, was initially set to expire after a year, but it was extended for an additional two years. It finally expired in 1855 after the political winds shifted back toward an antislavery legislature.

It wasn't unusual to find slaves in California. As many as a thousand worked in the mines or at other jobs, most brought by their owners before the state adopted its antislavery constitution in 1849.[7] Some came voluntarily, seeing an opportunity to buy freedom for themselves and their families. Slaves were generally allowed to work their own claims on evenings and Sundays.[8]

Most of the slaves were from the border states of Missouri, Kentucky, and Tennessee. But they were also brought from elsewhere. As many as two hundred slaves were from two North Carolina counties, Burke and McDowell.[9] Nathanial Ford brought two slaves from Polk County, Oregon, to mine gold in 1849, promising to free them after they returned to Oregon.[10]

White miners often saw slaves as unfair competition. When Thomas Jefferson Green—he of the "legislature of a thousand drinks"—brought fifteen slaves to the Yuba River in July 1849, white miners issued a declaration that "no slave or negro should own claims or even work in the mines." They ordered Green to remove his slaves by the following morning. The resolution had its intended effect—the slaves fled, and Green left.[11] Months later, the same group of miners ordered a Chilean man and his "peons" to leave, and when he refused, they hanged him. Miners were said to have cut the ears off another Chilean in a separate incident.[12]

California also drew many educated free blacks. Among them were Newport F. Henry of New York, described as a "confidential porter" to prominent white abolitionist Arthur Tappan; J. H. Townsend, formerly a New York editor; and Mifflin Wistar Gibbs of Philadelphia, a future attorney, judge, and diplomat who lectured with Frederick Douglass. These men and others, including many who obtained their freedom in California, became the leaders of the state's black community, which would come to the aid of Archy Lee.[13]

Archy Lee had been a house servant for the Stovall family. His owner had settlede temporarily in Sacramento while recovering from an illness. In the meantime, Stovall hired Lee out as a laborer and pocketed some, if not all, of Lee's earnings.

Sometime in December or early January 1858, Stovall prepared to return Archy Lee to Mississippi. But while being taken on a river steamer from Sacramento to San Francisco, he escaped and sought refuge at the Hotel Hacket, a Sacramento hotel owned by African Americans.[14] Stovall tracked him down and had him taken into custody as a runaway slave.

Advocates for Lee took the case to a district court, where Judge Robert Robinson ruled against Stovall and declared Lee a free man on January 23, 1858. But Stovall obtained a new warrant and had Lee rearrested. Stovall next appealed to the California Supreme Court, which heard the case at its January 1858 term.[15] The justices were Burnett and Chief Justice David S. Terry, a known proslavery sympathizer. The third seat was vacant, although it would be filled the following year by Stephen J. Field.

Stovall's attorney, James H. Hardy, argued before the court that Stovall had only been a visitor in California, giving him "a right of transit," and that he should be allowed to return home with his slave. Hardy also argued that even though California's constitution prohibited slavery, it was unenforceable because the legislature failed to enact any implementing legislation. Moreover, Lee's status as free or slave should properly be decided in Stovall's home state of Mississippi. "If the Negro is free, let it be asserted in a court competent to try the matter, and such a court can only be found in Mississippi," said Hardy.[16]

Lee was defended by Joseph W. Winans, who argued that California's Fugitive Slave Act was long expired at the time he escaped, and therefore could not possibly apply in his case.

Burnett, writing for the majority, rejected the argument that because Stovall was essentially a visitor to California he had the right to keep his slave property. He said the "right of transit" applied only to merchandise and inanimate objects, not slaves. He also noted that Stovall had worked for two months as a schoolteacher in Sacramento and had hired Lee out for work. "If the party engages in any business himself, or employs his slave in any business, except as a mere personal attendant upon himself, or family, then the character of visitor is lost, and his slave is entitled to freedom," Burnett said. He also said the constitution didn't require implementing legislation for the prohibition against slavery: "It is negative and restrictive in its terms and effect, and by its own force accomplishes the end aimed at . . . that the estate of slavery should not exist therein."[17]

So far, so good, for Archy Lee.

Shockingly, however, Burnett ordered Lee returned to Stovall as a slave. He ruled on February 11 that Stovall could be entitled to an exemption from the law—indeed he was exempt—because it was the first time California's antislavery law had been applied since the expiration of the state's Fugitive Slave Act. Thus, after rejecting every argument raised by Stovall's attorney, Burnett improbably ruled in Stovall's favor, suggesting Stovall was ignorant of California's laws:

> There are circumstances connected with this particular case that may
> exempt him [Stovall] from the operation of the rules we have laid
> down. This is the first case that has occurred under the existing law.
> . . . The petitioner had some reason to believe that the constitutional
> provisions would have no immediate operation. This is the first case;
> and under these circumstances we are not disposed to rigidly enforce
> the rule for the first time. But, in reference to all future cases, it is our
> purpose to enforce the rules laid down strictly, according to their
> true intent and spirit. Ordered that Archy be forthwith released from
> the custody of the chief of police and given into the custody of the
> petitioner, Charles A. Stovall.[18]

Burnett also found that relations with Mississippi, "a sister state," were more important than "the rights of the parties immediately concerned in this particular case." To Burnett, slavery was not the issue. "The institution [slavery] exists by positive law, and that positive law is paramount, and must be enforced." Citing the 1857 Dred Scott decision of the US Supreme Court—that African Americans did not have rights and could not be citizens—Burnett said it must be taken into account that "where slavery exists, the right of property of the master in the slave must follow as a necessary incident."[19] Justice Terry concurred.

Too bad for Archy Lee.

Reaction to the ruling was swift and furious. The *Sacramento Union* wrote on January 12 that its readers would be "astounded" at the contortions required to arrive at such a decision. "All of the law of the case is ruled against the petitioner [Stovall] and yet, because he is young and is in bad health, and his being the first case, it is ordered by court that Archy be delivered into his possession." Although this same newspaper had warmly endorsed Burnett's appointment as an associate justice months earlier, it said the ruling makes the court look "supremely ridiculous."

The *Union* followed with a second commentary on January 16, saying the ruling "caps the climax of all human absurdity and lowers the dignity of the Supreme Court to a degree wholly unparalleled . . . in the history of any state in the Union."[20]

Reaction of other newspapers throughout the state was much the same— they "unmercifully condemned" the ruling, according to the *Union*, which summarized their reactions.[21] Newspapers provided a reasonably accurate barometer of public sentiment at the time—indeed, they were the only barometer. The *Butte Record* of Oroville considered the ruling "a disgusting display of expediency in direct violation of law and facts." The *San Francisco Argus* said it "fills us with grief and shame," while the *San Joaquin Republican* denounced the ruling as "a mockery and trifling with justice."[22]

The *Alta* joined the parade of criticism on February 14, saying Burnett and Terry "have prostituted the supreme legal tribunal of California to a point of degradation from which it will not rise, until they cease to pollute the court chambers with their presence as judges." Not only had they "disgraced themselves," it went on, but they also "bought odium upon the state by this decision and rendered the supreme bench of California a laughing stock in the eyes of the world."[23]

How Burnett could not have seen this reaction coming is puzzling, but perhaps he did. The ruling was entirely consistent with policies he had advocated throughout his political life. As a jurist and lawyer, he was true to his calling in finding no legal justification for returning Archy Lee to slavery. But as a Southerner, he could not bring himself to affirm the rights of a black man against the interests of a fellow white man. His racism ran deep. "He wanted the law to serve his own ends," according to William Burg, a Sacramento historian and author.[24]

Archy Lee would not be returned to slavery, however. California's black community and another judge would see to that. Stovall sought to hide Archy Lee aboard the ship *Orizaba* on March 5. But before the ship could depart San Francisco, black supporters arranged to have him taken off. The *Orizaba* sailed without him.

Lee endured one more arrest and two more court rulings. In one of these, on March 17 in US District Court, a future US senator from Oregon, Edward D. Baker, who defended Lee, mocked Burnett with undisguised sarcasm: "Judge Burnett said he would set aside the constitution and the law, because Stovall was ignorant of our laws." To Baker, the decision amounted to "a reward for ignorance." Judge Thomas W. Freelon set Archy Lee free.[25]

Lee was next arrested on a charge of violating the federal Fugitive Slave Act and was brought before US Commissioner William Pen Johnston. Again, it was Baker who spoke for Lee: "If I were a judge, and called on to decide on comity . . . I would show some comity to the great principles of freedom of human liberty." Judge Johnston ruled Archy Lee a free man on April 14. This time, no one stopped him. A few weeks later, Lee joined a group of several hundred African Americans from California, led by Mifflin Wistar Gibbs, who resettled in British Columbia.[26]

One of the first cases to come before Burnett on the Supreme Court involved Samuel Brannan, with whom he'd had profitable real estate dealings. Although less dramatic than the Archy Lee case, *Brannan v. Mesick* was notable for several reasons, not least of which was that it brought together in a single courtroom the interests of all four of the principles in the Sacramento land sales: Brannan, Burnett, and the Sutters, father and son. William S. Mesick was a former Sacramento County clerk who initiated the case, which had already been heard once by Terry and the late chief justice, Hugh C. Murray.

The back-and-forth in the complicated case is difficult to follow. But it illustrates Brannan's machinations to control a substantial share of the property in fast-growing Sacramento during the 1850s. The senior Sutter's past debts had been paid with proceeds from Burnett's land sales, which should have put him in the financial clear. Unable to learn from past mistakes, however, Sutter was mired in debt again by May 1850. Similarly, with Burnett no longer around to advise him, August Sutter floundered in managing his own affairs. While recovering from an illness at Hock Farm, his father, anxious to have him out of the house, offered him $30,000 to go into business elsewhere.[27]

Relying on his father's promise, but without the money in hand, August invested in a venture in which he suddenly found himself in debt. Confronting his father about the promised money, August described "a very violent scene" after which the father once again deeded to his son his remaining lots and buildings in Sacramento, plus a half mile of riverfront land between Sacramento and Sutterville. This was accomplished in two transactions, on May 7 and May 11, for a dollar each.[28]

But the properties proved more of a worry for August than a benefit. According to a biography, "Free soilers squatted on choice lots and defied the owners to oust them." August also faced high taxes, imposed to pay for Sacramento's new flood-control levees. Then there were the complications resulting from his father's practice of selling the same lot twice.[29]

About this time, a German-born merchant, Julius Wetzlar, befriended August and persuaded him to sell his properties to a group of speculators headed by Brannan for $125,000. The other buyers were Samuel Bruce, James H. Grahame, and Wetzlar himself, who deviously played both sides of the street. He even charged young Sutter $1,000 for finding the buyers.[30] Included in the sale on June 21, 1850, were hundreds of town lots in Sacramento, the half square mile of riverfront land, and other miscellaneous properties.

Lacking property descriptions, Brannan and the others identified their properties through a process of elimination. They consulted a property map and deducted all Sutter lots not previously sold by Burnett and others. They then claimed the unsold lots as theirs, a legally dubious procedure that would later haunt them in the courts.[31] Meanwhile, unbeknownst to August and the buyers, the elder Sutter sold an interest in the riverfront property to two other investors, which would further complicate matters.

After signing the sales agreement, August left for the warmer climate of Acapulco to regain his health, believing he would be paid according to a fixed payment schedule. He was due $25,000 on July 1, 1850; $25,000 on October 30; and a final payment of $75,000 on July 1, 1851.[32] He received some of the initial payment, perhaps all. But when the second payment failed to arrive, August sent an agent to collect. The agent returned empty-handed, however, explaining that the Brannan group demanded a discount of $40,000 from the agreed price because the elder Sutter had sold some of same riverfront land to another buyer.

Without making any additional payments to August, the various owners wheeled and dealed their Sacramento property, dividing it among themselves, then subdividing the lots and reselling them at a substantial profit. Brannan took possession of 125 lots on 54 city blocks, plus 12 ten-acre lots between Sacramento and Sutterville. Wetzlar and the others emerged with similarly handsome bundles of properties.

A dismayed August returned to Sacramento in January 1851 to try to obtain the second payment. He already harbored a major grievance against Brannan, who two years earlier had effectively blackmailed him into forking over 200 town lots as the price of keeping Brannan and other merchants from moving their businesses to Sutterville. But he accepted the discounted price because he was broke.

The new agreement was signed on March 18, 1851.[33] August was paid with notes due July 1. But he would receive little if any actual money. By one account, young Sutter cleared only $3,500 after paying off claims against him, including fees to attorneys he said did little for him.[34] He soon fell ill again and returned to Acapulco and his new Mexican wife, Maria del Carmen Rivas, whom he married in 1850.

Mesick, the former county clerk, visited August in Mexico in July 1855 with a strategy to break the Brannan group's stranglehold on the Sutter land, while enhancing his own interests. Mesick convinced August to sell him some of the same properties he'd previously sold to the Brannan group. But unlike the vague property descriptions for the sales to the Brannan group, each block of land sold to Mesick was precisely identified in an agreement dated July 9, 1855. Mesick returned to California and filed a suit to expel a man named Thomas Sunderland from property Sunderland had purchased from Brannan.

Mesick's argument was twofold: first, the deed held by Brannan and the others was invalid because it failed to precisely describe the properties, and second, they lacked a valid claim to the property because they had never fully paid for it. A lower court threw the case out. But Mesick appealed to the California

Supreme Court, which ruled September 30, 1856—before Burnett joined the court—that the lower court was in error and returned the case for trial. The Supreme Court held that the Brannan group's deed was "void for want of a sufficient description of the premises conveyed.... There is nothing to distinguish them from the bulk of the property in the city."[35]

The *Sacramento Union* saw in the ruling a portent of doom for many Sacramento landowners, telling its readers: "The decision fell like a clap of thunder in a clear sky upon most of our citizens. . . . Nearly, if not all, of this property was in the hands of parties who had bought and paid a full price for it, under the firm belief that the title was a legal one." The newspaper also disparaged August: "If John A. Sutter, Jr. had been paid once for this property, and then sold it the second time, he must be a man lost to all sense of honor and honesty."[36]

At this insult to his son, the elder Sutter, whose careless business practices were responsible for his son's problems, rushed to his defense. In a letter to the *Union*, he claimed August had received "not more than twelve or thirteen thousand dollars" of what was promised in the 1850 agreement. "Out of the remaining sum he has been swindled," Sutter wrote. He insisted he was "not interested whatever" in getting some of the money for himself—although his own past behavior might suggest otherwise. He said his only interest was "to make the truth known to the public about this great swindling transaction."[37]

Brannan next won a ruling in Sixth District Court in July 1857 that his claims to the Sacramento properties were valid. District Judge A. C. Monson said that while the properties were inadequately described, this did not by itself invalidate Brannan's title. Importantly, Monson also held that August had been properly paid, if not in cash, then in "what is a legal requirement thereto."

Mesick appealed the district court's decision to the California Supreme Court, of which Peter Burnett was then a member, on July 24, 1857. Mesick alleged August had been cheated by Wetzlar, Brannan, and the others, even suggesting they drugged August during his illness at Hock Farm.[38]

The high court reversed the district court's decision and ruled largely in Mesick's favor. In a unanimous decision on May 25, 1858, the justices ruled that the Brannan deed was invalid. "It is shown by the plaintiff's witness that the money was not, in fact, paid; that Sutter [August] was induced to make a deduction of over forty thousand dollars, upon a representation that portions of the property conveyed had been previously deeded away by Sutter, which representation, it appears, was not true."[39]

Moreover, the justices said Wetzlar, who held power of attorney for August, had collected some of the money owed to August and "appropriated [it] to the use of Brannan and company." They also found "a strong presumption of fraud," singling out Wetzlar for "his manifest prevarication on many points" during his testimony. If Brannan wanted to further pursue his claim, the court said, he would need to prove at a new trial that he and his group had paid all the debt owed young Sutter.[40]

It is of more than passing interest that Burnett did not recuse himself in the case, as might be expected of a justice who had sold land for Sutter, and who was himself a major Sacramento landowner whose property rights had been challenged by squatters. For Brannan, proving he had fully paid August for the land was a hill too steep to climb. The Sacramento newspaper carried this brief item on July 2, 1858: "The Supreme Court in the case of *Brannan vs. Mesick* denied petition for rehearing by plaintiff."[41] Brannan's claim to the contested Sutter land in 1850 was over. He was not badly hurt, however, as nothing was said about refunding the money to buyers who had purchased land from him. Moreover, the court's decision was not entirely favorable to Mesick. The justices ruled that the titles were valid for owners who purchased property from the Brannan group in good faith.

But Mesick did come away with a handsome profit, as the *Union* said some of the new owners had paid him to clear their titles prior to the court's ruling. The newspaper accused Mesick of extortion: "we suppose no decision, however righteous, will enable those who have been victimized by the Mesick claim . . . to recover back their money." As for August, he received some modest additional payment from Mesick, but it's not clear that it amounted to more than several thousand dollars.[42] For August, insult followed injury. As his fortunes declined, his wife first sold her jewelry to help support them, and then divorced him.

The Sutters, father and son, who once owned all the land in Sacramento, came away from the land dealings largely empty handed. Brannan and Burnett, on the other hand, emerged mostly unscathed, and perhaps the experience forged the relationship that was soon to coalesce into a profitable enterprise for both men.

It was while serving on the court that Burnett received a surprise visit from his younger brother Glen, whom he thought was long dead in Oregon. Burnett recalled the scene: He was descending the stairs from the court's second floor offices—presumably located at the time in the B. F. Hastings Building at the corner of Second and J Streets—when he "observed a venerable old gentleman standing below. . . . I could only see the top of his head and his long gray hair as it extended below his hat." When he realized it was Glen, he said it was like seeing someone risen from the dead. "My feelings can be better imagined than described."[43]

Unbeknownst to Burnett, Glen had moved from Oregon to Knight's Landing in Yolo County, California, in 1861. Glen was in reasonably good health. He died in 1886, twenty years after his encounter with Peter.[44]

Chapter 25
Terry and Broderick at Ten Paces

The judicial career of Chief Justice David Terry, who voted with Burnett in the Archy Lee case, came to an ignominious and abrupt end when he shot and killed David Broderick, a US senator, in a duel on September 13, 1859. Never had there been a duel in California between two men as prominent as these. Burnett knew both men well. So it seems odd that, as an outspoken opponent of the "semi-barbarous" act of dueling, Burnett had little to say about the most famous of all the duels in California history.[1]

In a probable later reference to Terry, however, Burnett explained why duels seemed more numerous among politicians than other groups, except possibly army officers. "This arises in many cases from rivalship," he wrote. "It becomes desirable to kill off certain aspirants, to get them out of the way. Hence they are insulted. Those well skilled in such matters know much and what to say to produce a challenge."[2]

Terry, then 36, and Broderick, 40, were on opposite sides of the slavery debate. Broderick was an abolitionist who opposed the extension of slavery into the territories, while Terry belonged to the pro-South, proslavery, so-named Chivalry Wing of the California Democratic Party, led by William Gwin. Burnett evidently steered clear of the Chivalry Wing, but his vote on the Archy Lee case indicated that he, Terry, and Gwin were not far apart in their overall views of slavery.

Broderick and Terry were accidental adversaries. Their dispute started with Gwin. Broderick and Gwin were both elected to the US Senate in January 1857. While they had been past competitors for party dominance, they were compelled to cooperate in order to retake political control from the Know-Nothings, or American Party, who dominated California politics from 1854 to 1856 with their anti–Irish Catholic, anti-immigrant rhetoric.

Burnett supported Broderick even though they seemed strange bedfellows considering their differences over racial issues. "I have no confidence in Gwin as a politician," Burnett wrote. "I think he is not to be relied on. As for Broderick, I think he is frank, independent and straight forward."[3]

Gwin's first term in the US Senate had expired in 1855, and although he sought another term, he was not reelected. With neither Gwin nor other candidates able to gain a majority in the legislature, the seat remained vacant for nearly two years. It was the popular Broderick who opened the door for a second term for Gwin—Broderick had been easily elected to succeed the other incumbent, John Weller, on January 8, 1857.

Gwin was on the verge of defeat until Broderick responded to his appeal for help. Broderick's price was an agreement whereby Gwin would cede control of political patronage to Broderick, an understanding put in writing.[4] With the patronage agreement in hand, Broderick threw his backing to Gwin, who was elected to the Senate on January 11, 1857. Once Gwin was back in Washington, however, where he had far more support than Broderick, he quickly turned the tables on his rival, and commanded patronage through his close relationship with President Buchanan.

Gwin and Buchanan supported Kansas's proslavery Lecompton Constitution, which Broderick opposed. Broderick undermined any hopes he had for a working relationship with Buchanan when, in his maiden Senate speech on December 23, he denounced the president for attempting to "create civil war in Kansas" through the Lecompton Constitution.[5]

Broderick and Gwin were both Democrats, but they differed in just about every other way. The aristocratic Gwin was polished and diplomatic, comfortably at home in the corridors of power. His politics were as manipulative and quietly ruthless as Broderick's were hard edged and, occasionally, underhanded. Befitting their backgrounds, their bases of power were markedly different. Broderick drew his support from the working man, notably the Irish Catholic underclass to which he belonged. He was said to live "like a monk."[6] Gwin received backing from Southern political leaders and influential plantation owners, of which he was one. In the nation's capital, he and his wife hosted lavish balls and dinner parties—the kind of parties for which invitations were coveted, and which Broderick would seldom, if ever, find in his mailbox.

Through his influence with President Buchanan and the support of the Senate's proslavery Democrats, Gwin soon rendered Broderick powerless in

Former US Senator David C. Broderick, who blocked Peter Burnett's proposed black exclusion law while a California state senator. Broderick was fatally shot in 1859 in a duel with David Terry, chief justice on the California Supreme Court. Courtesy of the California History Room, California State Library, Sacramento.

Washington and in California as well. It was a replay of Gwin's political neutering of Fremont.

If there was to be a duel, the expectation was it would be between Broderick and Gwin. Back-and-forth insults grew progressively more heated. Broderick denounced Gwin as "dripping with corruption."[7] For his part, during the 1859 campaign for the party's nominations for office, Gwin menacingly denounced Broderick's campaign oratory. "What can you do with such an individual?" he asked. "If we club him, it will do no good; if we kill him it will only make him a martyr."[8]

Yet it was David Terry who faced Broderick in the early morning of September 13 at a well-known dueling field next to a barn along Lake House Road at Lake Merced, 7 miles west of San Francisco. Although unlawful in California, dueling remained an option to settle insults and irreconcilable disputes, both personal and political.

It is probably too much to say that Terry and Broderick had been friends, but they hadn't always been adversaries either. Broderick had defended Terry against charges in the near-fatal stabbing of a member of San Francisco's powerful Vigilance Committee, Sterling Hopkins, in 1856. Terry was jailed by the committee, which had been known to hang men for less. But he was released, in no small part due to Broderick, who was said to slip money to newspapers in return for favorable coverage of Terry.[9]

The Kentucky-born Terry was known for his hair-trigger temper. Sterling Hopkins probably wasn't the first to feel the blade of the bowie knife he carried. Terry, who arrived in California from Texas in December 1849, was once quoted as saying he intended to bring slavery to California, either by changing the state constitution or by dividing California into two states, one open to slavery.[10] He won election to the California Supreme Court as a Know-Nothing candidate in 1855, and was elevated to chief justice in 1857 following the death of Justice Murray.

The events that brought Broderick and Terry to the shores of Lake Merced escalated from the disagreement among badly divided Democrats over the Lecompton Constitution. Both men had also suffered stinging defeats in separate nominating campaigns for reelection, although their terms hadn't yet expired. Terry, speaking at a pro-Lecompton Democratic gathering in Sacramento in August 1859, blamed his defeat on anti-Lecompton Democrats, who he charged were "the personal chattels" of Broderick, who was beholden to the black abolitionist Frederick Douglass.[11]

Upon learning of Terry's remarks, Broderick responded with a verbal broadside of his own. He was overheard at a hotel breakfast the next morning calling Terry "a damned miserable wretch." He was reported as saying, "I have hitherto spoken of him [Terry] as an honest man—as the only honest man on the bench of a miserable, corrupt Supreme Court—but now I find I was mistaken. I take it all back. He is just as bad as the others."[12] There are less fiery versions of what was said.

Broderick's remarks were reported back to Terry, who wrote Broderick on September 9 demanding an unlikely apology.[13] With no apology forthcoming, Terry issued his challenge, accepted two days later by Broderick, bringing them to the barn on Lake House Road. The duel was no secret. The sheriff of San Mateo County, probably John W. Ackerson, interrupted the first scheduled duel on September 12, but he delayed it only a day.

At dawn on September 13, with a bright sun rising, a crowd of eighty or so friends and supporters watched as a coin was twice tossed to determine the choice of position and choice of weapons. The first toss fell Broderick's way, and he chose to stand with the sun at his back. The second toss favored Terry, who selected two French dueling pistols—smoothbore weapons with 10-inch barrels—which fired a single heavy lead ball. A gunsmith, Bernard Lagaorde, examined both pistols, and warned Broderick that "they were very delicate to the touch." The two men stood ten paces apart, weapons pointed at the ground, standing sideways, as little exposed as possible. At the command of "fire," they were instructed to await the count of one before shooting.

The count came. Broderick got off the first shot, but he was too hasty. The unfamiliar weapon's hair-trigger betrayed him. His ball struck the ground a foot short of Terry. One of Broderick's seconds, J. C. McKibbon, recalled that Broderick "appeared to look down with surprise at the course which his ball took." An instant later, Terry fired. His ball struck Broderick in the right shoulder, the impact raising a puff of smoke. Broderick slowly turned and fell to the ground as McKibbon and others rushed to his side.

Broderick was laid on a mattress in the back of a wagon and rushed to the home of a friend. The wound was at first not thought serious. Three days later, however, on September 16, the same day that San Francisco newspapers confidently predicted his recovery, Broderick died. The ball had penetrated his chest cavity, fractured his sternum, and passed through his left lung before coming to rest near his armpit.[14]

Broderick's death brought an outpouring of shock and grief; he had a huge following in San Francisco. Edward Baker, long a friend—who had kept a sleepless Broderick company the night before the duel—delivered the funeral oration before a crowd of thousands on September 18 in Portsmouth Square. Baker gave voice to what many suspected, that the duel was orchestrated to get rid of Broderick. He quoted a deathbed statement by Broderick that "I die because I was opposed to the extension of slavery and to a corrupt administration."[15]

Baker wasn't alone in suspecting Broderick was the victim of a conspiracy. In a September 18 editorial, the *Alta* called the duel a pretext for assassination. "What other inference can be drawn, whatever conclusion can be arrived at, than that there was a fixed and determined intention on the part of Terry and others, to force Mr. Broderick into a fight for the purpose of taking his life."[16]

Elisha Crosby linked Broderick's death to his outspoken opposition to a strategy of Terry and others to legalize slavery in California. "Broderick's denunciation of this scheme, I have no doubt, brought on the conflict which led to his assassination," Crosby wrote in his memoirs. "If Terry failed, somebody else was to kill him."[17]

Terry was arrested two days later in San Joaquin County and returned to San Francisco, where he was charged with the crime of dueling—ostensibly punishable by death when a combatant was killed. But he was released a week later, on September 23, after posting $10,000 bail.[18] Twenty years later, Terry would himself meet with violent death.[19] He was shot and killed near Stockton, California, in 1889 by a bodyguard to Judge Stephen J. Field, a justice on the US Supreme Court who had succeeded Terry as chief justice on the California court and also served with Burnett.[20]

As for Gwin, although he didn't fire the shot that killed Broderick, he received much of the blame. When he left San Francisco to return to Washington on September 20, the *Alta* wondered "whether he ever intends visiting the state again." Gwin would serve out his term, but he would not be nominated for another. His political career in California was over.

Chapter 26
Finally, the Good Life

Burnett sat out the Civil War. He was 54. He suffered from painful bouts of neuralgia, and probably lingering effects of malaria. But he left no doubt as to his Southern sympathies.

"I was born and reared in the slave section of the United States, and most of my relatives resided there," he wrote. "I knew well the sincerity and courage of the Southern people." Still, preserving the Union was paramount: "I could not fight against the grand old flag."[1] He voted for the pro-South ticket of John Breckinridge and Joseph Lane in 1860 but supported Abraham Lincoln for his second term in 1864.

When Burnett retired from the California Supreme Court in 1858, he also retired from public life. He devoted the next several years to reading and writing at his home in San Jose. Among his works in this period was a ninety-eight-page pamphlet with his thoughts and recommendations on how the United States should be restructured in the aftermath of the Civil War. Published in 1861, Burnett's *The American Theory of Government Considered with Reference to the Present Crisis* is a compilation of radical, bizarre, and patently unworkable ideas.

Burnett put the Civil War in the context of what he called the normal maturation of the American government. "We are in the midst of a mighty revolution; and are now passing through one of the ordinary, though painful stages in the progress of a people from youth to mature age." A Southern sympathizer certainly, but not an advocate of states' rights, Burnett believed the states had too much power while the federal government had too little. "The states should be strictly subordinate corporations, and only permitted to exercise such power as may be allowed by Congress."[2]

The changes Burnett urged included giving the president the power to appoint and replace state governors at will, subject to Senate approval. Theoretically, a new president could appoint new governors for all the states.

Senators would be elected for life. Burnett also wanted to give the president and Congress veto power over state legislation.

These and other changes, Burnett said, would remove the handicap of divided sovereignty, which he saw as the stumbling block to effective government. "Every citizen would then plainly know the government to which his allegiance was rightfully due."[3] An admirer of Alexander Hamilton, Burnett shared Hamilton's view of a strong central government.

Burnett maintained that defects and imbalances in the government, not slavery, were the causes of the Civil War. He considered slavery incidental to the conflict and suggested that whichever side prevailed, the antislavery North or the proslavery South, should determine the nation's overall policy toward "the vexed question" of slavery. In addition, the outcome "should be plainly stated in the Constitution."[4] The immorality of slavery was not an issue with him.

In a letter to the *Sacramento Union* on August 2, 1862, Burnett wrote that while Lincoln had done the right thing in waging war to preserve the Union, he could never support abolition so long as slavery was protected by the Constitution. Arguments that "higher law" should trump the Constitution did not wash.[5] By this time, most Western nations had long since abolished slavery, both at home and in their colonies: Spain in 1811, Great Britain in 1833, and France in 1848.

Burnett elaborated on his Civil War–era views in his *Recollections* and in letters to his brother George, arguing that the republican system of government would eventually collapse of its own weight. "The three principles of universal suffrage, elective offices and short terms . . . will in due time politically demoralize any people in the world."[6] He told his brother that a revolution was probably necessary sometime within the next half century to find a new direction for the country. "It may require several revolutions in succession," he wrote. "This I think most probable."

His brother seemingly rejected his ideas, because in Burnett's next letter, dated July 28, 1862, he admonished George for failing to understand him. "Although you have given this subject good attention, you have not fully understood," Burnett wrote, before restating his argument.[7]

Burnett was not one to remain closeted at home for long. Contrary to some of his earlier musings, he now said it was against his nature to retire.[8] He decided banking would suit him, bringing him once again into the orbit of Samuel Brannan. In early 1863—still the war years—officials of the newly incorporated Pacific

Accumulation Loan Company of San Francisco asked Burnett to help write its bylaws, after which they made him bank president, succeeding Brannan, who took a new role as treasurer.[9]

A biography of Brannan offers a somewhat different version of Burnett's involvement, saying Burnett was one of the bank's founders along with Brannan and Joseph Winans, the attorney who defended Archy Lee before the Supreme Court.[10] Brannan had earlier founded another bank, in 1857, simply called "Samuel Brannan's Bank," at the corner of Montgomery and California Streets. Brannan was ridiculed for an ill-advised scheme to issue his own paper currency, which he hoped would catch on with the public. It didn't. That bank failed after two years.[11]

In banking, Burnett had finally found a world he understood, one dominated by money, numbers, and interest rates. It was an environment that didn't wholly depend for success on personal relationships or political networking. Not to say that relationships and networking weren't helpful, but they weren't Burnett's strength. To Burnett, success depended on sound banking practices, which required decision-making that left no room for sentiment.

As the new bank president, Burnett faced the immediate challenge of increasing the bank's assets. He suspended the lucrative dividends paid to bank directors and imposed a moratorium on salaries for fifteen months. He changed what he described as defects in the charter and bylaws, and gave the bank a new name, Pacific Bank, with offices at 404 Montgomery Street, probably in the same building as Brannan's old bank.

Burnett directed the bank staff as if he were a drill sergeant. "The discipline in a bank must be as rigid as that in an army," wrote Burnett, whose own military experience was limited to a brief time as a grunt in the Missouri and Oregon militias. "If an employee willfully and deliberately disobeys orders, he should be discharged."[12] One has to wonder whether Burnett was recalling his difficulties of having his orders followed while he was captain of the 1843 wagon train to Oregon.

According to a history of California banking, Burnett became one of the "prominent bankers of San Francisco" during the 1860s and 1870s, during which time he transformed Pacific Bank into "one of the most solid financial institutions in San Francisco." But after Burnett retired in 1880, "the new owners failed to live up to the ideals established by Burnett and his associates." The bank collapsed in the Panic of 1893, an economic depression during which many banks failed.[13]

Peter Burnett about age 72,
toward the end of his San
Francisco banking career.
Courtesy of the Oregon
Historical Society.

Burnett's affection for banking is reflected in the space it receives in his autobiography—thirty-one pages compared to only a few pages on being governor. He cited examples of his uncompromising decision-making. In one example, he said he was approached by "a most admirable man" whose loan was overdue. Burnett liked him. "He exhibited the truest financial feeling and honor, and told me that he would pay the note within two days if I would permit the endorser to waive." But rules were rules. Two days were two days too long. "I assured him of my kindest feeling toward him, and of my fullest confidence in his good faith, but the rule of the bank must be carried out."[14] He didn't mention whether his decision cost the man his home or business, but that wasn't his concern.

Burnett believed that a borrower's lifestyle could reveal a good credit risk. "If a man borrows money, and at the same time is found insuring his life for the benefit of his family, or improving a homestead, or living above his means, or driving fine horses, or doing any other thing incompatible with the condition of an honest debtor, those who lend him money will be very apt to receive a notice to attend a meeting of creditors."[15]

In a rare instance of giving praise to someone else, Burnett said Brannan should receive much of the credit for the bank's success. "It is but simple justice to Samuel Brannan to state that he is the father of the bank. . . . With all his faults, he has many noble qualities and has done much for California."[16]

Burnett moved with his wife to San Francisco, where they rented a home for $50 a month; his son John and daughter Romietta lived nearby with their families. Burnett was still affected by neuralgia. "I find my nerves are not so steady," he wrote George, although he said he felt better in San Francisco's moist climate.[17]

When Burnett finished his autobiography on September 26, 1878, he was still bank president, living with Harriet, his wife of fifty years, in the rented home in San Francisco. He'd finally given up his goal of becoming a millionaire, although he and his wife were enjoying the comfortable lifestyle typical of a successful banker. And so he wrote: "When a man has reached the point of independence, where he is secure of the necessaries of life with reasonable effort, he is as rich as any one, if he only knew it." Now, for the first time, he knew it. He could look forward to a contented retirement. Religion had come to dominate his life.

Chapter 27
Retreating to Religion

In a life with few lasting commitments, one stood out in Peter Burnett's later years—his commitment to the Roman Catholic Church. He had converted to Catholicism in Oregon, after John McLoughlin exposed him to the church. His belief seems to have been reinforced by his vigil at the deathbed of Judge James Jones in 1851.

Burnett devoted four pages of his autobiography to an account of Jones's death, impressed by his young friend's late-in-life religious fervor. He wrote of one visit, perhaps the final one, when Jones had "wasted away to a skeleton." He said the young man held up a cross to reveal his conversion, voicing regret he had waited so long. He quoted Jones as then telling him, "'The greatest sin I have ever committed—that which has given me more pain, and that which I deplore more than all the others—is the fact that I deferred repentance to near the end of my existence.'"[1]

Burnett broke down in tears. He must have had Jones in mind when he wrote in a book on Catholicism that one of the many proofs that the Catholic Church is the true church was that "there is no known instance where a Roman Catholic changed his faith upon a dying bed, while thousands of Protestants have done so."[2] Of course, he had no way of knowing whether this was true.

It was during his post-governor period that Burnett wrote what he regarded as the seminal work of his life, *The Path Which Led a Protestant Lawyer to the Catholic Church.* One doesn't have to be Roman Catholic to admire the effort Burnett put into this book, published in 1859 by Benziger Brothers of New York, described as the printer to the Holy Apostolic See. The book is dedicated to Most Reverend John B. Purcell, Archbishop of Cincinnati, who had played a pivotal role in Burnett's decision to become a Catholic. While still in Oregon, Burnett read a series of debates from 1837 between Purcell and

Alexander Campbell, a founder of the Disciples of Christ. He said Purcell's arguments "laid the foundation of my conversion to the Old Church."[3]

Although the book's title suggests it is largely about Burnett's path to the church, his actual conversion is confined to the preface. The remaining 741 pages are about the church and his repudiation of criticisms of Catholicism. The book runs the gamut of issues relating to the church and its doctrine, among them:

> On miracles: He who takes the position that a miracle is impossible must assume one of two things to be true: either that there is no creator, or, two, that admitting to the existence of such a creator, in creating the world and giving to it and its inhabitants certain properties and laws, he resolved in advance, never for any purpose, or any occasion, to interfere in any manner with the legitimate efforts of this order.[4]
>
> On charges against certain Popes: All those Catholic writers I have read cheerfully admitted that the conduct of some individual Popes had been scandalous and wicked, while they insisted that the great majority were worthy of the station they filled, and many of them martyrs and saints of the first character.[5]

As with all of Burnett's writing, the book is excessively wordy. He paid from his own pocket to have it published—$2,500 for a thousand copies.[6] The book was well received within the church, reflected in a review in the Catholic journal *Brownson's Quarterly Review* that said it "must rank among the graver and more important contributions to Catholic literature made in this country."[7]

While little of Burnett's correspondence has survived, in part because he didn't often make copies, his letters to Purcell were preserved in church archives. In one letter, Burnett blamed Protestants for encouraging the Civil War, saying it was part of a Protestant strategy to combat Catholicism—slavery was simply a convenient excuse. Never much of an optimist, Burnett predicted the Union would fall apart and be replaced by a stronger government that would undertake severe persecutions of Catholics. "We may look out for trials and sufferings," he said.[8]

Despite Burnett's commitment to the church, he appeared unable to sway all of his children. His wife and son-in-law converted, but his two youngest sons, John and Armstead, resisted. While enrolling John, about 14, and Armstead, about 13, at an unnamed Catholic school—likely Santa Clara College, now Santa Clara University—in 1852, he warned the school they might present problems because of their hostility to the church.[9] "Mrs. Burnett and myself were Protestants until they were about the ages of eleven and nine, and consequently they may still retain some prejudices against our religion," he wrote. "Your own discretion will enable you to understand their feelings."[10]

Harriet died September 19, 1879, a year after the Burnetts celebrated their fiftieth wedding anniversary. Burnett resigned from the bank the following January, telling his family that he wanted to retire before people would be saying he "didn't have sense enough to know that he was old." It was a rare jest for the largely humorless Burnett. He was then 72 and had moved from the rental home in San Francisco to live with his son John W. Burnett and his family in their home at 1713 Larkin Street in San Francisco.

The former governor lived out his life with his son's family in San Francisco, evidently comfortable and content. "Life is private, tranquil and happy and I spend my time in a peaceful hopeful preparation for death," he wrote in 1885.[11] It was during this period that he also wrote his final book, *Reasons Why We Should Believe in God, Love God and Obey God.*

Burnett must have been pleased when the *New York Times* ran a lengthy review of his autobiography, *Recollections*, although the newspaper's praise was muted. The unnamed reviewer focused on Burnett's Oregon experience, saying the book should be read by foreign students "as a record of the ancestry, early life and adventures of a plain American."[12] But the reviewer seemed taken aback at the suggestion the nation needed another revolution. "Curious to relate, this backwoods trader, lawyer and California banker and politician does not believe that the present form of American government can last as it is. He thinks that the three principles of universal suffrage, elective offices and short terms will in due time politically demoralize any people in the world." The review mentioned little about Burnett's experience in California, offering only these few words: "The strictly California portion of his life cannot be entered into; it must be sufficient to state that, coming from a representative of a large and efficient class of Americans, the straightforward account of ex-Gov Burnett will be found unusually instructive. He was witness to, and participant in, most of the scenes that make the short history of California more eventful than that of any other of the newer states of the union."[13]

In his last years, Peter Burnett followed a "strictly methodical" routine, according to a written account by his granddaughter, Sarah L. Burnett. He set aside "so much time for prayer and religious reading, so much for outdoor exercise, so much for general reading and for the family." He also tended the family garden.[14]

Burnett told an interviewer in 1894, a year before his death, that his hands shook so much from palsy he was unable to do any more serious writing. "I lost the power to write almost entirely," he said. "My hands gave out." He was devoting his final years "to a preparation for death . . . a man should prepare for death before he died, I am doing that now."[15]

Sarah Burnett reported that her grandfather didn't talk much about his experiences. His explanation, she said, was that he didn't want to "become tiresome." But another reason may have been that there was nothing in his political past he wanted to savor, and he felt it best left to distant memory. His solace was his faith. Sarah recalled once seeing Burnett on his knees in the parish church "gazing into that other Land . . . to explore in vision before the time had come when he would be called to cross its frontier." The last time he left the house was to attend mass.[16]

Peter Hardeman Burnett died May 17, 1895, with family members at his bedside, among them his last surviving brother, Thomas. A mass was held three days later at St. Ignatius Church in San Francisco. According to a newspaper account, a long line of carriages followed Burnett's hearse from his son's home on Larkin Street, proceeding along Van Ness Avenue to the church, where "immense crowds" had gathered. Honorary pallbearers included US senator and former governor George Clement Perkins. The incumbent governor, James Budd, was among those attending the service. Burnett was buried next to Harriet in the Santa Clara Mission Cemetery.[17]

The San Francisco Call offered a much more positive assessment of Burnett's career than newspapers had given Burnett immediately following his exit from public life. As governor, the newspaper said, Burnett was "one of the most popular men of the time" who exhibited "a wonderful amount of energy and developed a grasp of affairs that was truly masterful." His resignation as governor, it concluded, was for the sole purpose of "saving his fortune," imperiled by the squatter riots and fires in Sacramento and San Francisco.[18]

Burnett's wealth had diminished over the years. He left an estate valued at $67,000, most in US government bonds. One explanation for the decline may have been losses in untimely real estate investments. In his will, dated August

Burnett's portrait hangs with other California governors in the corridors of the state capitol. His is the nearest in this photo, across the hallway from the governor's suite of offices. Photo by the author.

24, 1891, he left $5,000 to the Catholic Church for charitable purposes, dividing the remainder in equal amounts between his daughters, Romietta Wallace and Martha Ryland, and his two daughters-in-law, Mary Burnett, Dwight's wife, and Ellen Burnett, John's wife. To Dwight, he willed his watch, and to John, with whom he had lived, he bequeathed "my furniture, library and garden and other implements."[19] Dwight and John were named executors.

Burnett had one final request. He wanted his headstone engraved with the words "I believe in God, Love God and I will obey God."[20]

Peter Burnett would have been pleased by the postmortem respect given him by Governor Budd, who credited him with playing the lead role in achieving statehood for California. "Peter Burnett amply proved himself to be the right man in the right place, and it was largely his personal efforts and addresses to the people at large, through the medium of the daily press, that helped formulate the civil government of California."[21] It was the kind of validation that had eluded Burnett throughout his public life.

Epilogue

Peter Hardeman Burnett had obvious flaws as a political leader, of which his onerous racial policies were the most egregious. But as someone who played a leading role in establishing the American governments on the Pacific Coast, he should not be considered a complete failure.

It's beyond puzzling why Burnett has been virtually ignored by contemporary historians who write the region's history. To the degree he is mentioned at all, it is because he mentions himself. Virtually every reference to Burnett cites his own autobiography as the source for information about him.

Burnett was a compelling figure. He had an unsullied reputation for honesty and was untouched by the corruption endemic in early California politics. His intelligence was never in question—although it didn't always translate into common sense. He was articulate, and impressive in appearance. He stood tall, as they say, and others quickly identified him as a leader. Burnett's long résumé illustrates his appeal for positions of responsibility.

But Burnett was hampered by an inability to work with others. He was humorless, egotistical, defensive to a fault, and seemed to lack a sense of loyalty outside of his family. He may also have been imperious toward underlings—mistakes were the fault of others; if there was any credit to go around, he wanted it for himself. These were not attributes conducive to winning friends and exercising effective leadership. Supporters quickly tired of him. Tragically for Burnett's career, he was a leader who could not lead.

Burnett's closed personality may well have stemmed from the humiliations he suffered in his adolescence. From an impoverished home life, he was suddenly plunged into living with wealthy and successful relatives whom he may not have known, or at least not well. He was ashamed of his shabby dress, unable to even afford a hat to replace one taken as a prank. Girls he might have liked ignored him.

Beyond identifying him as a conservative, Burnett's political philosophy is difficult to categorize. Formerly an admirer of the rural-based political philosophy of Thomas Jefferson, he came later in life to favor the strong central government approach of Alexander Hamilton. Praising Hamilton's writing in *The Federalist*, Burnett believed Hamilton to have "had the clearest mind and the most logical power, and to have been the greatest statesman of our country."[1]

Burnett held judicial positions in both Oregon and California, where he was sworn to uphold the law. Yet he was not above deviating from the law when it suited him. He argued forcefully for self-government in both Oregon and California. Even so, his initial reaction on arriving in Oregon was to question why it needed any government at all. And in his first address to the elected California legislature, he questioned whether it should pass any laws prior to statehood.

One of Peter Burnett's last decisions before leaving the California Supreme Court in 1858 was to join in the majority ruling that California's new Sunday closing law was unconstitutional because it amounted to governmental interference in the free exercise of religion, a ruling that any libertarian today might applaud. "If there be but a single individual in the state who professes a particular faith, he is as much within the sacred protection of the constitution as if he agreed with the great majority of his fellow citizens," he said in a concurring opinion.

But any extrapolation from the opinion on the Sunday closing law, that Burnett must have been a strict constitutionalist, fades in the shadow of his ruling in the Archy Lee case. No matter how clear California law was in prohibiting slavery—and it was clear without a doubt—Burnett could not bring himself to rule in favor of a former slave against the claim of his former master. He said on several occasions he opposed slavery, yet he returned a free black man to slavery.

Burnett had much changed over time from the vindictive young man who plotted the death of someone breaking into his store. But he would never outgrow his prejudices or, more importantly, his attempts to impose them on others. He argued relentlessly for excluding African Americans from the West Coast, and he opposed Chinese immigration. The "sacred protection" he championed in the Sunday closing ruling was sorely limited.

We can, and should, put Burnett's racism in the context of attitudes that were common among emigrants from the South, and many from the North as well. But even in that context, his views were extreme and difficult to explain.

Had he somehow forgiven himself for the fatal shooting of a black slave in Bolivar, Tennessee, by believing that African Americans were truly "others" and "less than"? It may be a stretch to connect that incident with his racism, but something ignited the fierce prejudice within him that arguably contributed to his difficulties as a politician and leader.

Contrary to the image Burnett sought to project, he was not one to roll up his sleeves. He said he welcomed hard work, but he was quick to walk away when the work became too difficult or tiresome. His modus operandi was to withdraw rather than endure criticism and rectify his mistakes or change his behavior.

When, toward the end of his life, Burnett seemed to be adding up the pluses and minuses of his long career, he wanted his involvement with the Sutters to be recognized among his successes. In his letter to August Sutter in 1894, Burnett rightly claimed that after paying Sutter's debts, he had returned a sound, debt-free enterprise to the Sutter family. But he apparently felt this hadn't been sufficiently appreciated. In typical braggadocio, he told August, "Under all the circumstances, I think I have a just right to claim that I saved the estate from great embarrassment if not from final ruin."[2]

Perhaps it was Burnett's racism, perhaps his personality, perhaps his reluctance to see a job to completion, but history scarcely remembers California's first elected governor. Rarely has he received more than a paragraph or two in current California histories.

"I am not sure as to why that may be the case," speculated Dylan McDonald about why Burnett is not well remembered in histories of California. "Perhaps his views on race have pushed people away and that the names of others in the birth of modern California offered historians more fertile ground. Maybe he is just lost among the many names of the period—Sutter, Brannan, Fremont, Gwin, etc."[3]

Burnett has had a few modest public recognitions. His portrait hangs in the California state capitol in Sacramento a short distance down the south hallway from the rotunda. The portrait is positioned just 15 feet from the entrance to the governors' suite of offices, a prominent location that Burnett would no doubt applaud.

"Some people think he looks like Paul Newman," said Robert Dreyer, a guide for the Capital State Museum Association. When tourists occasionally ask about Burnett's portrait, Dreyer tells them, not quite accurately, "He was the first governor before statehood. After statehood, he didn't agree with

California being a nonslave state and resigned. He didn't hang around too long, and went back to Oregon." Of course, Burnett never went back to Oregon. Dreyer can tell people a lot more about Ronald Reagan, whose larger-than-life statue is on the next floor down.

Burnett's name is among dozens engraved on a frieze circling the ceiling in the Oregon House of Representatives in Salem. Burnett Avenue near Haight-Ashbury in San Francisco is named for him, as are several schools in California, including the Peter Burnett Elementary School in Sacramento. But Burnett Street in Sacramento evidently is named for another Burnett.

Burnett might have received public recognition for his gift of a quarter block at 7th and K Streets to the Catholic Church in Sacramento that is now St. Rose of Lima Park. Burnett donated the property for the St. Rose of Lima Church in July 1849 and chaired the committee to build it. The church later moved to another location. Burnett's name does not appear in the park, however.[4]

The "partner's desk" Burnett used in his private law practice is on display in a re-creation of the former governor's office at the Roberto Adobe and Suñol House Museum in San Jose, along with a dress Harriet may have worn to the inaugural ball on December 27, 1849.[5] They are on permanent loan from Burnett's great-great-granddaughter Francisca Burnett Allen, an assistant district attorney for Santa Clara County.

St. Rose of Lima Park at 7th and K Streets in Sacramento, the property donated by Peter Burnett in 1849 for a Catholic church. There is no mention in the park of Burnett being the original donor. Photo by William Burg.

Burnett's achievement in rising from a child of poverty to governor of California is remarkable in its own right. Not to be discounted is the path he blazed for his family to follow into the legal profession. Francisca Allen is the fifth in a direct line of attorneys that started with Burnett. Her great-grandfather was Burnett's son, John May Burnett. Allen's son, also named John, is the sixth in the line of attorneys. Her husband, Douglas, also is an attorney. Another of Peter Burnett's sons, Dwight, became an attorney, and his daughters, Martha and Romietta, married attorneys.

Allen said she is proud to have the former governor among her ancestors. While she can't condone his racist policies, she sees them in the context of the times. She is saddened that several schools have dropped Burnett's name in recent years. The former Burnett Child Development Center in San Francisco is now the Leola M. Harvard Early Education School, named for the city's first African American principal. And the former Peter H. Burnett Elementary School in Long Beach is renamed Bobbie Smith Elementary School, for the first African American member of the Long Beach area school board.

"People are running all over him now, but it was different then," Allen said. "We shouldn't judge him by our morals of today."[6]

It may signify nothing at all, but in 1885, after wealth and fame had lost their lure, and he no longer needed a more "emphatic" name, Burnett wrote a personal genealogy in which he spelled the last names of his four brothers with a single "t." He wrote his own name as Peter Hardeman Burnet.

Appendix A
Moving On: Men of Ambition

Some of the prominent men with whom Burnett engaged during his career fared well as their lives played out, but most did not. These men were largely risk takers and speculators, good at accumulating fame and wealth. poor at keeping it.

JESSE APPLEGATE

Jesse Applegate didn't sign the Oregon Constitution, objecting to its exclusion clause and other discriminatory provisions. He rejected an invitation to a reunion of convention delegates in 1868, calling the constitution "a disgrace."[1]

Never a wealthy man, Jesse Applegate lost what property he did have through unwise investments. He sought to regain some wealth by raising sheep near Clear Lake in California's Siskiyou County, but he lost the entire herd of 1,800 sheep during a severe winter in 1874. "It seemed no matter what Jesse did to recoup his losses in his old age, failure seemed his lot in life," wrote a biographer.[2]

Known as the "Sage of Yoncalla," Applegate wrote frequently about Oregon history. He lived much of his life in a modest three-room cabin on Mt. Yoncalla in Oregon's Douglas County, although he would lose his home to creditors near the end of his life.

In 1886, following the death of his wife, Cynthia Ann, in 1881, Applegate was declared "unsane and unsafe to be at large." He spent a year in the state infirmary for the insane, after which he lived with his children.[3] Applegate died on April 22, 1888.

SAMUEL BRANNAN

It was easy come, easy go for Samuel Brannan. For a time, he was a wealthy man, one of the wealthiest in the American West. But his weaknesses eroded his fortune, and when he died in 1889, there was hardly anything left.

The *San Francisco Examiner* wrote that Brannan had fallen victim to swindlers and succumbed to his vices. One of those vices was a passion for actresses, notably Lola Montez. "He lavished a fortune on the fiery and vivacious Lola Montez when she was the rage in San Francisco."[4]

Brannan was regarded as San Francisco's leading citizen for fifteen years, improving "everything he purchased." His fortunes turned, however, in part because of his wasted investment in 2,000 acres of property in the Napa Valley, which he developed into Calistoga Hot Springs. His economic difficulties were compounded by his drinking—it was rumored he was seldom seen sober after midday.[5]

Brannan's wife, Ann Eliza Brannan, her patience with his infidelities and misadventures finally run out, divorced him on November 11, 1870, after twenty-six years. She alleged he was "addicted to open and notorious intemperance."

Following Brannan's death in 1889, an obituary in the *Deseret Evening News* in Salt Lake City described Brannan as having once achieved "some prominence" in the Mormon Church, but "his course and habits were not consistent with the life of a Latter-day Saint."[6]

JOHN CHARLES FREMONT

During the war, President Lincoln gave Fremont command of the Department of the West in July 1861, with headquarters in St Louis. But Fremont made numerous missteps that dismayed Lincoln, including issuing an emancipation proclamation for the region under his command.[7]

With the war in Fremont's region also not going well, he was removed from his command after just three months. He was also charged with insubordination and corruption and subjected to a formal investigation by Congress, although he was absolved of blame. Lincoln next assigned Fremont to a post in West Virginia, which similarly did not go well. He was demoted, after which he resigned in protest.

President Rutherford B. Hayes appointed Fremont governor of the Arizona Territory in 1878. But Fremont was accused of being inattentive to his responsibilities, and he resigned under pressure three years later.[8]

Heavily in debt, Fremont sold his California estate, Las Mariposas, in 1863. His personal life also was in shambles, with rumors of marriage infidelities. His wife, Jessie, lived apart in California in his later years, although she remained loyal as a defender of his reputation.

Shortly before Fremont's death, Congress granted him a long-sought military pension of $6,000 a year, a pension that ended with his death in 1890.[9] Jessie Fremont received a special widow's pension of $2,000 a year.[10] She died in 1902.

WILLIAM MCKENDREE GWIN

No longer in Congress and his loyalty in question, William Gwin was arrested in New York on November 11, 1861, on suspicion of treason, but he was released after President Lincoln intervened on his behalf.[11]

After a failed effort as a mediator to avoid the Civil War, Gwin sent his wife, Mary, to Paris, while he retired to his Mississippi plantation. The plantation was destroyed during the Battle of Vicksburg in 1863, after which Gwin joined his family in Paris. He conspired with Napoleon III in an unsuccessful effort to establish a colony in Mexico.

Returning to the United States, Gwin was again arrested for his secessionist activities and imprisoned in Mississippi.[12] Following his release, he returned to California, where he died in 1885.

LANSFORD WARREN HASTINGS

Lansford Hastings went to California seeking fame and fortune. He was never to acquire a fortune, but he would gain a measure of fame, albeit probably unwanted, as developer of the ill-conceived Hastings Cutoff.

Will Bagley wrote that Hastings never accepted responsibility for the tragedy of the Donner-Reed Party, and only in later years was he blamed for misleading the emigrants who took his cutoff.

Following the Donner tragedy, Hastings went into business with John Sutter. He was appointed judge for the northern district of California in 1848 and elected a delegate to the California Constitutional Convention in 1849.

During the Civil War, he sided with the South and was commissioned a major in the Confederate Army. Following the war, Hastings pursued an improbable scheme to establish a confederate colony in Brazil. He died in 1870.

PETER LASSEN

Danish-born Peter Lassen was another of the restless adventurers so common in early California. Like John Sutter, he worked first with the Mexican government, then with the Americans.

The cutoff that took his name fell mostly into disuse after the disastrous experience of the 1849 emigration, dashing his hopes of developing a city around his Mexican land grant in Tehama County. Financial setbacks caused Lassen to lose his ranch in 1850. He was murdered while on a silver mining expedition near western Nevada's Black Rock Mountains in 1859 at age 58.

Lassen may have had more places named for him in California than any of his contemporaries, among them Lassen National Forest, Lassen Volcanic National Park, Lassen County, Lassen Peak, Lassen Community College, and, of course, the Lassen cutoff. He is also remembered with a memorial near his birthplace in Farum, Denmark.

MORTON M. MCCARVER

As restless as any of the early pioneers, Morton McCarver continued advancing in his career, unlike so many others who rose to prominence only to fade away.

Following the 1849–50 floods that devastated much of Sacramento, McCarver turned his property losses into a profit. He remained long enough for the rebuilding to begin, then sold his properties for a tidy profit of $30,000.[13]

McCarver also purchased a ship for coastal trade between California and Oregon, a profitable venture with several partners. He returned to Oregon City, where he built a nine-room mansion and later served as a general in the Rogue River wars in southern Oregon in 1855.[14]

McCarver followed gold strikes to the Fraser River in British Columbia and to eastern Oregon and Idaho, selling goods to miners. In 1868, he settled in Puget Sound, where he planned and established the city of Tacoma in 1868. This time, his city planning proved a major success.

McCarver died in 1875 and is buried in a Tacoma cemetery he had himself planned. There's nothing to indicate he ever forgave Burnett for his betrayal.

DR. JOHN MCLOUGHLIN

The "white headed eagle" and his wife, Marguerite, lived out their lives in a two-story wooden Colonial home they built on the banks of the Willamette River. McLoughlin finally became an American citizen in 1849 and was elected to a term as mayor of Oregon City in 1851.

A portion of McLoughlin's controversial land claim at Oregon City was restored to his children by the Oregon's Legislative Assembly in 1862, a recognition that McLoughlin had been unjustly treated.[15]

In 1957, the Oregon legislature officially designated McLoughlin the "Father of Oregon" for the help and support he gave to early settlers in defiance of the orders of his British superiors. A statue of McLoughlin was placed in National Statuary Hall in the US Capitol in 1853, a gift from Oregon.

The McLoughlin house was moved in 1909 to a cliff overlooking Willamette Falls. Open to tours, the restored home is administered by the US Park Service as part of the Fort Vancouver National Historic Site. McLoughlin, who died in 1857, and his wife are buried on the property. McLoughlin Boulevard, a major Portland thoroughfare, takes his name.

JAMES FRAZIER REED

Irish-born James Frazier Reed was named guardian of George and Tamsen Donner's children following the tragedy of the Donner-Reed Party.[16] Reed settled with his family in San Jose in 1848 after succeeding at mining gold around Placerville in El Dorado County.

He had enough money to begin buying real estate, and over the next several years became a wealthy man. He helped underwrite the construction of the first legislative chambers in San Jose in 1850. When the legislature considered moving, Reed offered to sell four city blocks to raise money for a new capital building in exchange for the legislature remaining in San Jose. The legislature moved anyway, to Vallejo.[17]

GENERAL BENNET C. RILEY

After skillfully executing the transition to a civilian government, Brevet Brigadier General Riley was promoted to full colonel and assigned command of the First Infantry, stationed on the Rio Grande. But poor health prevented Riley from assuming his new post. He moved to Buffalo, New York, where he died in 1853.

One historian wrote that Riley deserved a great deal of credit, not just for his role in the transition but also as a military officer who served with distinction. "He was no startling innovator, no tactical or strategical genius. . . . He was the epitome of the professional field officer, a man to execute the orders given him without going off on private wars of his own."[18] Fort Riley and Riley County, both in Kansas, are named in his honor.

THE SUTTERS

John A. Sutter left California for good in 1864, bereft of his once considerable land holdings. The US Supreme Court in 1858 had upheld his land grant from

Mexican Governor Alvarado but rejected his claim to the much larger grant from Governor Micheltorena.

The rulings made little practical difference to Sutter, however, as he owned little of the land, and none of it in Sacramento. He had sold or given away—or was finagled out of—more property than the two grants combined. What little remained was sold at a sheriff's auction in 1857.[19]

On one hand, the ruling in favor of the Alvarado grant was reassuring to those in Sacramento who had purchased the former Sutter lots. On the other hand, it disappointed the squatters who challenged the validity of Sutter's grant and whether the grant extended to Sacramento.

Sutter was allowed to keep six hundred acres of his Hock Farm property, a concession by his creditors. For a time, he made a go of it with a vineyard. In 1865, however, a thief set fire to Sutter's house and some of his fields, in apparent revenge for his deeds being exposed—and punished—by Sutter. Virtually all Sutter's possessions, collected over forty years, were destroyed, including his extensive library.[20]

With his wife, Anna, and three of his son's children, Sutter moved to a German-speaking community in Lititz, Pennsylvania, in 1879, and it became their home for the remainder of their lives. Sutter had received a stipend of $250 a month, approved by the California legislature in 1864. It was money Sutter insisted was owed him as repayment of the taxes he paid on the defunct Micheltorena grant.

Sutter spent the last fifteen years of his life lobbying Congress for a special pension of $50,000 as a reward for services to the nation. It was after being informed of yet another rejection in 1880 that a distraught Sutter collapsed and died in a room in Washington's old Mades Hotel.[21]

Sutter was buried in the Moravian Cemetery in Lititz. John Fremont delivered the eulogy at the well-attended funeral, their past differences overlooked, if not forgotten.[22]

One of Sutter's greatest admirers and a former congressman, John Bidwell, said that if Fremont was to be forever known as the "pathfinder," then Sutter should be known as "the discoverer." He said, "No pioneer ever did so much for this state as Sutter." Bidwell added, "More, I verily believe no pioneer ever did so much for the United States, and that few men in modern times have done so much for the world at large, as General Sutter."[23]

August Sutter never stopped looking after his father's well-being. He provided the money for his parents to build an impressive two-story brick home in Lititz. But not forgetting his father's proclivity for losing money, he put the home and other money in his mother's name.

August lived the remainder of his life in Mexico, where President Grant named him US consul in Acapulco in 1870. He also worked as cashier and bookkeeper for the Pacific Mail Steamship Company. August died in 1897.

Appendix B
Estimated Immigration on the Oregon Trail, 1840–60

Year	Number of Immigrants to Oregon	Number of Immigrants to California
1840	13	0
1841	24	34
1842	125	0
1843	875	38
1844	1,475	53
1845	2,500	260
1846	1,200	1,500
1847	4,000	450
1848	1,300	400
1849	450	25,000
1850	6,000	44,000
1851	3,600	1,100
1852	10,000	50,000
1853	7,500	20,000
1854	6,000	12,000
1855	500	1,500
1856	1,000	8,000
1857	1,500	4,000
1858	1,500	6,000
1859	2,000	17,000
1860	1,500	9,000
Total	**53,062**	**200,335**

Source: Unruh, *Plains Across*, 119–20.

Appendix C
Oregon's Exclusion Act and Lash Law, June 18, 1844

AN ACT IN REGARD TO SLAVERY
AND FREE NEGROES AND MULATTOES

Be it enacted by the Legislative Committee of Oregon as follows:

Section 1. That slavery and involuntary servitude shall be forever prohibited in Oregon.

Section 2. That in all cases where slaves shall have been, or shall hereafter be, brought into Oregon, the owners of such slaves respectively shall have the term of three years from the introduction of such slaves to remove them out of the country.

Section 3. That if such owners of slaves shall neglect or refuse to remove such slaves from the country within the time specified in the preceding section, such slaves shall be free.

Section 4. That when any free negro or mulatto shall have come to Oregon, he or she (as the case may be), if of the age of eighteen or upward, shall remove from and leave the country within the term of two years for males and three year for females from the passage of this act; and that if any free negro or mulatto shall hereafter come to Oregon, if of the age aforesaid, he or she shall quit and leave the country within the term of two years for males and three years for females from his or her arrival in the country.

Section 5. That if such free negro or mulatto be under the age aforesaid, the terms of time specified in the preceding section shall begin to run when he or she shall arrive at such age.

Section 6. That if any such free negro or mulatto shall fail to quit the country as required by this act, he or she may be arrested upon a warrant issued by some justice of the peace, and, if guilty upon trial before such justice, shall receive upon his or her bare back not less than twenty nor more than thirty-nine stripes, to be inflicted by the constable of the proper county.

Section 7. That if any free negro or mulatto shall fail to quit the country within the term of six months after receiving such stripes, he or she shall again receive the same punishment once in every six months until he or she shall quit the country.

Section 8. That when any slave shall obtain his or her freedom, the time specified in the fourth section shall begin to run from the time when such freedom shall be obtained.

AMENDED DECEMBER 19, 1844

Section 1. That the sixth and seventh sections of said act are hereby repealed.

Section 2. That if any such free negro or mulatto shall fail to quit and leave the country, as required by the act to which this is amendatory, he or she may be arrested upon a warrant issued by some justice of the peace; and if guilty upon trial before such justice had, the said justice shall issue this order to any officer competent to execute process, directing said officer to give ten days' public notice, by at least four written or printed advertisements, that he will publicly hire out such free negro or mulatto to the lowest bidder, on a day and at a place therein specified. On the day and at the place mentioned in said notice, such officer shall expose such free negro or mulatto to public hiring; and the person who will obligate himself to remove such free negro or mulatto from the country for the shortest term of service, shall enter into a bond with good and sufficient security in Oregon, in a penalty of at least one thousand dollars, binding himself to remove said negro or mulatto out of the country within six months after such service shall expire; which bond shall be filed in the clerk's office in the proper county; and upon failure to perform the conditions of said body, the attorney prosecuting for Oregon shall commence a suit upon a certified copy of such bond in the circuit court against such delinquent and his sureties.

Appendix D
California Fugitive Slave Act of 1852: An Act Respecting Fugitives from Labor and Slaves Brought to This State Prior to Her Admission into the Union

Section Four: Any person or persons held to labor or service in any state or territory of the United States, by the laws of such state or territory, and who were brought or introduced within the limits of this state previous to the admission of this state as one of the United States of America, and who shall refuse to return to the state or territory where he, she, or they owed such labor or service, upon the demand of the person, or persons, his or their agent, or attorney, to which such labor or service was due, such person or persons so refusing to return, shall be held and deemed fugitives from labor within the meaning of this act, and all the remedies and rights, and provisions herein given to claimants of fugitives who escaped from any other state into this state, are hereby given and conferred upon claimants of fugitives from labor within the meaning of this section; provided, the provisions of this section shall not have force and effect after the period of twelve months from the passage of this act.

Notes

PREFACE

1 Lenox, *Overland to Oregon*, 12.

CHAPTER 1

1 Burnett, *Recollections*, 37. The whiskey was named for a river in western Pennsylvania.
2 Burnett, *Recollections*, 40–41.
3 Burnett, *Recollections*, 41.
4 Burnett didn't provide dates for the shooting or the inquest. Janette Tigner, director of the Hardeman County Library in Bolivar, Tennessee, told me on February 24, 2016, that she researched available newspapers and other documents from the period but was unable to locate any record of the shooting.
5 Burnett, *Recollections*, vi.
6 Three other girls died before age 5.
7 Peter Burnett's typewritten genealogy, March 2, 1885, Burnett Letters, Bancroft Library, Berkeley, California.
8 By 1860, the price of a healthy male slave in Missouri had increased to about $1,300.
9 Hardeman, *Wilderness Calling*, 36.
10 Burnett, *Recollections*, 3–4.
11 Burnett, *Recollections*, 7.
12 Paxton, *Annals of Platte County*, 37.
13 US Slave Census for 1840.
14 Burnett, *Recollections*, 31. Emphasis added.
15 Burnett, *Recollections*, 18. Honey was valued as a sweetener.
16 When Missouri was admitted to statehood in 1821, the border was then a straight line that intersected the confluence of the Missouri and Kaw Rivers, now the Kansas River. Lands west of the border were ostensibly off-limits to settlers and reserved for the Native American tribes, among them the Iowas, Sax, and Fox.
17 Burnett, *Old California Pioneer*, 8–9. Constantia's first husband, James M. Miller, was killed by lightning about 1821.
18 Burnett, *Recollections*, 23.
19 Burnett, *Recollections*, 24.
20 Burnett, *Recollections*, 23.
21 Burnett, *Recollections*, 26.
22 Burnett, *Recollections*, 1.

CHAPTER 2

1 Burnett, *Recollections*, 30.
2 Burnett, *Recollections*, 30.
3 Burnett, *Recollections*, 38.
4 Burnett, *Recollections*, 42.
5 *Sacramento City Directory for 1851*, 100.
6 Burnett apparently rented the dwelling for $25 a year. *Sacramento City Directory for 1851*, 100.
7 Burnett, *Recollections*, 41.
8 Burnett, *Old California Pioneer*, 22.
9 Burnett, *Recollections*, 48.

CHAPTER 3

1 Burnett would have become an attorney through a process called

"reading for the law," usually done under the supervision of another attorney. The best-known self-educated lawyer was Abraham Lincoln, who advised an aspiring attorney, Isham Reaves, in 1855 to "get the books and read and study them till you understand them in their principle features; that is the main thing." Lincoln recommended beginning with William Blackstone's four-volume *Commentaries on the Laws of England* (1765–69), considered a basic primer for attorneys. "Lincoln's Advice to Lawyers," Abraham Lincoln Online.

2 Burnett, *Recollections*, 50.

3 Fuenfausen, "Slavery in Clay County." Thornton served in the military and was a judge and a Missouri state representative. He grew hemp and owned a ferry on the Missouri River. He was listed in 1840 as owner of twenty slaves.

4 The economic collapse had many causes, including land speculation and a fall in cotton prices, but the final blow occurred when New York banks suspended so-called specie payment, or repayment in gold and silver of the full value of bank notes. Banks failed, and unemployment soared as high as 25 percent in places. The recession lasted until the mid–1840s and was one of the inducements for emigrants to head west on what became known as the Oregon Trail.

5 Burnett, *Recollections*, 50.

6 The interest was not exorbitant at the time, considering a credit crunch from the impending economic collapse.

7 Burnett, *Recollections*, 51.

8 *Far West*, August 25, 1836.

9 *Far West*, August 25, 1836.

10 Kinney, *Mormon War*, 7.

11 Kinney, *Mormon War*, 76.

12 Kinney, *Mormon War*, 79–78. The passages are from Daniel 2:44–45:

"And in the days of these kings the God of heaven will set up a kingdom which shall never be destroyed nor shall its sovereignty be left to another people. It shall break in pieces all these kingdoms and bring them to an end, and it shall stand for ever; just as you saw that a stone was cut from a mountain by no human hand, and that it broke in pieces the iron, the bronze, the clay, the silver and the gold. A great God has made known to the king what shall be hereafter. The dream is certain, and its interpretation sure."

13 LeSueur, *1838 Mormon War*, 117–18.

14 LeSueur, *1838 Mormon War*, 141–43.

15 Kinney, *Mormon War*, 158. The order was officially rescinded on June 25, 1976, by Governor Christopher S. Bond, with "deep regret for the injustice and undue suffering" the order had caused.

16 Kinney, *Mormon War*, 159.

17 In the Militia Act of 1792, Congress required all able-bodied white men between ages 18 and 45 to serve in a local militia company. The law was amended in 1862 to include all able-bodied males.

18 Burnett, *Recollections*, 60.

19 Burnett, *Recollections*, 61–62.

20 Krakauer, *Under the Banner of Heaven*, 103.

21 LeSueur, *1838 Mormon War*, 183. Others who were court-martialed included Sydney Rigdon, Hyrum Smith, and Lyman Wight (181). LeSueur makes clear that the precise circumstances of the court-martial are unknown or in dispute.

22 Burnett, *Recollections*, 63.

23 LeSueur, *1838 Mormon War*, 257.

24 Paxton, *Annals of Platte County*, 15.

25 Burnett, *Recollections*, 54.

26 Burnett, *Recollections*, 57.

27 Burnett, *Recollections*, 67.

28 Burnett, *Recollections*, 66–67.

29 Kinney, *Mormon War*, 187.

30 LeSueur, *1838 Mormon War*, 244.

31 LeSueur, *1838 Mormon War*, 35, 255–59. An unknown number were allowed to remain after severing ties with the church.

32 Krakauer, *Under the Banner of Heaven*, 105.

33 Krakauer, *Under the Banner of Heaven*, 120–21.

34 Krakauer, *Under the Banner of Heaven*, 127.

35 Krakauer, *Under the Banner of Heaven*, 131.

36 "Missouri History Not Found in Textbooks," 469.

37 Atchison was a US senator from Missouri from 1843 to 1855. He was a fierce proslavery advocate who owned many slaves.

38 Burnett, *Recollections*, 69. The population of Platte County in 1840 was 8,913, including 858 slaves.

39 Burnett, *Recollections*, 71.

40 Burnett, *Recollections*, 194.

41 Paxton, *Annals of Platte County*, 43.

CHAPTER 4

1 Burnett, "Letters of Peter H. Burnett," 190, 191.

2 Dale, "Organization of the Oregon Emigrating Companies," 209. The first of these was the American Society for Encouraging the Settlement of the Oregon Territory, organized in 1829 in Boston, although nothing came of its efforts to promote an emigration (207).

3 *Congressional Globe* 29, no. 1 (1846): 918.

4 Fremont, *Report on an Exploration*. Fremont was married to Missouri Senator Thomas Hart Benton's daughter Jessie.

5 Fremont, *Report on an Exploration*, 57.

6 Bagley, *South Pass*, 24. The pass is the lowest point through the Rocky Mountains, at 7,412 feet.

7 Drury, *Where Wagons Could Go*, 194. There has been recent speculation that the missionaries crossed the Continental Divide not at South Pass, but 20 miles north over a steeper ridge in the Wind River Mountains known as the Lander Cutoff. See Bagley, *South Pass*, 99.

8 Drury, *Where Wagons Could Go*, 194.

9 See Appendix C for yearly immigration totals for Oregon and California.

10 Unruh, *Plains Across*, 91.

11 *Ohio Statesman*, March 14, 1843.

12 *Ohio Statesman*, April 16, 1843.

13 Prosch, *McCarver and Tacoma*, 20; *Ohio Statesman*, April 26, 1843.

14 Lenox, *Overland to Oregon*, 12–13.

15 Burnett, *Recollections*, 97.

16 Paxton, *Annals of Platte County*, 19. An early county history listed "Burnett Brothers" as merchants in the even smaller nearby town of Martinsville, 7 miles southeast of Weston, in 1836. It merged with Platte City in 1840.

17 Burnett, *Recollections*, 98.

18 Geer, *Fifty Years in Oregon*, 218. Geer's parents emigrated to Oregon in 1847 and settled near the well-known Waldos in what are now called the Waldo Hills east of Salem in Marion County. Geer was Oregon's governor from 1899 to 1903. He gave no attribution for the quote.

19 Burnett, *Recollections*, 98.

20 Settlers arriving before December 1, 1850, were entitled to the maximum.

21 *Liberty Tribune*, March 27, 1847.

22 Unruh, *Plains Across*, 115.

23 Mattes, *Great Platte River Road*, 107.

24 Nesmith, "Address," 46, 52.

25 Nesmith, "Address."

26 Hardeman, *Wilderness Calling*, 163. Tharpe, *Encyclopedia of Frontier Biography*, 531. John Gantt had a checkered career in the US Army, serving as captain in the Sixth Infantry at frontier posts prior to being court-

martialed and dismissed in 1829 for falsifying pay records. He formed his own fur-trading company, Gantt and Blackwell, with trapper Jefferson Blackwell, trading with the Arapahoe and Cheyenne tribes from a trading post on the Arkansas River. Because of his baldness, Gantt was called "Bald Head" by the tribes. After the trading post failed in 1834, he began a third career as a guide to emigrant wagon trains.

27 Unruh, *Plains Across*, 110.

28 Dary, *Oregon Trail*, 86.

29 Burnett, *Recollections*, 103.

30 Dary, *Oregon Trail*, 87.

31 Prosch, *McCarver and Tacoma*, 29.

32 Burnett, "Letters of Peter H. Burnett," 410. Burnett frequently gave evasive reasons for resigning some of his responsibilities.

33 Mattes, *Great Platte River Road*, 36, 65. Mattes wrote that the dissension that occurred in the 1843 wagon train was unusual for Oregon-bound wagons, although not so unusual among wagons headed to California. "The Oregon companies, with strong family bonds, held together better than the Californians, who were united only in their lust for gold." The trails to both destinations were generally not for the very young or the very old. Ninety-five out of every one hundred emigrants were between ages 15 and 50. According to Mattes, at least half of Oregon emigrants were women and children, while those bound for California were almost exclusively male, either bachelors or men traveling without their families.

34 Applegate, *Day with the Cow Column*, 372–73.

35 Applegate, *Day with the Cow Column*, 381.

36 Burnett, *Recollections*, 110.

37 Burnett, *Recollections*, 113.

38 Burnett, *Recollections*, 115. This would have been Pacific Springs, a 36-mile-long stream on the western slopes of South Pass, whose waters eventually flow into the Pacific.

39 Whitman, *Letters of Narcissa Whitman*, 24. The stockade was said to enclose 80 square feet. Emigrants could obtain supplies, blacksmith services, and fresh cattle at Fort Hall.

40 Burnett, *Recollections*, 108.

41 Unruh, *Plains Across*, 110.

42 Prosch, *McCarver and Tacoma*, 26.

43 Ford, "Pioneer Road-Makers," 11.

44 Burnett, *Recollections*, 124–26.

45 Burnett, *Recollections*, 126–27.

46 Burnett, *Recollections*, 126–27.

47 Applegate, *Recollections of My Boyhood*, 45.

48 Mary Burslie Mertz Davis, interviewed in The Dalles, April 29, 2016. Davis and her husband, Dennis, are both docents at Fort Dalles's two-story Surgeon's House, built in 1856 and maintained as a museum and historic site. Sixty years have not silenced the falls in Davis's memory. "People went to sleep to that roar and woke up to that roar." When the last ripple of the rapids disappeared, "the silence was deafening." The only roar people hear today are from trucks passing on Interstate 84, or the clattering of the frequent freight and coal trains rumbling through the city of nearly fourteen thousand.

49 Celilo Falls was submerged in 1957 behind The Dalles Dam, one of three dams constructed in this stretch of the river to generate hydroelectric power and to provide passage for inland shipping from the Pacific to Lewiston, Idaho. The others are the Bonneville Dam in 1938, and the John Day Dam in 1971. The dams flooded Native American villages and fishing sites, along with submerging the rapids.

50 Ford, "Pioneer Road-Makers," 15. Emigrants built the rafts using six to eight logs in 20-foot lengths that were lashed together. The wagons were dismantled and loaded onto the rafts, to be reassembled downriver.

51 Bancroft, *History of Oregon*, 409.

52 Applegate, *Recollections of My Boyhood*, 105.

53 Ford, "Pioneer Road-Makers," 21.

54 Nokes, *Breaking Chains*, 18.

55 Burnett, *Recollections*, 115.

56 Ford, "Pioneer Road-Makers," 8.

57 Nesmith, "Diary of the Emigration of 1843," 52–53.

58 Lenox, *Overland to Oregon*, 46; Mattes, *Great Platte River Road*, 91.

59 Mattes, *Great Platte River Road*, 280.

60 Mattes, "Council Bluffs Road," 15, 21. He estimated deaths from all causes on the various trails conservatively at twenty thousand over a period of 25 years, or 10 deaths for every mile of the 2,000-mile journey from the Missouri River to the Pacific Coast. Mattes also argued the trails should be collectively known as the Great Platte River Road until South Pass, after which the Oregon, California, and Mormon Trails would be so designated.

61 Nesmith, "Diary of the Emigration of 1843," 49.

62 Tate, *Great Medicine Road*, 131–133.

63 Applegate, *Recollections of My Boyhood*, 52–53. This was Memaloose Island, the name derived from a Chinook word for "death." Meriwether Lewis and William Clark also passed this island in 1805 and called it "Sepulcher Island." American Indian tribes along the Columbia buried their dead above ground, wrapped in robes or tule mats. Memaloose was one of several burial islands. Most have been submerged behind dams, although a large part of Memaloose remains above water and is easily seen from shore. The Native American remains were relocated during the 1930s. Memaloose State Park is nearby on the Oregon side of the river.

64 David Harrelson, manager of the Grand Ronde Historic Preservation Department, interviewed June 9, 2016. See also Lynch, *Free Land for Free Men*, 24. The Clackamas, Clowewallas, and Kalapuyas would be made nearly extinct by an illness they called "cold sick," brought by crewmen on the ship *Owyhee*, which sailed into the Willamette in 1829. Lynch estimated that 90 percent of the tribes were wiped out: "The epidemic so depleted the tribes that open Indian opposition to white men in the Willamette Valley was broken forever." Her estimates are in line with those of other historians. According to Lynch, by 1851, there were only eighty-eight Clackamas remaining. Their name is remembered in the Clackamas River, a major tributary of the Willamette, as well as Clackamas County, which includes Oregon City and the traditional lands of the falls-area tribes.

65 White, *American Ulysses*, 487.

66 Lynch, *Free Land for Free Men*, 74–75, 236.

67 Nineveh Ford counted twelve houses in the area of the falls when he arrived in 1843. He commented that the immigrants were well-received by residents.

68 The valleys are of loess soil, wind-blown glacial dust, and silt accumulated over millions of years and reaching depths of up to 150 feet in eastern Washington. The Missoula floods swept great quantities of the soil down the Columbia River toward the Pacific in a series of floods thousands of years ago, when Ice Age dams on Montana's Clark River collapsed, releasing their enormous reservoirs. The backwaters from the

floods diverted the loess down the 90 miles of the Willamette Valley, and also into the Tualatin Valley, west of today's Portland, leaving the rich soil behind as the waters receded. The floods, reaching depths up to 500 feet and rushing downriver at breakneck speed, greatly widened and reshaped the gorge of the Columbia River, now known as the Columbia River National Scenic Area. For more on the Missoula floods and their the causes, effects, and consequences, see Allen et al., *Cataclysms on the Columbia*.

69 According to records on display at the End of the Oregon Trail Museum in Oregon City. The land office was established in 1851.

70 Oregon City's population in 2015 was just under thirty-six thousand.

71 The letter was written by P. L. Edwards, who emigrated overland with missionary Jason Lee in 1834 and taught at Lee's mission school north of present-day Salem. He returned east in 1838 and at some point must have become acquainted with Burnett, although Burnett didn't mention him. The contents of the letter are unknown.

72 Brown, *Brown's Political History of Oregon*, 117. See also "History," Historic The Dalles.

73 Burnett, *Recollections*, 127.

74 Mattes, *Great Platte River Road*, 53.

75 Whitman, *Letters of Narcissa Whitman*, 33.

76 Descriptions from Gray, *History of Oregon*, 150. Carey, *General History of Oregon*, 245. The Columbia Barracks, a US military post overlooking Fort Vancouver, was established in 1849. The fort was destroyed by fire in 1866 after being abandoned by the Hudson's Bay Company in 1860—a replica fort has been constructed near the site. The original Columbia Barracks are well preserved.

77 Prosch, *McCarver and Tacoma*, 29.

78 Carey, *General History of Oregon*, 382–83.

79 Burnett, *Recollections*, 40.

80 Gray, *History of Oregon*, 65.

81 Unruh, *Plains Across*, 5.

82 Mattes, *Great Platte River Road*, 13, 70.

83 Johnson, *Founding the Far West*, 110.

84 Cornelius Gilliam had been sheriff in Clay County, Missouri, and a Missouri state senator. He was involved in military operations to expel the Mormons from Missouri, and also served as an officer with the Missouri Volunteers in several conflicts with Native American tribes. The wagon train he led from Missouri included about 300 wagons. In Oregon, he commanded the Oregon Rifles in the Cayuse War following the Whitman massacre in 1847. He accidently shot and killed himself while returning from combat in 1848. See Doyle, "Cornelius Gilliam (1798–1848)." Ford was a four-term county sheriff in Howard County, Missouri, and a member of the Missouri legislature. He was a major landowner and slaveholder who led about 350 emigrants to Oregon in a wagon train that traveled near Gilliam. In Oregon, he was a prominent Democrat and served five terms in the Provisional and Territorial legislatures. See Nokes, *Breaking Chains*, 33–34.

85 Minto, "Motives and Antecedents of the Pioneers," 43.

86 Cleland, "John Bidwell's Arrival in California," 112.

87 Tate, *Great Medicine Road*, 76.

CHAPTER 5

1 Burnett, *Recollections*, 250.

2 Drury, *Where Wagons Could Go*, 107.

3 Whitman, *Letters of Narcissa Whitman*, 79.

4 Whitman, *Letters of Narcissa Whitman*, 142, 149.

5 Whitman, *Letters of Narcissa Whitman*, 224.

6 Victor, *Early Indian Wars of Oregon*, 95.

7 Victor, *Early Indian Wars of Oregon*, 94. Fort Walla Walla, also known as Fort Nez Perce, was on the east bank of the Columbia River. It was built as a fortified trading post in 1818 and was separate from the military Fort Walla Walla, established in 1856.

8 *Oregon Spectator*, December 10, 1847. Oregon's first newspaper, first published in Oregon City on February 5, 1846.

9 *Oregon Spectator*, December 10, 1847.

10 Victor, *Early Indian Wars of Oregon*, 139.

11 Burnett, *Recollections*, 210.

12 Victor, *Early Indian Wars of Oregon*, 215. The book includes the muster rolls for the Cayuse War.

13 Victor, *Early Indian Wars of Oregon*, 149. George Burnett served a term in the Oregon legislature from Yamhill County in 1868. He died in 1878. See also Lang, *History of the Willamette Valley*, 653.

14 Victor, *Early Indian Wars of Oregon*, 180. Victor, a respected historian writing in the late 1890s, offered no source for these quotations.

15 Lansing, "Whitman Massacre Trial"; and Carey, *General History of Oregon*, 508–9. Joseph Lane was the territorial governor when the trial commenced, but he resigned after the sentences were handed down to accept a new position as territorial delegate in Washington, DC. The new acting governor, Kintzing Pritchett, reportedly planned to issue a reprieve to allow an appeal. But Judge Pratt ruled there was a twenty-five-day waiting period before Pritchett could issue his pardon, and he declined to wait.

16 Whitman, *Letters of Narcissa Whitman*, 234.

17 Griffin, *Oregon American and Evangelical Unionist*, 38, 40.

CHAPTER 6

1 Burnett, *Recollections*, 239.

2 Gray, *History of Oregon*, 261.

3 Holman, "Brief History of the Oregon Provisional Government," 134.

4 The overland trip included the remarkable survival story of the one woman in the expedition, Marie Dorion, a Native American of the Iowa tribe, who traveled with her two small children and gave birth to a third en route, enduring the journey better than most of the men.

5 Stark, *Astoria*, 178.

6 Stark, *Astoria*, 74–75.

7 Stark, *Astoria*, 214. McKay's widow, Marguerite, would marry John McLoughlin in 1812. His son Thomas McKay would guide Peter Burnett into California in 1848.

8 Stark, *Astoria*, 209–13.

9 Stark, *Astoria*, 176–77.

CHAPTER 7

1 Prosch, *McCarver and Tacoma*, 12–13.

2 Prosch, *McCarver and Tacoma*, 13. Nothing was said about who put up the money for these improvements. McCarver had "hundreds of lots and acres" in Iowa, however, and he may have come away with a sufficient profit to help finance Linnton.

3 Eight miles of the eastern slopes of the Tualatin Mountains, also known as the West Hills, are preserved as a 5,100-acre Portland city park called Forest Park, one of the largest forested parks within any American city. The tallest of the mountains is Cornell Peak, at 1,270 feet.

4 Prosch, *McCarver and Tacoma*, 30–31.

5 There is still today a town of Linnton (population 541 in 2010) on a narrow strip of land between heavily traveled Highway 30 and the Willamette River, north of Portland's industrial district. But it's a far cry from the vibrant port city envisioned by Burnett and McCarver. Its most distinctive feature to the thousands of commuters who drive to jobs in Portland was for years an abandoned and windowless three-story stone block building, a former gas manufacturing plant built by the Portland Gas & Coke Company in 1912. Fenced off and unusable because of decades of ground contamination, the soot-blackened building was topped with a clock tower that tells no time—the hands disappeared long ago. Plans were approved in 2015 to tear the building down, although preservationists intervened in a probably futile attempt to have it preserved as a historic site. Senator Linn is better honored in the names of the upscale Portland suburb of West Linn, and Linn County in the fertile Willamette Valley, the destination of early settlers.

6 Oregon Provisional and Territorial Land Claim Records, 1845–1849, No. 60793, April 14, 1846, 7:166, Oregon State Archives, Salem.

7 Burnett, *Recollections*, 139.

8 Burnett, *Recollections*, 183.

9 Burnett, *Recollections*, 183. Oliphant, "Minutes of West Union Baptist Church," 247.

10 The congregation was dissolved in 1878, but the building was well maintained over the years. It became active again in the 1980s, and services are regularly held there today. Surrounded by farmland on three sides, the building retains its original belfry, siding, doors, and other major features. The adjacent cemetery, one of the oldest in Oregon, holds about three hundred graves.

11 Oregon Provisional and Territorial Land Claim Records, 7:165. Efforts were not successful to locate an actual deed of sale from Burnett to Cornelius, despite the aid of clerks in the Washington County recorder's office in Hillsboro.

12 Letter from Burnett to Father Stephen Beauchamp, San Francisco, June 29, 1849, Burnett Files, California State Library, Sacramento. Burnett wrote that Smith was unlikely to take possession of the property because he was "a great drunkard and will soon kill himself."

13 Peter Burnett carried on an extensive correspondence with George. The letters are in possession of Peter's great-great-granddaughter, Emily Douville, of Antioch, California, who generously shared their contents. Burnett almost certainly wrote Harriet during their long separations and corresponded with other members of his family, but those letters have not been located, if they still exist.

14 Hardeman, *Wilderness Calling*, 186; Oregon Provisional and Territorial Land Claim Records.

15 Burnett, *Recollections*, 187–88.

16 Burnett, *Recollections*, 193.

17 Carey, *General History of Oregon*, 244–47.

18 Holman, "Brief History of the Oregon Provisional Government," 91. Holman died in 1927. He was the grandson of John Holman, an 1843 emigrant. By coincidence, at the time of this writing, the news broke that Holman's elegant 1872 home in northwest Portland was targeted for destruction to make way for new development. Although neighbors campaigned to save the historic home, it was torn down in October 2016.

19 Burnett, *Recollections*, 143.

20 Burnett, *Recollections*, 144.

21 Morrison, *Outpost*, 382–83.

22 Prosch, *McCarver and Tacoma*, 31.

23 Morrison, *Outpost*, 388–89.

24 Morrison, *Outpost*, 390.

25 Organic Act, Article 3, Sections 1 & 2, cited in Brown, *Brown's Political History of Oregon*, 167.

26 Burnett, *Recollections*, 142.

27 Carey, *General History of Oregon*, 246.

28 Morrison, *Outpost*, 466.

29 Gray, *History of Oregon*, 334.

30 Burnett, *Recollections*, 189–90.

31 Burnett, *Recollections*, 189.

32 Burnett, *Old California Pioneer*, 114.

33 Gray, *History of Oregon*, 375.

34 Drury, *Where Wagons Could Go*, 161.

35 Carey, *General History of Oregon*, 243.

36 Nesmith, "Diary of the Emigration of 1843," 58.

37 Oregon is also represented by Methodist missionary Jason Lee.

CHAPTER 8

1 Burnett, "Letters of Peter H. Burnett," October 28, 1843.

2 Burnett, "Letters of Peter H. Burnett," August 18, 1845.

3 *Tribune*, August 21, 1847.

4 Burnett, *Recollections*, 177–78.

5 Unruh, *Plains Across*, 119–20.

6 Burnett, *Recollections*, 169.

7 Brown, *Brown's Political History of Oregon*, 155.

8 Gray left Waiilatpu for the Willamette Valley prior to the massacre of the Whitmans.

9 Carey, *General History of Oregon*, 346.

10 Gray, *A History of Oregon*, 375.

11 Bancroft, *History of Oregon*, 429.

12 George Abernethy, formerly of New York, was elected governor in 1845 and served until Oregon gained territorial status in 1848. Abernethy arrived in Oregon with his family in 1840 on the ship *Lausanne*, which made the voyage around Cape Horn. He had been recruited by Methodist missionary Jason Lee to join the Methodist mission and manage the mission's store in Oregon City. The Abernethy Bridge on Interstate 205 is named for him.

13 *Platte Argus*, November 4, 1844.

14 *Jefferson City Inquirer*, November 26, 1845. Burnett's letter to the Missouri paper was dated December 9, 1944.

CHAPTER 9

1 The Northwest Ordinance established the Northwest Territory, the region northwest of the Ohio River ceded to the United States in the 1783 Treaty of Paris, which marked an end to the Revolutionary War.

2 Carey, *General History of Oregon*, 342.

3 Gray, *History of Oregon*, 378; Burnett, *Recollections*, 193.

4 Burnett, letter to the *Jefferson City Inquirer*, written from Willamette Falls, Oregon, December 25, 1844, and printed October 23, 1845.

5 The 1830 slave census listed Daniel Waldo of Gascade, Missouri, with four slaves, all male.

6 Nokes, *Breaking Chains*, 105.

7 Gray, *History of Oregon*, 378.

8 Gray, *History of Oregon*, 379.

9 The ban on slavery presumably didn't apply to slaves brought into Oregon during the period the 1844 law was in effect, which gave slave owners three years to free their slaves. "Presumably" is the best that can be said, since the 1844 law was never tested in court.

10 Rucker, *Oregon Trail*, 232.

11 Prosch, *McCarver and Tacoma*, 37. McCarver was speaker in both the 1844 and 1845 committees, but he evidently deferred to Burnett and Applegate for leadership.

12 *Holmes v. Ford* was the 1852 habeas corpus suit brought in Second District Court in Polk County. A copy of the trial record is on file in the Polk County Courthouse in Dallas, Oregon, and is reprinted in Lockley,

"Case of Robin Holmes vs. Nathaniel Ford," 134–35.

13 Williams, *Political History of Oregon*, 6. A native of New York, Williams was appointed to Oregon's Territorial Supreme Court by President Franklin Pierce in 1852. He was elected a US senator from Oregon, serving 1865–71, and was appointed US attorney general by President Ulysses Grant, serving 1871–75. He was also nominated by Grant for chief justice of the US Supreme Court, but he was not confirmed.

14 Nokes, *Breaking Chains*, 154–55. The former slave, Reuben Shipley, paid part of Ford's demand before being persuaded by white friends that he didn't need to pay. Shipley was brought to Oregon from Miller County, Missouri, in 1853, by his white owner, Robert Shipley, an ancestor of mine. He was freed after helping his owner develop a farm near Philomath in Benton County, Oregon. Reuben Shipley became a successful farmer. In 1863, he and Mary Jane donated three acres for a cemetery, which was open to blacks as well as whites. Known as the Mt. Union Cemetery, it is still in operation today at Philomath. The Shipleys are buried there, as are some of my relatives.

15 Nokes, *Breaking Chains*, 100.

16 Burnett, *Recollections*, 128.

CHAPTER 10

1 Grover, "Oregon Acts and Laws Passed by the House of Representatives at a Meeting Held In Oregon City, August, 1845," in *Oregon Archives and Public Papers of Oregon*, 52. Governor Abernethy's pay was $300 a year.

2 Grover, *Oregon Archives and Public Papers of Oregon*, 115. The legislature decided on Burnett at a closed session, so it's not known if there were other candidates.

3 Actions of Supreme Court of Oregon's Provisional Government, 1844–1848, 47–90, Supreme Court Library, Salem, Oregon. Courtesy of Stephen Dow Beckham.

4 The Massachusetts-born Lovejoy first traveled to Oregon in 1842 with the Elijah White expedition and went as far as the Whitman mission at Waiilatpu. He was persuaded to accompany Marcus Whitman on his trip east and returned in 1843 with the Burnett-organized wagon train. He is remembered as one of the founders of the City of Portland, but he lost a coin toss in 1845 with Francis Pettygrove from Portland, Maine, to decide whether to name the city Portland or Boston.

5 *Oregon Spectator*, January 7, 1847.

6 Lang, *History of the Willamette Valley*, 647. Skinner had a distinguished judicial career in Oregon. He helped negotiate treaties with Willamette Valley tribes in 1850–51. See McArthur, "Alonzo A. Skinner (1814–1877)."

7 *Oregon Spectator*, August 6, 1846.

8 Brown, *Brown's Political History of Oregon*, 460.

9 Burnett, *Recollections*, 206.

10 Burnett, *Recollections*, 191.

11 Burnett, *Recollections*, 193.

12 Rucker, *Oregon Trail*, 232–33.

13 Bancroft, *History of Oregon*, 431.

14 *Weekly Tribune*, January 20, 1846. We have only Burnett's account of Hill's letter, as early editions of the Boonville paper in which it was published evidently no longer exist.

15 *Weekly Tribune*, August 15–16, 1846. Hill took Burnett's seat in the Territorial Legislature after Burnett resigned. The City of Hillsboro, west of Portland, is named for Hill, who had a donation land claim there.

16 *Weekly Tribune*, August 15–16, 1846.

17 Burnett, *Recollections*, 150. By this time, the remaining Kalapuya had been moved with other western Oregon tribes to the Grand Ronde Reservation

18 Carey, *General History of Oregon*, 247.

19 There were an estimated eighty independent Chinookan villages, linked by marriage, along the Lower Columbia from Astoria to Cascade Locks, with a combined population of fifteen thousand. Most of the villages were wiped out by epidemics of malaria and other fevers in the early 1830s. See Zenk et al., "Chinookan Villages of the Lower Columbia," 6–37.

20 Nokes, *Breaking Chains*, 35. The number of Kalapuya language speakers was reduced from about two thousand in 1806—a figure reported by the Lewis and Clark expedition—to about three hundred in 1844. See also Ruby and Brown, *Indians of the Pacific Northwest*, and Juntunen and Dasch, *World of the Kalapuya*. The last known fluent speaker of the Kalapuya language died on the reservation in 1954.

21 David Harrelson, interviewed on June 9, 2016. The Kalapuya bands included the Tualatins, Molallas, Yamhills, Yoncallas, and Mary's River. According to Harrelson, although the number of Kalapuya has rebounded, no effort is made to keep a separate count for the Kalapuya or other tribes on the reservation, as most members are descendants of multiple tribes or bands. In a development reflecting the new influence of the tribes, the Grand Ronde Tribal Council and the City of Portland agreed on December 16, 2016, to a historic memorandum of understanding for lands ceded to the city by the tribes and now occupied by the city. This understanding commits the parties to cooperate and consult on decisions of mutual interest

concerning the former tribal lands. See the publication of the Confederated Tribes of the Grand Ronde, *Smoke Signals*, December 16, 2016.

CHAPTER 11

1 Burnett, *Recollections*, 253.

2 Carey, *History of Oregon*, 506n12.

3 Burnett, *Recollections*, 254.

4 *Oregon Statesman*, October 12, 1848, cited in Carey, *History of Oregon*, 506. The US Census put Oregon's 1850 population at 13,294 whites, of whom 8,138 were males. See also Nemec, "Oregon Fever."

5 Nemec, "Oregon Fever."

6 Starr, *California*, 81–82. Improvements to ease the isthmus crossing were swift in coming. In 1850, William Henry Aspinwall established a port called Aspinwall, today's Colon, for his new California shipping line, the Pacific Mail Steamship Company, which also was the eastern terminus for a railroad completed in 1855. Panama became an independent country in 1903.

7 The US Census put the 1850 population at 92,000, but figures for San Francisco and some other Bay Area communities were lost and not included. The total for 1860 was 378,994.

8 Starr, *Americans and the California Dream*, 52.

9 Burnett, *Recollections*, 254. I have been unable to locate this letter. Alphonso Boone, the grandson of frontiersman Daniel Boone, traveled to Oregon in 1846, taking the difficult Applegate Trail into southern Oregon. He and former Missouri governor Lilburn Boggs had traveled together as far as Fort Hall, where Boggs turned off toward California. Boone and his family operated Boone's Ferry across the Willamette River south of

Portland. The ferry was replaced in 1954 by the I-5 bridge, named Boone's Bridge. Alphonso Boone went to California in 1849 to mine gold. He died of an illness in 1850 at Long Bar on the Yuba River.

10 Burnett, *Recollections*, 194. Brown, *Oregon Blue Book*, 318.

11 Burnett, *Recollections*, 254.

12 Burnett, *Recollections*, 254–55.

13 Burnett to James Hughes in Liberty, Missouri, March 1847, quoted in Morgan, *Overland in 1846*, 686–89.

14 Hazelett, "'To the World!!,'" 212.

15 Hazelett, *Wagons to the Willamette*, 145–51.

16 Thornton, *Oregon and California in 1848*, 1:225–26. Thornton also wrote an account of the Donner Party tragedy in volume 2 of his history.

17 Burnett, *Recollections*, 258.

18 He was probably a member of the Pit tribe, so named because of the large holes the natives dug along the Pitt River to trap deer and other game. Neither the Burnett Party nor the Lassen Party were menaced by the Pit tribe, although an emigration in 1849 was frequently harassed, with several emigrants killed and many cattle lost or stolen.

19 Burnett, *Recollections*, 262.

20 Unruh wrote in *Plains Across* that shortcuts almost never proved to be a good bet for the emigrants (341). Those who proposed the cutoffs were in it for profit. Emigrants persuaded to leave the established trails "learned a harsh lesson about western travel; that no matter how loudly praised by their discoverers and promoters, cutoffs usually lengthened the distance to be covered, and increased travel hardships."

21 Buck, *Guide to the Lassen Trail*, 2015. Benton City was abandoned by its few occupants and is now largely a ghost town.

22 Burnett, *Recollections*, 263.

23 Buck, *Guide to the Lassen Trail*, 156.

24 Burnett, *Recollections*, 260–70. The Lassen Cutoff would be the major emigrant trail into California for just a single year, 1849. As many as nine thousand emigrants took the cutoff, believing it to be easier and shorter, and also to avoid the Donner Pass crossing into California, where tragedy befell the Donner Party in 1846. But the cutoff proved disastrous for many. The trail was much longer than advertised, 228 miles instead of a promised 110 miles. Food supplies ran out; many suffered from near-starvation, diarrhea, and even scurvy from the poor diet. One emigrant recalled chewing acorns for moisture; another remembered drinking water "delightfully tinctured with the flavour of the carcasses of some dead oxen." The party faced near-constant harassment by the Pit tribe. An emigrant who fell behind to repair a wagon was found dead with eighteen arrows in his body. For more, read Buck's *Guide to the Lassen Trail*.

25 *California Star*, December 12, 1848. The *Star* was California's first newspaper, established by Mormon immigrants Samuel Brannan and Orrin E. Smith in the second-story loft of a grist mill at Clay and Kearney Streets in San Francisco. The first issue was published on October 24, 1847. The last issue was published the following year.

CHAPTER 12

1 Long Bar was a productive mining site until 1852. "Oroville Area and the Gold Rush of 1849," 43, 53.

2 Burnett, *Recollections*, 272.

3 J. W. Long sketch; see "Pantoscope."

4 Burnett may have confused two productive mining sites with similar names. There was a Long's Bar on the Feather River, which evidently was

named for the Longs, who had a store and hotel there—and a Long Bar on the Yuba River, which more likely was named for the elongated bar at the site. Long's Bar on the Feather River has since been submerged by the reservoir behind the Oroville Dam.

5 Burnett, *Recollections*, 273–74.

6 Burnett, *Recollections*, 286.

7 Starr, *Americans and the California Dream*, 7.

8 Lewis, *Sutter's Fort*, 40.

9 Hurtado, *John Sutter*, 10.

10 Hurtado, *John Sutter*, 20.

11 Lewis, *Sutter's Fort*, 43. California at the time was a province of Mexico called Alta California and included all the modern states of California, Nevada, and Utah, as well as parts of Arizona, Wyoming, Colorado, and New Mexico.

12 One league equals approximately 5,760 acres, or 3.5 square miles.

13 Lewis, *Sutter's Fort*, 83.

14 Severson, *Sacramento*, 35.

15 Sutter, *New Helvetia Diary*, xiii

16 Sutter, *New Helvetia Diary*, viii–ix.

17 The distinctive bell, which remained at Fort Ross, melted in a fire that destroyed the chapel in 1973. A duplicate was cast in Belgium for the rebuilt chapel using metal from the original. "Fort Ross Chapel."

18 Sutter, *New Helvetia Diary*, xii.

19 Lewis, *Sutter's Fort*, 145.

20 Sutter and Watson, *Diary of Johann Augustus Sutter*, January 28, 1848.

21 Sutter and Watson, *Diary of Johann Augustus Sutter*, January 28, 1848.

22 Lewis, *Sutter's Fort*, 165.

23 Hurtado, *John Sutter*, 237.

24 Bancroft, *History of California*, 4:179.

25 Pisani, "Squatter Law in California."

26 Sutter, Jr., *Sutter Family*, 13.

27 Sutter, Jr., *Sutter Family*, 88, 93.

28 Burnett, *Recollections*, 287. A document in Burnett's files at the California State Library in Sacramento cites an agreement between Burnett and young Sutter dated December 30, 1848, "to place all town property in the hands of said Burnett for sale and to give to said Burnett one fourth of the proceeds from the sale." Burnett evidently cited the agreement to support his case for a final settlement with the senior Sutter. Document in the Burnett Files, California State Library, Sacramento.

CHAPTER 13

1 Johnson, *Unfortunate Emigrants*, 43.

2 Johnson, *Unfortunate Emigrants*, 294–96. Foster owned property and a store on the Yuba River at Foster's Bar, a prosperous mining site named for him that apparently made him a wealthy man. According to Bancroft's history, mining on the Yuba River was among the most productive in California, with miners typically earning $60 to $100 per day.

3 Burnett, *Old California Pioneer*, 164.

4 Johnson, *Unfortunate Emigrants*, 55.

5 Burnett, *Recollections*, 277.

6 The 1846 wagon train ended up taking four different paths: some wagons took the Hastings Cutoff, others followed the established California Trail to California, others took the Applegate Trail into Oregon, and still others continued along the established Oregon Trail into Oregon.

7 In addition to the Donner-Reeds and J. Quinn Thornton, other well-known 1846 emigrants that started the journey with Russell from Independence included former Missouri governor Lilburn Boggs, and Alphonso Boone, grandson of the famed Daniel Boone. Boggs took the California Trail to California, while Boone followed the Applegate Trail into Oregon.

8 Brown, *Brown's Political History of Oregon*, 108. Hastings was elected to replace White as wagon train captain after White angered the other emigrants with decisions such as killing their dogs because the barking disturbed the livestock. See Medorem Crawford's recollections in Tate, *Great Medicine Road*, 93. After about eight months in Oregon, Hastings led a party of forty or so men on a pack trail to California. They were said to have indiscriminately attacked Native Americans along the way, killing as many as forty. See Bagley, "Lansford Warren Hastings," 14.

9 Bagley, *Scoundrel's Tale*, 116. See also Sutter, *New Helvetia Diary*, 26.

10 Hurtado, *John Sutter*, 175.

11 Hurtado, *John Sutter*, 169.

12 Hastings, *Emigrants' Guide to Oregon and California*, 137. Dale Morgan, the noted western historian, said Hastings was largely responsible for elevating California over Oregon as the preferred destination for 1846 emigrants. "He had focused attention upon California as no one had before." Excerpts from the guide ran in eastern newspapers. See Morgan, *Overland in 1846*, 50.

13 Clyman, "Journal of James Clyman," 33. Korns's excellent article includes journal entries and recollections of Clyman and several of the emigrants, including Heinrich Lienhard and James Reed. A sad incident for Clyman was the loss of his spaniel "Lucky," which was fatally scalded when it tried to drink from a hot springs in the salt desert. "I felt more for his loss than any other animal I ever lost in my life, as he had been my constant companion in all my wanderings." See Morgan, *Overland in 1846*, 50.

14 Korns, "From Fort Bridger," 45.

15 Johnson, *Unfortunate Emigrants*, 22.

16 Korns, "From Fort Bridger," 176.

17 Korns, "From Fort Bridger," 133.

18 The distance from Fort Bridger to the Humboldt River on the Hastings Cutoff was roughly the same as from Fort Hall, about 550 miles. But the cutoff required at least an extra five days, according to a study by Richard L. Rieck, because of the steep elevations and descents, plus frequent stream crossings. "Geography of the California Trails," 27–32.

19 Korns, "From Fort Bridger," 195.

20 Korns, "From Fort Bridger," 198. According to Dale Morgan, Hastings had never intended to direct them down Weber Canyon. Morgan said the Harlan-Youngs and Lienhard went into the canyon by mistake. The route Hastings would recommend to the Donner-Reeds was the same path he'd taken earlier with Clyman. Morgan said if the mix-up hadn't occurred, there would have been more men to work on the recommended road, and the Donner Party could have avoided spending so much of its precious time building the road on its own. Morgan, *Overland in 1846*, 418, 420.

21 Korns, "From Fort Bridger," 133.

22 Korns, "From Fort Bridger," 198.

23 Rieck, "Geography of the California Trails," 29.

24 Korns, "From Fort Bridger," 224.

25 Korns, "From Fort Bridger," 211.

26 Korns, "From Fort Bridger," 218.

27 Tate, *Great Medicine Road*, 211.

28 Korns, "From Fort Bridger," 218.

29 Johnson, *Unfortunate Emigrants*, 243.

30 Johnson, *Unfortunate Emigrants*, 36.

31 Hurtado, *John Sutter*, 205.

32 Johnson, *Unfortunate Emigrants*, 44.

33 Grebenkemper and Johnson, "Forensic Canine Search for the Donner Family Winter Camps," 56–67.

34 Grebenkemper and Johnson, "Forensic Canine Search for the Donner Family Winter Camps," 71.

35 Johnson, *Unfortunate Emigrants*, 48.

36 Unruh, *Plains Across*, 368.

37 Johnson, *Unfortunate Emigrants*, 55.

38 Thornton served for less than a year as presiding judge in Oregon. He resigned in November 1847 to accept an assignment from Governor Abernethy to go to Washington, DC, to advocate for territorial status for Oregon. It was while stopping over in San Francisco that he interviewed Donner Party survivors.

39 Thornton, *Oregon and California in 1848*, 2:150.

40 Mary Ann Graves to Levi Fosdick, May 22, 1847, quoted in Johnson, *Unfortunate Emigrants*, 129.

41 Hurtado, *John Sutter*, 205.

42 Burnett, *Recollections*, 282.

43 Burnett, *Recollections*, 282.

44 Thornton, *Oregon and California in 1848*, 199–200.

45 Johnson, *Unfortunate Emigrants*, 294–95.

46 Hurtado, *John Sutter*, 206.

CHAPTER 14

1 Bagley, *Scoundrel's Tale*, 16.

2 Bagley, *Scoundrel's Tale*, 149, 173.

3 Young would become church president in December 1847, the first since Joseph Smith was assassinated. Young served until his death in 1877 at age 76.

4 Bagley, *Scoundrel's Tale*, 364. Young at the time was president of the Quorum of Twelve Apostles, the church's governing body.

5 Bagley, *Scoundrel's Tale*, 91.

6 Bancroft, *History of California*, 169. Another account said the Mormons abandoned New Hope when they learned the overland Mormons would not be continuing to California. See the website of the San Joaquin County Historical Society and Museum, accessed October 22, 2017, sanjoaquinhistory.org.

7 Bagley, *Scoundrel's Tale*, 116.

8 Bagley, *Scoundrel's Tale*, 85–86.

9 Hastings to Larkin, March 3, 1846, quoted in Korns, "From Fort Bridger," 23.

10 Bagley, *Scoundrel's Tale*, 180.

11 Brannan to Badlam, March 13, 1849, quoted in Bagley, *Scoundrel's Tale*, 185.

12 Hittel, *History of California*, 2:595. Mormon Island was the site of another major gold discovery on the American River, 25 miles north of Coloma. This discovery drew a preponderance of Mormons— earning the island its name— including the workers from Sutter's sawmill at Coloma. Brannan wrote that Sutter had tried to collect 10 per cent of the gold the men were finding near the mill, claiming it was his property. But the Mormon workers weren't having it and developed their own profitable mining site at Mormon Island. *Deseret News*, June 5, 1872.

13 Bagley, *Scoundrel's Tale*, 264–65.

14 Cross, *Financing an Empire*, 1:224.

15 Cross, *Financing an Empire*, 1:76.

16 Cross, *Financing an Empire*, 1:234. C. C. Smith was a former business partner of Brannan's.

17 Bagley, *Scoundrel's Tale*, 27, 185.

18 Bagley, *Scoundrel's Tale*, 278.

19 Bagley, *Scoundrel's Tale*, 28.

20 Bagley, *Scoundrel's Tale*, 342.

21 The *Star* merged in 1849 with the *Californian* to become the *Daily Alta California*, for many years the leading newspaper in California. Brannan sold his interest in 1850 for $125,000. The newspaper was published until 1891. See Cross, *Financing an Empire*, 1:324.

22 Bagley, *Scoundrel's Tale*, 17.

23 *Salt Lake Daily Tribune*, March 24, 1877, 4.

24 Bagley, *Scoundrel's Tale*, 297.

25 Bagley, *Scoundrel's Tale*, 322.

CHAPTER 15

1 Among the lieutenants who deserted Sutter was John Gantt, guide for the 1843 wagon train.

2 Hurtado, *John Sutter*, 190. Sutter was no doubt referring to the anticipated thousands of Mormons. Although he initially looked forward to their immigration, he may have concluded the Americans were a threat; moreover, he was trying to curry favor with the new government.

3 Sutter, *New Helvetia Diary*, March 6, 1844. Sutter's diary entry for Pico is off by a year. Pio de Jesus Pico became governor in 1845 following the short-lived Californio revolt, during which Sutter fought on the losing side with Governor Micheltorena. Pico was the last Mexican governor before the American occupation, serving from 1845 to 1846.

4 Hurtado, *John Sutter*, 192–93.

5 Severson, *Sacramento*, 43. Hastily designed on a piece of muslin, the flag featured a star and a grizzly bear over the words "California Republic." A version of the flag was adopted in 1911 as California's official state flag.

6 Chaffin, *Pathfinder*, 325–26.

7 Chaffin, *Pathfinder*, 220–21.

8 Chaffin, *Pathfinder*, 330.

9 Polk and Quaife, *Diary of James K. Polk*, 1:35.

10 Polk and Quaife, *Diary of James K. Polk*, 1:36.

11 Merry, *Country of Vast Designs*, 195.

12 Merry, *Country of Vast Designs*, 258.

13 Merry, *Country of Vast Designs*, 250–51.

CHAPTER 16

1 Hurtado, *John Sutter*, 64, 92.

2 Sutter Jr., "Statement Regarding Early California Experiences," in Ottley, *Sutter Family*, 13.

3 Eifler, *Gold Rush Capitalists*, 52.

4 Sutter Jr., "Statement Regarding Early California Experiences," in Ottley, *Sutter Family*, 24.

5 Eifler, *Gold Rush Capitalists*, 53.

6 Although Burnett claimed the prices and four-lot limit was his idea, others suggested August set the terms. See Eifler, *Gold Rush Capitalists*, 53.

7 Peter H. Burnett, Ledger of 1849 Sacramento Land Sales and Sutter Debt Payments, Society of California Pioneers, Sacramento.

8 Eifler, *Gold Rush Capitalists*, 55. Eifler said the hotel was a former flour mill moved to the site.

9 Burnett, Ledger of 1849 Sacramento Land Sales.

10 Gudde, *Sutter's Own Story*. See also Sutter Jr., "Statement Regarding Early California Experiences," in Ottley, *Sutter Family*, 22–23.

11 Most historians credit William H. Warner and General William Tecumseh Sherman with laying out the town grid in 1848. See Burg, *Sacramento's K Street*, 17.

12 Prosch, *McCarver and Tacoma*, 54–55. With two other partners, Prosch established the *Seattle Post-Intelligencer* in 1881.

13 Peter H. Burnett to John A. Sutter Jr., January 18, 1894, Files of the Society of California Pioneers, Sacramento.

14 Burnett, Ledger of 1849 Sacramento Land Sales.

15 Sutter, *Statement Regarding Early California Experiences*, 93–94.

16 Gudde, *Sutter's Own Story*, 222. See also Hurtado, *John Sutter*, 247.

17 Franklin, "Forgotten Chapter in California's History," 322.

18 Sutter Jr., "Statement Regarding Early California Experiences," in Ottley, *Sutter Family*, 30.

19 Burnett, *Recollections*, 335.

20 Sacramento County Deeds, Book F, 490–91, 498, Center for Sacramento History, Sacramento, California.

21 Burnett, *Recollections*, 341.

22 Sacramento County Deeds, Book F, 79–82.

23 Hurtado, *John Sutter*, xx, viii.

24 Franklin, "Forgotten Chapter in California's History," 323.

25 William Burg, interviewed in Sacramento, July 25, 2017. Burg is a historian in the Office of Historic Preservation in the California Department of Parks and Recreation. He is the author of several books about early Sacramento, including *Sacramento's K Street*.

CHAPTER 17

1 Burnett, *Recollections*, 204.

2 Melendy and Gilbert, *Governors of California*, 19–22. The number of military governors depends on the historical status of General Persifor Frazer Smith, who served in the role of governor for two months in 1849 but did not consider himself governor, although others did.

3 Pico, who led a force of "Californios," signed the so-named Treaty of Cahuenga with Fremont on January 13, 1847, which ended the fighting in California. Pico later obtained American citizenship and was elected to the California Assembly, and then to the California Senate, representing Los Angeles.

4 Melendy and Gilbert, *Governors of California*, 21.

5 Riley, often referred to as general, was appointed brevet brigadier general during the Mexican War, an appointment that did not confer the benefits of a full general.

6 Cooke, *Conquest of New Mexico and California*, 283. The several hundred members of the Mormon Battalion arrived after most of the fighting had ended and served mainly as an occupying force until disbanded.

7 Chaffin, *Pathfinder*, 148–49.

8 Chaffin, *Pathfinder*, 380.

9 Crosby, *Reminiscences of California and Guatemala*, 33–34.

10 Benton, "To the People of California," *Alta*, January 11, 1849, 2.

11 Benton, "To the People of California."

12 Franklin, "Forgotten Chapter in California's History," 136.

13 *Alta*, January 25, 1849, 1. According to Burnett, Samuel Brannan introduced the motion to prohibit slavery.

14 The *Alta*'s January 4 issue was the first for the newspaper, whose editor and publisher was Edward Gilbert, a veteran of the war with Mexico. Published initially thrice weekly, it resulted from the merger of two earlier newspapers, the *California Star*, founded by Samuel Brannan, and the *Californian*, founded by Robert Semple. The *Alta*, as it quickly became known, was California's must-read newspaper.

15 *Alta*, January 18, 1849.

16 The number of Polk's slaves is uncertain. He inherited some slaves from his father. According to the Hauenstein Center for Presidential Studies at Grand Valley State University in Allendale, Michigan, Polk was one of twelve American presidents who owned slaves. Eight presidents owned slaves while in office: Washington, Jefferson, Madison, Monroe, Jackson, Tyler, Polk, and Taylor. See "Slaveholding Presidents."

17 Buchanan, "Important Letter," *Alta*, March 15, 1849, 1.

18 Cross, *Financing an Empire*. Naglee's Bank was operated by Henry M. Naglee and Richard H. Sinton as Naglee & Sinton and was considered San Francisco's first bank, established January 9, 1849; it folded in September 1850.

19 White, *American Ulysses*, 212–13.

20 "Seen the elephant" was a popular nineteenth-century Americanism denoting experience gained at considerable cost or hardship.

21 Burnett, *Recollections*, 305.

22 Burnett, *Recollections*, 306–7.

23 Burnett, "The Rights of the People," *Alta*, April 26, 1849, 1.

24 Burnett, "The Rights of the People."

25 Riley, "To the People of California," *Placer Times*, June 23, 1849, 1.

26 Riley, "To the People of California."

27 Bancroft, *History of California*, 277.

28 Burnett, *Recollections*, 319. Burnett is not listed among the fifteen original members elected on February 21, 1849, so he must have been added later. See Dwinelle, *Colonial History of the City of San Francisco*, 112.

29 Bancroft, *California*, 278.

30 Burnett, *Recollections*, 320.

31 Burnett to Samuel Thurston, August 7, 1850, Peter Burnett Papers, 1849–1895, Bancroft Library, Berkeley, California.

32 Starr, *California*, 91.

33 Quinn, *Rivals*, 24.

34 Burnett, *Recollections*, 333–34. An online search of the J. Bennet Riley Papers at the Bancroft Library turned up no mention of Burnett.

35 Burnett, *Recollections*, 339.

36 Burnett, *Recollections*, 346.

37 Burnett, *Recollections*, 340. Alviso became part of San Jose in 1868.

CHAPTER 18

1 Starr, *California*, 74.

2 Richards, *California Gold Rush*, 39. The 1840 US Slave Census listed William M. Gwin of Vicksburg, Warren County, Mississippi, with twenty-three slaves. Richards said Gwin had multiple plantations, with several he rented out, and nearly two hundred slaves. He was appointed by President Jackson as US marshal for Mississippi, a lucrative position. But most of his wealth evidently came through land speculation. Warren County tax rolls for 1840 listed the value of Gwin's 2,000 acres at $14,000, on which he owed a tax of $3,500.

3 Quinn, *Rivals*, 66.

4 Crosby, *Reminiscences of California and Guatemala*, 38–39.

5 Bancroft, *History of California*, 284.

6 Quinn, *Rivals*, 69.

7 Browne, *Report of the Debates in the Convention of California*, 133–34.

8 Browne, *Report of the Debates in the Convention of California*, 134, 139.

9 Browne, *Report of the Debates in the Convention of California*, 139.

10 Browne, *Report of the Debates in the Convention of California*, 139.

11 Browne, *Report of the Debates in the Convention of California*, 176.

12 Browne, *Report of the Debates in the Convention of California*, 125.

13 Crosby, *Reminiscences*, 49.

14 Browne, *Report of the Debates in the Convention of California*, 432–34. A career army officer, Major General Halleck was appointed by President Lincoln in 1862 as general-in-chief of the Union armies during the Civil War. But Halleck had little combat experience, and his command was considered a disappointment. Leincoln replaced him with General Ulysses A. Grant in 1864. See "Major General Henry Wager Halleck."

15 Mexican President Vicente Guerrero formally abolished slavery in 1829.

16 Browne, *Report of the Debates in the Convention of California*, 441.

17 Browne, *Report of the Debates in the Convention of California*, 458.

18 Browne, *Report of the Debates in the Convention of California*, 446.

19 Starr, *California*, 94.

20 *Alta*, January 12, 1851.

21 Burnett, *Recollections*, 346.

22 Burnett, *Recollections*, 348.

23 Sutter, who never liked Burnett, said Burnett beat him only because he started campaigning sooner. "Burnett had been in the mountains several days ahead of me; otherwise he never would have defeated me." From Gudde, *Sutter's Own Story*, 229.

24 Hall, *History of San Jose*, 203.

25 Hall, *History of San Jose*, 204.

26 Bancroft, *History of California*, 305.

27 Hall, *History of San Jose*, 353. Burnett's homes are long gone.

CHAPTER 19

1 *Alta*, December 12, 1849.

2 Hall, *History of San Jose*, 202–7. The legislative chambers were built to fulfill a guarantee that in exchange for being named the capital, San Jose would construct suitable chambers. James Reed, a Donner-Reed Party survivor, was one of a dozen businessmen who loaned the city $34,000 to cover construction costs. The building burned in 1853, but the legislature had already moved the capital to Vallejo in 1852. The capital went next to Benicia in 1853 and finally to Sacramento, effective in 1854.

3 *Alta*, December 28, 1849.

4 Text of Burnett's address in the *Alta California*, December 26, 1849.

5 *Alta*, December 29, 1849.

6 Hittell, *History of California*, 2:806–7.

7 Bancroft, *History of California*, 643–44.

8 Crosby, *Reminiscences of California and Guatemala*, 62.

9 Crosby, *Reminiscences of California and Guatemala*, 62.

10 McPherson, "William McKendree Gwin," 127; Browne, *Report of the Debates in the Convention of California*, 445

11 Crosby, *Reminiscences of California and Guatemala*, 46–47.

12 Journal of the Senate of the State of California, First Session, Puebla de San Jose, December 15, 1849, http://clerk.assembly.ca.gov/sites/clerk.assembly.ca.gov/files/archive/DailyJournal/1849/Volumes/1849_50_jnl.pdf#page=1, 129.

13 Hittell, *History of California*, 804–5.

14 Journal of the Senate of the State of California, 137.

15 Journal of the Senate of the State of California, 229.

16 Bagley, *Scoundrel's Tale*, 249.

17 Dwinelle, *Colonial History of the City of San Francisco*, 104.

18 Crosby, *Reminiscences of California and Guatemala*, 111.

19 Bancroft, *History of California*, 196–97.

20 The alcalde under Mexican law was roughly equivalent to mayor, but with greatly expanded powers, combining the roles of judge, jury, and chief executive.

21 *Minutes of the Proceedings of the Legislative Assembly of the District of San Francisco*, 24. Hereafter referred to as *Legislative Assembly*.

22 "Along the Wharves," Maritime Heritage Project website, accessed October 23, 2017, maritimeheritage.org/news/wharves.html.

23 *Legislative Assembly*, 54.

24 The Pennsylvania-born Geary was elected alcalde of San Francisco on January 8, 1850, and became the city's first mayor. He went on to a distinguished career as governor of the Kansas Territory in 1856, a brigadier general for the Union Army in the Civil War, and two-term governor of Pennsylvania in 1867 and 1873.

25 *Legislative Assembly*, 103.

26 *Legislative Assembly*, 80–83.

27 *Legislative Assembly*, 66, 70, 83.

28 *Legislative Assembly*, 104.

29 *Legislative Assembly*, 219.

30 *Legislative Assembly*, 123.

31 Burnett to Horace Hawes, February 8, 1850, Burnett Papers, Bancroft Library, Berkeley, California.

32 *Legislative Assembly*, 239.

33 *Legislative Assembly*, 240–41.

34 *Legislative Assembly*, 162.

35 *Legislative Assembly*, 242–43.

36 *Alta*, January 4, 1850.

37 *Legislative Assembly*, 178.

38 Burnett to Edward J. Kewen, March 4, 1850, Burnett Papers, Bancroft Library, Berkeley, California.

39 *Legislative Assembly*, 188.

40 *Legislative Assembly*, 246.

41 *Alta*, March 21, 1850.

42 Bagley, *Scoundrel's Tale*, 309.

43 *Alta*, April 3, 1850.

44 *Alta*, April 3, 1850.

45 Bagley, *Scoundrel's Tale*, 249.

CHAPTER 20

1 Pisani, "Squatter Law in California," 287.

2 Pisani, "Squatter Law in California," 287.

3 Crosby, *Reminiscences of California and Guatemala*, 71.

4 Pisani, "Squatter Law in California," 305.

5 Taylor, *El Dorado*, 209.

6 *Alta*, June 27, 1850.

7 Eifler, *Gold Rush Capitalists*, 147–48.

8 Eifler, *Gold Rush Capitalists*, 147.

9 Bagley, *Scoundrel's Tale*, 310.

10 Severson, *Sacramento*, 78.

11 Severson, *Sacramento*, 79; see also Eifler, *Gold Rush Capitalists*, 153–55. Robinson later moved to Kansas, where he was elected its first governor in 1861.

12 Burnett to General Winn, August 15, 1850, Burnett Papers, Bancroft Library, Berkeley, California.

13 Eifler, *Gold Rush Capitalists*, 158–59, 165. Shopkeeper William Prince claimed they were not squatters. According to Prince, "it now turns out there were no squatters there at all. One man had been sick a month that they killed, and the others were Allen's family and some hired laborers and neighbors."

14 Bancroft, *History of California*, 329–35.

15 *Alta*, August 25, 1850.

16 Ryland emigrated from Missouri in 1849. He served two terms in the California Legislative Assembly, in 1854 and 1866, and was assembly speaker in 1868.

17 Ryland to Larkin, July 19, 1850, Burnett Papers, Bancroft Library, Berkeley, California. Larkin was a longtime California resident and prominent businessman who was US consul at Monterey during the Mexican administration, from 1843 until California statehood. He served as a delegate to the 1849 constitutional convention.

18 Ryland to Larkin, July 19, 1850.

19 Burnett, *Recollections*, 371.

CHAPTER 21

1 Grenier, "Officialdom," 142.

2 Grenier, "Officialdom," 142–43.

3 Grenier, "Officialdom," 145–46. This was the same Thomas Green whose slaves were chased out of mining camps along the Yuba River in July 1849. Green, originally from North Carolina, served in legislatures in three states: North Carolina, Florida, and California. He also served in the congress of the Texas Republic before it became a state. He emigrated to California in 1849.

4 Grenier, "Officialdom," 148.

5 Burnett to unnamed commander, March 4, 1850, Burnett Papers, Bancroft Library, Berkeley, California.

6 Burnett to General Bean, June 1, 4, September 4, 1850, Burnett Papers, Bancroft Library, Berkeley, California.

7 Secrest, *When the Great Spirit Died*, 49–50.

8 *Sacramento Daily Union*, May 13, 1851. The newspaper was published from 1851 to 1899. Johnson's Ranch was a ranch of 320 acres along the Bear River in Yuba County, part of a 22,000-acre Mexican land grant. It was acquired by William Johnson and Sebastian Keyser at an auction after the original grantee died. The English-born Johnson was a sailor who arrived in California in 1842 from the Sandwich Islands; Keyser was an Austrian-born fur trapper. Johnson married Mary Murphy, a survivor of the Donner-Reed Party; the marriage soon ended in divorce. The city of Wheatland is on land that was part of Johnson's Ranch.

9 Sioli, *History of El Dorado County*, 157–59.

10 Sioli, *History of El Dorado County*, 158.

11 Osborn, "John Calhoun Johnson," 44.

12 Green to Burnett, in *Journals of the Legislature of the State of California*, 763.

13 Green to Burnett, in *Journals of the Legislature of the State of California*, 764.

14 Secrest, *When the Great Spirit Died*, 65.

15 Green to Burnett, in *Journals of the Legislature of the State of California*, 764–65.

16 Sioli, *History of El Dorado County*, 158. It's impossible to sort through the conflicting details of these incidents with any degree of certainty. There are no timely first-hand accounts of militia activities beyond the brief, and sometimes self-serving and exaggerated, official correspondence. Newspaper accounts and recollections shared decades later were notoriously unreliable.

17 General Green to Burnett, May 25, 1850, with copy of letter to "Indian Chiefs Weima, Buckler, Poollal," in *Journals of the Legislature of the State of California*, 764–65. Weima was considered one of the chiefs opposed to war. He turned over the body of Samuel Hoyt to the militia following the attack on the sawmill.

18 Green to Burnett, in *Journals of the Legislature of the State of California*, 765–66.

19 Burnett to Green, in *Journals of the Legislature of the State of California*, 768.

20 Secrest, *When the Great Spirit Died*, 68.

21 Secrest, *When the Great Spirit Died*, 68.

22 Burnett to Sheriff Rogers, October 25, 1850, Burnett Papers, Bancroft Library, Berkeley, California.

23 *Alta*, December 15, 1850.

24 *Journals of the Legislature of the State of California*, 734–35.

25 Kooshdaaka, "Bloody Island Massacre"; Larson, "Bloody Island Atrocity." Descendants of Lucy Moore established the Lucy Moore Foundation to commemorate the massacre and to foster understanding between the races. For more on this horrific slaughter by US troops, see the recent excellent account by Madley, *American Genocide*, 103–45.

26 Starr, *California*, 55.

27 Bancroft, *History of California*, 336.

28 Richards, *California Gold Rush*, 110.

29 Richards, *California Gold Rush*, 117.

30 Hammond, "Speech of Hon. James H. Hammond."

31 The SS *Oregon* was launched in 1848 and was one of several ships operated by the Pacific Mail Steamship Company, which had a government

contract to transport mail between
Panama and California.

32 Burnett, *Recollections*, 375.

CHAPTER 22

1 Burnett, *Recollections*, 367.

2 Burnett, *Recollections*, 377–78.

3 Letter to George Burnett, September
2, 1850. Courtesy of Emily Douville.

4 *Marysville Daily Herald*, November 15,
1850. Published from 1850 to 1858.

5 *California Daily Courier*, November
27, 1850.

6 *Alta*, November 29, 1850.

7 *Sacramento Transcript*, December 2,
1850. Published from 1850 to 1851.

8 "Senate Journal," in *Journals of the
Legislature of the State of California*,
11–37.

9 *Sacramento Transcript*, January 10–13,
1851.

10 "Assembly Journal," in *Journals of the
Legislature of the State of California*,
815.

11 *Alta*, January 1, 1851.

12 "Senate Journal," in *Journals of the
Legislature of the State of California*,
11.

13 "Senate Journal," *in Journals of the
Legislature of the State of California*, 33.

14 "Senate Journal," *in Journals of the
Legislature of the State of California*, 13.

15 "Senate Journal," *in Journals of the
Legislature of the State of California*, 14.

16 "Senate Journal," *in Journals of the
Legislature of the State of California*, 18.

17 "Senate Journal," *in Journals of the
Legislature of the State of California*,
19–21.

18 "Senate Journal," *in Journals of the
Legislature of the State of California*, 23.

19 "Senate Journal," *in Journals of the
Legislature of the State of California*,
36–37.

20 *Alta*, January 8, 1851.

21 *Alta*, January 11, 1851.

22 *Alta*, January 12, 1851.

23 *Alta*, January 12, 1851.

24 *Alta*, December 12, 1852.

25 *San Francisco Herald*, January 31,
1851. Published from 1850 to 1851.

26 *San Francisco Herald*, January 31,
1851.

27 *Sacramento Transcript*, January 11,
1851.

28 *Sacramento City Directory for 1851*,
103.

29 Quinn, *Rivals*, 96.

30 Quinn, *Rivals*, 99.

31 Williams, *David C. Broderick*, 34.

32 Burnett to General Jonas Winchester
in Grass Valley, California, March 21,
1854, Burnett Files, California State
Library, Sacramento. Winchester was
a former state printer appointed by
Burnett while governor.

33 Burnett, *Recollections*, 354–55.

34 The US Census put the Chinese
population in the United States in
1880 at 105,465, of whom 75,132
were in California and 9,510 in
Oregon.

35 Twenty-five Chinese coal miners were
massacred in labor violence at Rock
Spring, Wyoming, in 1885; as many as
thirty-four Chinese gold miners were
massacred in Oregon's Hells Canyon
in 1887. For details on these and other
crimes, see Nokes, *Massacred for Gold*.

36 Burnett, *Recollections*, 357. Emphasis
added.

37 Burnett, *Recollections*, 356.

38 "Assembly Journal," in *Journals of the
Legislature of the State of California*,
840–41.

39 *Sacramento Transcript*, January 14,
1851.

40 Crosby, *Reminiscences of California and
Guatemala*, 39.

41 *Sacramento Transcript*, January 11,
1851.

42 Hardeman, *Wilderness Calling*, 225.

43 Letter to George Burnett, September
2, 1850.

CHAPTER 23

1 Burnett, *Recollections*, 393.

2 Burnett, *Recollections*, 408.

3 Burnett to Mrs. Elizabeth Rogers in Sacramento City, December 26, 1851, Burnett Files, California State Library, Sacramento.

4 Burnett to George Burnett, July 27, 1862. Courtesy of Emily Douville.

5 There is some confusion about the date of Armstead's death. Burnett's letter is clearly dated July 27, 1862, but elsewhere he listed Armstead's death as May 26, 1862, the same date as recorded in other family records. Burnett may have been the source for these records.

6 Emily Douville graciously shared the letters with the author.

7 Burnett, *Recollections*, 378–79.

8 William T. Wallace, originally from Kentucky, was California's attorney general from 1856 to 1858, was a justice on the California Supreme Court from 1870 to 1879, and was chief justice from 1872 to 1879.

9 Burnett, *Recollections*, 335–36.

10 Severson, *Sacramento*, 89–90.

11 Severson, *Sacramento*, 72.

12 *Placer Times*, January 19, 1850.

13 Severson, *Sacramento*, 72, 106, 130. *Placer Times*, January 19, 1850.

14 Severson, *Sacramento*, 106, 130.

15 Burnett, *Recollections*, 391–92.

16 Burnett to Winchester, March 21, 1854.

17 Burnett, *Recollections*, 398.

18 Burnett to George Burnett, June 19, 1854. In the same letter, Burnett said he'd been to four different doctors within the space of ten days but now felt "almost well." He didn't say which of his several ailments were bothering him, but it may have been the onset of the neuralgia that would affect him for the next several years.

19 Burnett, *Recollections*, 401–3.

20 Burnett, *Recollections*, 401–3.

21 *New York Times*, September 23, 1857, 1. The wreckage was located in 1957 in mile-deep water off the coast of South Carolina. Much of the gold has been recovered, although not without considerable controversy. See William J. Broad, "Out of Wreckage, Lives Emerge," *New York Times*, July 29, 2014.

22 Captain Herndon was also known for leading a successful exploration into the Amazon in 1851. He is remembered with a monument on the grounds of the US Naval Academy in Annapolis. The inscription reads: "Captain William Lewis Herndon 1818–1857, Naval Officer, Explorer, Merchant Captain. In command of the *Central America*, homebound with California gold seekers, Captain Herndon lost his life in a gallant effort to save ship and lives during a cyclone off Hatteras, September 12, 1857." Herndon, Virginia, takes his name.

23 Burnett, *Old California Pioneer*, 238.

24 Burnett, *Old California Pioneer*, 238.

CHAPTER 24

1 *Sacramento Union*, October 6, 1857. In a complicated game of musical chairs, Burnett promptly resigned the seat and was appointed by Governor Johnson to the longer-term seat vacated by the death of Chief Justice Hugh Murray. After a delay, Stephen J. Field was then appointed by Johnson to fill Burnett's vacated seat. The third member of the court was David Terry, who became chief justice.

2 *Sacramento Union*, January 14, 1857.

3 Smith, *Freedom's Frontier*, 77.

4 Fugitive Slave Act of 1852, Calif. Stat. (passed Jan. 5, 1852, ended May 4, 1852).

5 Smith, *Freedom's Frontier*, 70.

6 Smith, *Freedom's Frontier*, 71.

7 Smith, *Freedom's Frontier*, 29.

8 Smith, "Remaking Slavery in a Free State," 47.

9 Smith, "Remaking Slavery in a Free State," 37.

10 Nokes, *Breaking Chains*, 65.

11 Smith, *Freedom's Frontier*, 47.

12 Richards, *California Gold Rush*, 68.

13 Lapp, *Blacks in Gold Rush California*, 39.

14 Lapp, *Blacks in Gold Rush California*, 148.

15 "*Ex Parte Archy*," in *Reports of Cases Determined in the Supreme Court of California*, 9:146.

16 "*Ex Parte Archy*," 156.

17 "*Ex Parte Archy*," 170.

18 "*Ex Parte Archy*," 181.

19 "*Ex Parte Archy*," 162–63.

20 *Sacramento Union*, January 12 and 16, 1858.

21 Newspapers at the time provided the most accurate barometer of public opinion—indeed the only barometer.

22 *Sacramento Union*, January 18, 1858.

23 *Alta*, February 14, 1858.

24 William Burg, interviewed July 25, 2017.

25 Lapp, *Blacks in Gold Rush California*, 150.

26 Lapp, *Blacks in Gold Rush California*, 152–53. See also Kilian, "Gibbs, Wiflin Mistar (1823–1915)." Gibbs was among those who returned from Canada to the United States following the Civil War. Settling in Arkansas, he was elected a city judge in Little Rock in 1873, becoming the nation's first elected black judge. President William McKinley appointed him as US consul to Madagascar in 1897.

27 Sutter, *Statement Regarding Early California Experiences*, 104.

28 Sutter, *Statement Regarding Early California Experiences*, 109.

29 Sutter, *Statement Regarding Early California Experiences*, 35.

30 Sutter, *Statement Regarding Early California Experiences*, 111.

31 *Sacramento Union*, September 30, 1856.

32 Sutter, *Statement Regarding Early California Experiences*, 112.

33 Sutter, *Statement Regarding Early California Experiences*, 121.

34 Sutter, *Statement Regarding Early California Experiences*, 41.

35 *Sacramento Union*, September 30, 1856.

36 *Sacramento Union*, October 1, 1856.

37 *Sacramento Union*, October 7, 1856.

38 "*Brannan v. Mesick*," in *Reports of Cases Determined in the Supreme Court of California*, 10:95.

39 *Sacramento Union*, May 26, 1858.

40 *Sacramento Union*, May 26, 1858.

41 *Sacramento Union*, July 2, 1858.

42 *Sacramento Union*, May 26, 1858.

43 Burnett, *Recollections*, 450. The B. F. Hastings Building was for many years the western terminus of the Pony Express.

44 Glen Burnett was well known as a circuit preacher in Oregon. He founded Bethel Church in Polk County and helped establish Bethel College in 1855. The college later merged in what is today Western Oregon University in Monmouth, Oregon. See Dailey, "Pioneer Preacher Profile: Glen Owen Burnett."

CHAPTER 25

1 Duels were not uncommon among prominent men in California. Edward Gilbert, who served a single term as one of California's first two congressmen, was killed in a duel on August 2, 1852, near Sacramento by California State Senator James W. Denver, later the governor of Kansas. Denver, Colorado, is named for him.

2 Burnett, *Old California Pioneer*, 54.

3 Burnett to General Jonas Winchester, Grass Valley, California, March 21, 1854. Burnett Files, California State Library, Sacramento.

4 Quinn, *Rivals*, 225.

5 Quinn, *Rivals*, 241.

6 Quinn, *Rivals*, 203.

7 Quinn, *Rivals*, 257.

8 Williams, *David C. Broderick*, 219.

9 Richards, *California Gold Rush*, 5. Broderick was aligned with the men targeted by the Vigilance Committee.

10 Richards, *California Gold Rush*, 4–5.

11 Richards, *California Gold Rush*, 5. See also Quinn, *Rivals*, 256.

12 Quinn, *Rivals*, 256.

13 *Alta*, September 18, 1859. The newspaper carried this account five days after the duel.

14 *Alta*, September 18, 1859. See also Williams, *David C. Broderick*, 238.

15 *Alta*, September 19, 1859. Baker, a friend of Lincoln's, was elected a US senator from Oregon in 1860. He was killed October 21, 1861, at the Battle of Ball's Bluff in Loudoun County, Virginia, while serving in the Union Army.

16 *Alta*, September 19, 1859.

17 Crosby, *Reminiscences of California and Guatemala*, 63.

18 *Alta*, September 24, 1859.

19 Richards, *California Gold Rush*, 235.

20 Richards, *California Gold Rush*, 236–37. Terry joined the Confederate Army during the Civil War, serving as a brigadier general. The confrontation with Field resulted from a ruling by Field denying a claim by Terry's third and much younger wife, who had sought alimony from a previous marriage. Terry and Field encountered one another at a restaurant at the small town of Lathrop, near Stockton. Terry slapped Field, and was in turn shot dead by Field's bodyguard, David Neagle.

CHAPTER 26

1 Burnett, *Recollections*, 405.

2 Burnett, *American Theory of Government*, iii, 68, 71.

3 Burnett, *American Theory of Government*, 71.

4 Burnett, *American Theory of Government*, 82.

5 *Sacramento Union*, September 1, 1862. Burnett letter to *Sacramento Union*, August 2, 1862.

6 Burnett, *Recollections*, 88.

7 Letter to George Burnett, July 28, 1862.

8 Burnett, *Recollections*, 407.

9 Burnett, *Recollections*, 405–6.

10 Bagley, *Scoundrel's Tale*, 347.

11 Cross, *Financing an Empire*, 223.

12 Burnett, *Recollections*, 437.

13 Cross, *Financing an Empire*, 621, 791.

14 Burnett, *Recollections*, 436.

15 Burnett, *Recollections*, 429.

16 Bagley, *Scoundrel's Tale*, 347.

17 Letter to George Burnett, November 3, 1865.

CHAPTER 27

1 Burnett, *Recollections*, 378.

2 Burnett, *The Path*, 740.

3 Burnett, *The Path*, vii.

4 Burnett, *The Path*, 233.

5 Burnett, *The Path*, 367.

6 Colvert, *Letters of Peter Burnett*, 159.

7 "Burnett's Path to the Church," *Brownson's Quarterly Review*, April 1860. The review was probably written by Orestes Augustus Brownson, himself a Catholic convert, who published the quarterly as a Catholic journal of opinion from 1844 to 1864.

8 Colvert, *Letters of Peter Burnett*, 170.

9 Burnett to an unnamed recipient at Santa Clara College, April 26, 1852. Santa Clara College was established in 1851 by the well-known Jesuit missionary Father John Nobili at the Spanish-built Santa Clara Mission. The school offered classes for elementary and high school students in addition to college-level courses. It later became Santa Clara University.

10 Colvert, *Letters of Peter Burnett*, 143.

11 Burnett genealogy, typewritten copy, dated March 2, 1885, written by Burnett. Burnett Papers, Bancroft Library, Berkeley, California.

12 "A Pioneer's Recollections," *New York Times*, April 15, 1880.

13 "A Pioneer's Recollections."

14 Burnett, "Last Years of Peter H. Burnett."

15 "The Home Life of Peter H. Burnett," *San Francisco Call*, February 11, 1894. The *Call* was published from 1890 to 1913.

16 Burnett, "Last Years of Peter H. Burnett."

17 *San Francisco Call*, May 21, 1895, 1.

18 *San Francisco Call*, May 19, 1895.

19 Several of Burnett's books are on display with his desk and other items at the Roberto Adobe and Suñol House Museum in San Jose. Burnett's great-great-granddaughter Francisca Burnett Allen said his library may not have remained intact. Telephone interview, February 28, 2017.

20 "Strong Sentiments Bequeathed by the Ex-Governor in His Will," *San Francisco Call*, May 29, 1895.

21 *San Francisco Call*, May 18, 1895.

EPILOGUE

1 Burnett, *Recollections*, 88–89.

2 Burnett to Sutter Jr., January 18, 1894. Society of California Pioneers, San Francisco.

3 Dylan McDonald e-mail, July 17, 2017.

4 Walsh, *Hallowed Were the Gold Dust Trails*, 408; William Burg, interviewed July 25, 2017. See also the property deed dated July 17, 1849, Burnett Files, California State Library, Sacramento.

5 Bernal, "Governor Burnett's Office in Suñol House."

6 Francisca Burnett Allen interview, February 28, 2017.

APPENDIX A

1 Nokes, *Breaking Chains*, 181.

2 Neiderheiser, *Jesse Applegate*, 280.

3 Neiderheiser, *Jesse Applegate*, 296, 300.

4 *San Francisco Examiner*, January 15, 1888, quoted in Bagley, *Scoundrel's Tale*, 406–7.

5 Bagley, *Scoundrel's Tale*, 17.

6 *Deseret Evening News*, May 18, 1889, 9.

7 Chaffin, *Pathfinder*, 464.

8 Chaffin, *Pathfinder*, 485–86.

9 Chaffin, *Pathfinder*, 496.

10 Chaffin, *Pathfinder*, 498.

11 Richards, *California Gold Rush*, 234.

12 Quinn, *Rivals*, 297.

13 Prosch, *McCarver and Tacoma*, 63.

14 Prosch, *McCarver and Tacoma*, 63.

15 Carey, *General History of Oregon*, 254.

16 Morgan, *Overland in 1846*, 253.

17 Hall, *History of San Jose*, 244.

18 Young, *First Military Escort*, 174.

19 Hurtado, *John Sutter*, 314.

20 Hurtado, *John Sutter*, 320–21.

21 Hurtado, *John Sutter*, 338–39.

22 Hurtado, *John Sutter*, 390.

23 Hurtado, *John Sutter*, 344.

Bibliography

BOOKS

Allen, John Eliot, Marjorie Burns, and Scott Burns. *Cataclysms on the Columbia: The Great Missoula Floods*. Portland, OR: Ooligan Press, 2009.

Applegate, Jesse. *A Day with the Cow Column*. Chicago: Caxton Club, 1934.

———. *Recollections of My Boyhood*. Chicago: Caxton Club, 1934.

Bagley, Will. *South Pass: Gateway to a Continent*. Norman: University of Oklahoma Press, 2014.

———. *Scoundrel's Tale: The Samuel Brannan Papers*. Spokane, WA: A. H. Clark, 1999.

Bancroft, Hubert Howe. *History of California*, vols. 4–6. San Francisco: History Company, 1886–88.

———. *History of Oregon, 1834–1848*, Vol. 1. San Francisco: History Company, 1886.

Barber, Katrine. *Death of Celilo Falls*. Seattle: University of Washington Press, 2005.

Barnes, H. Edgar, and Byron A. Milner. *Selected Cases in Constitutional Law*. Philadelphia: Lyon and Armor, 1910.

Brown, J. Henry. *Brown's Political History of Oregon: Provisional Government*, vol. 1. Portland, OR: Lewis & Dryden, 1892.

Brown, Kate, Secretary of State. *Oregon Blue Book: Almanac and Fact Book, 2011–2012*. Salem, OR: Archives Division, Office of the Secretary of State, 2011–12.

Browne, Ross. *Report of the Debates in the Convention of California on the Formation of the State Constitution in September and October*. Washington, DC: John T. Towers, 1850.

Buck, Donald E., and Denise Moorman. *A Guide to the Lassen Trail and Burnett Cutoff*. Reno, NV: Trails West, 2015.

Burg, William. *Sacramento's K Street: Where Our City Was Born*. Charleston, SC: History Press, 2012.

Burnett, Peter H. *The Path Which Led a Protestant Lawyer to the Catholic Church*. New York: Benziger Brothers, 1859.

———. *The American Theory of Government Considered with Reference to the Present Crisis*. New York: D. Appleton, 1861.

———. *Recollections and Opinions of an Old Pioneer*. New York: D. Appleton, 1880.

———. *An Old California Pioneer*, foreword by Joseph A. Sullivan. Oakland, CA: Biobooks, 1946. [From a previously published Appleton 1880 edition of a Burnett manuscript dated August 16, 1878.]

Carey, Charles H. *General History of Oregon*. Portland, OR: Binford & Mort, 1971.

Chaffin, Tom. *Pathfinder: Jon Charles Fremont and the Course of American Empire*. Norman: University of Oklahoma Press, 2014.

Clyman, James. "The Journal of James Clyman May 2–June 7, 1846." In *From Fort Bridger: The Pioneering of the Immigrant Trails across Utah, 1846–1850*, edited by J. Roderick Korns. Utah Historical Quarterly 19. Salt Lake City: Utah State Historical Society, 1951.

Colvert, Dominic. *The Letters of Peter Burnett: Realism and the Roots of California*. Antioch, CA: Solas Press, 2013.

Cooke, Philip St. George. *The Conquest of New Mexico and California: An Historical and Personal Narrative*. New York: G. P. Putnam's Sons, 1878.

Crosby, Elisha Oscar. *Reminiscences of California and Guatemala from 1849 to 1864*. San Marino, CA: Huntington Library, 1945.

Cross, Ira B. *Financing an Empire: History of Banking in California*, vols. 1 and 2. San Francisco: S. J. Clarke, 1927.

Dary, David. *The Oregon Trail: An American Saga*. New York: Alfred A. Knopf, 2004.

Drury, Clifford Merrill. *Where Wagons Could Go: Narcissa Whitman and Eliza Spalding*. Lincoln: University of Nebraska Press, 1963.

Dwinelle, John Whipple. *The Colonial History of the City of San Francisco*. San Francisco: Towne & Bacon, 1867.

Eifler, Mark A. *Gold Rush Capitalists: Greed and Growth in Sacramento*. Albuquerque: University of New Mexico Press, 2002.

Fremont, J. C. *A Report on an Exploration of the Country Lying between the Missouri River and the Rocky Mountains on the Line of the Kansas and Great Platte Rivers*. US 27th Cong., 3d Sess. 243, 1843.

Geer, T. T. *Fifty Years in Oregon: Experiences, Observations and Commentaries upon Men, Measures and Customs in Pioneer Days and Later Times*. New York: Neale, 1912.

Gray, W. H. *A History of Oregon 1792–1849*. Portland, OR: Harris & Holman, 1870.

Grenier, Judson A. "Officialdom: California State Government, 1849–1879." In *Taming the Elephant: Politics, Government and Law in Pioneer California*. Berkeley: University of California Press, 2003.

Griffin, Rev. J. S., ed. *Oregon American and Evangelical Unionist, 1848–1849*. Tualatin Plains: Oregon Territory, 1848.

Grover, La Fayette. *The Oregon Archives and Public Papers of Oregon*. Salem, OR: Asahel Bush, 1853.

Gudde, Erwin G. *Sutter's Own Story: The Life of General John Augustus Sutter and the History of New Helvetia in the Sacramento Valley*. New York: G. P. Putnam's Sons, 1936.

Hall, Frederic. *History of San Jose and Its Surroundings with Biographical Sketches of Early Settlers*. San Francisco: A. L. Bancroft, 1871.

Hardeman, Nicholas Perkins. *Wilderness Calling: The Hardeman Family in the American Westward Movement, 1750–1900*. Knoxville: University of Tennessee Press, 1977.

Hastings, Lansford W. *The Emigrants' Guide to Oregon and California*. Cincinnati: Ohio: G. Conclin, 1845. [Reprint, Bedford, MA: Applewood Books, 1994.]

Hazelett, S., and J. Stafford. *Wagons to the Willamette: Captain Levi Scott and the Southern Route to Oregon*. Pullman: Washington State University Press, 2015.

Hittell, Theodore H. *History of California*, vol. 2. San Francisco: N. J. Stone, 1898.

Hurtado, Albert L. *John Sutter: A Life on the North American Frontier*. Norman: University of Oklahoma Press, 2006.

Jessett, Thomas E. *The Indian Side of the Whitman Massacre*. Fairfield, WA: Ye Galleon Press, 1969.

Johnson, David Alan. *Founding the Far West: California, Oregon and Nevada, 1840–1890*. Berkeley: University of California Press, 1992.

Johnson, Kristin. *Unfortunate Emigrants: Narratives of the Donner Party*. Logan: Utah State University Press, 1966.

Johnston-Dodds, Kimberly. *Early California Laws and Policies Related to California Indians*. Sacramento: California State Library, September 2002.

Journals of the Legislature of the State of California at Its Second Session Held at the City of San Jose, Commencing on the Sixth Day of January, and Ending on the First Day of May 1851. Sacramento: Eugene Casserly, California State Printer, 1851.

Juntunen, Judy Rycraft, and May D. Dasch. *The World of the Kalapuya: A Native People of Western Oregon*. Philomath, OR: Benton County Historical Society, 2005.

Kinney, Brandon G. *The Mormon War: Zion and the Missouri Extermination Order of 1838*. Yardley, PA: Westholme, 2011.

Klindt, Philip. *Win-Quat: A Brief History of The Dalles*. The Dalles, OR: Wasco County Historical Museum, 2011.

Knuth, Priscilla. *"Picturesque" Frontier: The Army's Fort Dallas*. Portland: Oregon Historical Society Press, 1987.

Korns, J. Roderick, ed. *From Fort Bridger: The Pioneering of the Immigrant Trails across Utah, 1846–1850*. Utah Historical Quarterly 19. Salt Lake City: Utah State Historical Society, 1951.

Krakauer, Jon. *Under the Banner of Heaven; A Story of Violent Faith*. New York: Doubleday, 2003.

Lang, Henry O. *History of the Willamette Valley, Being a Description of the Valley and Resources, with Account of Its Discovery and Settlement by White Men, and Its Subsequent History: Together with Personal Reminiscences of Its Early Pioneers*. Portland, OR: Himes & Lang, 1885.

Lapp, Rudolph M. *Blacks in Gold Rush California*. New Haven, CT: Yale University Press, 1977.

Lenox, Edward Henry. *Overland to Oregon: In the Tracks of Lewis and Clark, 1843*. Oakland, CA: Dowdle Press, 1904.

LeSueur, Stephen C. *The 1838 Mormon War in Missouri*. Columbia: University of Missouri Press, 1987.

Lewis, Oscar. *Sutter's Fort: Gateway to the Gold Fields*. Englewood Cliffs, NJ: Prentice-Hall, 1966.

Lynch, Vera Martin. *Free Land for Free Men: A Story of Clackamas County*. Portland, OR: Artline, 1973.

Madley, Benjamin. *An American Genocide: The United States and the California Indian Catastrophe, 1846–1873.* New Haven, CT: Yale University Press, 2016.

Mattes, Merrill J. *The Great Platte River Road.* Lincoln: University of Nebraska Press, 1969.

Melendy, H. Brett, and Benjamin F. Gilbert. *The Governors of California: Peter H. Burnett to Edmund G. Brown.* Georgetown, CA: Talisman Press, 1965.

Merry, Robert W. *A Country of Vast Designs: James K. Polk, the Mexican War and the Conquest of the American Continent.* New York: Simon & Schuster, 2009.

Minutes of the Proceedings of the Legislative Assembly of the District of San Francisco, from March 12, 1849 to June 4, 1849 and a Record of the Proceedings of the Ayuntamiento or Town Council of San Francisco from August 6, 1849 until May 3, 1850. San Francisco: Town & Bacon, 1860.

Morgan, Dale, ed. *Overland in 1846: Diaries and Letters of the Oregon-California Trail,* vols. 1 and 2. Georgetown, CA: Talisman Press, 1963.

Morrison, Dorothy Nafus. *Outpost: John McLoughlin and the Far Northwest.* Portland: Oregon Historical Society Press, 1999.

Neiderheiser, Leta Lovelace. *Jesse Applegate: A Dialogue with Destiny.* Mustang, OK: Tate Publishing, 2010.

Nelson, Robert. *Enemy of the Saints: The Biography of Governor Lilburn W. Boggs of Missouri.* Baltimore: Publish America, 2011.

Nesmith, James W. "Address." In *Transactions of the Third Annual Reunion of the Oregon Pioneer Association, Salem.* Portland: Oregon Historical Society Library, 1876.

Nokes, R. Gregory. *Massacred for Gold: The Chinese in Hells Canyon.* Corvallis: Oregon State University Press, 2009.

———. *Breaking Chains: Slavery on Trial in the Oregon Territory.* Corvallis: Oregon State University Press, 2013.

Owens, Kenneth, ed. *John Sutter and a Wider West.* Lincoln: University of Nebraska Press, 1994.

Paxton, W. M. *Annals of Platte County, Missouri, from Its Exploration Down to June 1, 1897 with Genealogies of Its Noted Families and Sketches of Its Pioneers and Distinguished People.* Kansas City, MO: Hudson-Kimberly, 1897.

Polk, James K., and Milo Milton Quaife. *The Diary of James K. Polk during His Presidency, 1845–1849,* vol. 1. Chicago: A. C. McClurg, 1910.

Prosch, Thomas W. *McCarver and Tacoma.* Seattle: Lowman & Hanford, 1906.

Quinn, Arthur. *The Rivals: William Gwin, David Broderick, and the Birth of California.* New York: Crown, 1994.

Reports of Cases Determined in the Supreme Court of California, vols. 9 and 10. San Francisco: Bancroft-Whitney, 1906.

Rich, E. E., ed. *John McLoughlin's Fort Vancouver Letters, First Series, 1825–1838,* and *Second Series, 1839–1844.* London: Champlain Society for the Hudson's Bay Record Society, 1941, 1943.

Richards, Leonard L. *The California Gold Rush and the Coming of the Civil War.* New York: Vintage Books, 2008.

Ruby, Robert H., and John H. Brown. *Indians of the Pacific Northwest*. Norman: University of Oklahoma Press, 1981.

Rucker, Maude Applegate. *The Oregon Trail: Some of Its Blazers*. New York: Walter Neale, 1930.

Sacramento City Directory for 1851. Sacramento, CA: Center for Sacramento History, 1851.

Secrest, William B. *When the Great Spirit Died: The Destruction of the California Indians*. Sanger, CA: World Dancer Press, 2003.

Severson, Thor. *Sacramento: An Illustrated History, 1839 to 1874, from Sutter's Fort to Capital City*. Sacramento: California Historical Society, 1973.

Sioli, Paoli, ed. *History of El Dorado County, California with Illustrations and Biographical Sketches of Its Prominent Men and Pioneers*. Oakland, CA: Paoli Sioli, 1883.

Smith, Stacey L. *Freedom's Frontier: California and the Struggle over Unfree Labor; Emancipation and Reconstruction*. Chapel Hill: University of North Carolina Press, 2013.

Stark, Peter. Astoria: *John Jacob Astor and Thomas Jefferson's Lost Pacific Empire*. New York: HarperCollins, 2014.

Starr, Kevin. *Americans and the California Dream, 1850–1915*. New York: Oxford University Press, 1973.

———. *California: A History*. New York: Modern Library, 2007.

Sutter, John A. *New Helvetia Diary: A Record of Events Kept by John A. Sutter and His Clerks at New Helvetia, California, from September 9, 1845, to May 25, 1848*. San Francisco: Grabhorn Press, 1939.

Sutter, John A., and Douglas S. Watson. *The Diary of Johann Augustus Sutter, Excerpts for 1838–1848, Part II*. San Francisco: Grabhorn Press, 1932.

Sutter, John A., Jr. "Statement Regarding Early California Experiences, February 27, 1855." In *The Sutter Family and the Origins of Gold-Rush Sacramento*, edited by Allan Ottley, introduction by Albert L. Hurtado. Norman: University of Oklahoma Press, 2002.

Tate, Michael L., ed. *The Great Medicine Road: Narratives of the Oregon, California, and Mormon Trails, Part I: 1840–1848*. Norman, OK: A. H. Clark, 2014.

Taylor, Bayard. *El Dorado; Or, Adventures in the Path of Empire*. New York: Alfred A. Knopf, 1949.

Tharpe, Dan L. *Encyclopedia of Frontier Biography*, vol. 2. Glendale, CA: A. H. Clark, 1988.

Thornton, J. Quinn. *Oregon and California in 1848*. New York: Harper and Brothers, 1848. [Major portions excerpted and edited in Johnson, *Unfortunate Emigrants*.]

Unruh, John, Jr. *The Plains Across*. Urbana: University of Illinois, 1979.

Victor, Frances Fuller. *The Early Indian Wars of Oregon, vol. 1, The Cayuse War*. Corvallis, OR: Taxus Baccata Books, 2007. [Based on the original work published in 1894.]

Walsh, Henry L. W. *Hallowed Were the Gold Dust Trails*. Santa Clara, CA: University of Santa Clara Press, 1946.

White, Ronald C. *American Ulysses: A Life of Ulysses S. Grant*. New York: Random House, 2016.

Whitman, Narcissa. *The Letters of Narcissa Whitman.* Fairfield, WA: Ye Galeon Press, 1986.

Williams, David A. *David C. Broderick: A Political Portrait.* San Marino, CA: Huntington Library, 1969.

Young, Otis E. *The First Military Escort on the Santa Fe Trail 1829: From the Journal and Reports of Major Bennet Riley and Lieutenant Philip St. George Cooke.* Glendale, CA: A. H. Clark, 1952.

ARTICLES

Bagley, Will. "Lansford Warren Hastings: Scoundrel or Visionary." *Overland Journal* 12 (Spring 1994).

Bernal, Paul. "Governor Burnett's Office in Suñol House." *Trail Blazer: Journal of the California Pioneers of Santa Clara County* 55, no. 3 (September 2014).

Boggs, William M. "A Short Biographical Sketch of Lilburn Boggs by His Son." *Missouri Historical Review* 4 (1910): 107–8.

Browne, J. Ross. "A Quarter of a Century." *Overland Monthly and Old West Magazine* 15 (October 1875).

Burnett, Peter H. "Letters of Peter H. Burnett." *Quarterly of the Oregon Historical Society* 3, no. 4 (December 1902).

Cleland, Robert G. "John Bidwell's Arrival in California." *Annual Publication of the Historical Society of Southern California* 10 (2015).

Dailey, Charles. "Pioneer Preacher Profile: Glen Owen Burnett." Pioneer History: Churches of Christ and Christian Churches in the Pacific Northwest website, accessed November 26, 2017. http://ncbible.org/nwh/ProBurnett.html.

Dale, Harrison C. "The Organization of the Oregon Emigrating Companies." *Quarterly of the Oregon Historical Society* 16, no. 3 (1915).

Doyle, Susan Badger. "Cornelius Gilliam, 1798–1848." In *The Oregon Encyclopedia.* Oregon Historical Society; online ed. https://oregonencyclopedia.org/articles/gilliam_cornelius/#.WfOHWEyZOu4.

"Fort Ross Chapel." Fort Ross Conservancy website, accessed October 20, 2017. http://www.fortross.org/chapel.htm.

Franklin, William E. "The Political Career of Peter Hardeman Burnett." PhD diss., Stanford University, 1954.

———. "Peter H. Burnett and the Provisional Government Movement." *California Historical Society Quarterly* 40 (1961).

———. "A Forgotten Chapter in California's History: Peter H. Burnett and John A. Sutter's Fortune." *California Historical Society Quarterly* 41 (1962).

Fuenfausen, Gary Gene. "Slavery in Clay County," accessed December 3, 2017. littledixie.net/slavery_in_clay_county.htm.

Grebenkemper, John, and Kristin Johnson. "Forensic Canine Search for the Donner Family Winter Camps at Alder Creek." *Overland Journal* 33 (Summer 2015).

Hamblin, Joan S. "Voyage of the Brooklyn." Ensign (July 1997): https://www.lds.org/ensign/1997/07/voyage-of-the-brooklyn?lang=eng.

Hammond, James Henry. "Speech of Hon. James H. Hammond, of South Carolina, on the Admission of Kansas, under the Lecompton Constitution: Delivered in the Senate of the United States, March 4, 1858." American Antiquarian Society Online, accessed October 27, 2017. http://www.americanantiquarian.org/Freedmen/Manuscripts/cottonisking.html.

Hazelett, Stafford. " 'To the World!!' The Story Behind the Vitriol." *Oregon Historical Quarterly* 116 (Summer 2015).

"History." Historic The Dalles website, accessed November 24, 2017. historicthedalles.org/history/.

Holman, Frederick V. "A Brief History of the Oregon Provisional Government and What Caused Its Formation." *Oregon Historical Quarterly* 13 (June 1912).

Johnston-Dodds, Kimberly. "California Militia and 'Expeditions against the Indians,' 1850–1859." California State Military Museums website, accessed October 27, 2017. http://www.militarymuseum.org/MilitiaandIndians.html.

Kilian, Crawford. "Gibbs, Wiflin Mistar (1823–1915)." In BlackPast.org; online ed. blackpast.org/aaw/gibbs-mifflin-wistar-1823-1915.

Kooshdaaka, Gordon. "The Bloody Island Massacre." Website of the Manataka American Indian, accessed October 24, 2017. http://www.manataka.org/page2199.html.

Lansing, Ronald B. "Whitman Massacre Trial." In *The Oregon Encyclopedia.* Oregon Historical Society; online ed. https://oregonencyclopedia.org/articles/whitman_massacre_trial/#.WfONPEyZOu4.

Larson, Elizabeth. "Bloody Island Atrocity Remembered at Saturday Ceremony." *Lake County News,* May 12, 2007.

"Lincoln's Advice to Lawyers," Abraham Lincoln Online, accessed November 24, 2017. http://www.abrahamlincolnonline.org/lincoln/speeches/law.htm.

Lockley, Fred. "The Case of Robin Holmes vs. Nathaniel Ford." *Oregon Historical Quarterly* 23 (June 1922).

"Major General Henry Wager Halleck." California Military Museum website, accessed October 23, 2017. http://militarymuseum.org/Halleck.html.

Mattes, Merrill J. "The Council Bluffs Road." *Overland Journal* 35 (Spring 2017). [Reprint from Nebraska History, 1984.]

McArthur, Scott. "Alonzo A. Skinner (1814–1877)." In *The Oregon Encyclopedia.* Oregon Historical Society; online ed. https://oregonencyclopedia.org/articles/skinner_alonzo_1814_1877_/#.Wenm50yZP-Y.

McPherson, Hallie Mae. "William McKendree Gwin: Expansionist." PhD diss., University of California, Berkeley, 1931.

Minto, John. "Motives and Antecedents of the Pioneers." *Oregon Historical Quarterly* 5 (March 1904).

"Missouri History Not Found in Textbooks." *Missouri Historical Review* 24 (April 1930).

Nemec, Bethany. "Oregon Fever." End of the Oregon Trail: Historic Oregon City website, November 28, 2016. https://www.historicoregoncity.org/2016/11/28/oregon-fever/.

Nesmith, James W. "Diary of the Emigration of 1843." *Oregon Historical Quarterly* 7 (December 1906).

"Newspaper Excerpts Relating to the Oregon Emigration Movement, 1842–1843." *Oregon Historical Quarterly* 4 (December 1903).

Oliphant, J. Orin. "Minutes of West Union Baptist Church." *Oregon Historical Quarterly* 36 (September 1935).

"The Oregon Meeting." *Oregon Historical Quarterly* 103 (December 2002).

"The Oroville Area and the Gold Rush of 1849." *Diggins* 43 (Fall 1999).

Osborn, Ellen. "John Calhoun Johnson: California Pioneer and Trail Blazer." *Overland Journal* 33 (Summer 2015).

"Pantoscope: Pencil Sketches Made Crossing the Plains to California in 1850–51." *Diggins* 43 (Fall 1999). [Originally published 1927.]

Pisani, Donald J. "Squatter Law in California, 1850–1858." *Western Historical Quarterly* 25 (Fall 1994).

Reick, Richard L. "Geography of the California Trails, Part II." *Overland Journal* 12 (1994).

Royce, Josiah. "The Squatter Riot of 1850 in Sacramento." *Overland Monthly* 6 (September 1885).

"Slaveholding Presidents." Hauenstein Center at Grand Valley State University website, accessed October 23, 2017. http://hauensteincenter.org/slaveholding/.

Smith, Stacey L. "Remaking Slavery in a Free State: Masters and Slaves in Gold Rush California." *Pacific Historical Review* 80 (October 2011).

Williams, George H. "Political History of Oregon, 1853–65." *Oregon Historical Quarterly* 2 (March 1901).

Zenk, Henry, Yvonne Hajda, and Robert Boyd. "Chinookan Villages of the Lower Columbia." *Oregon Historical Quarterly* 117 (Spring 2016).

Acknowledgments

I am deeply beholden to Emily Arques Douville of Antioch, California, and also to her cousin Francisca Burnett Allen of San Jose, two great-great-granddaughters of Peter Burnett. It was through them that I obtained access to personal correspondence I had been led to believe didn't exist. It took a bit of sleuthing. Here's how it happened:

I couldn't imagine that someone as verbose as Peter Burnett would not have written numerous personal letters over his lifetime to friends and family. But only a few random letters could be found. None of the researchers I queried at various museums and historical societies knew of any significant cache of letters, and for a long time I was unable to locate a family source who might be helpful.

Having almost given up, I chanced during an Internet search to read in a 2014 issue of *Trailblazer*, a publication of the Journal of the California Pioneers of Santa Clara County, that Burnett's desk had recently been put on display at the Roberto Adobe and Suñol House Museum in San Jose. The desk was on loan from a Burnett descendant, Francisca Burnett Allen.

I tracked down the author of the article, Judge Paul Bernal, the museum board chairman, who kindly helped me contact Ms. Allen. She didn't herself have any correspondence, but she had recently learned that her cousin Emily Douville possessed some letters. She put me in contact with Ms. Douville, who confirmed that she had about twenty letters written by Peter to his brother George in Lafayette, Oregon.

Ms. Douville generously agreed to text me copies of many of the letters, no easy task as they were ponderously long, faded with time, and difficult to read, especially those written as Burnett grew older and his hands became progressively afflicted by palsy. It was in these letters to his brother that I learned of Burnett's deep sadness at the death of two of his children, his mounting frustration as governor of California, his struggle with illness, and his second-guessing of his desire for great wealth. Ms. Douville received the letters from her late mother, who kept them locked in a safe for many years. She had intended to write a book about Burnett but never did.

Judge Bernal, who is also the official historian of the City of San Jose, deserves additional thanks for sending photographs of Burnett's desk and other family artifacts on display at the museum.

Acknowledging the many others who provided valuable help with this book is a distinct pleasure. The only downside is that I may fail to recognize someone who deserves my public thanks. But those who were helpful, either directly or indirectly, and in no particular order, include the following:

My wife, Candise, who joined me on a research trip to the Bancroft Library in Berkeley and remained ever patient and supportive for this book, as she did for my other books. Also, my son, Deston, who drove me to Sacramento, exploring en route the 1848 Burnett Road from Oregon to the Sacramento Valley, and on to Sutter's Fort and Sacramento for additional research. He helped me find the ruts remaining from the old Burnett Road near Tulelake, California.

A very special thanks goes to Timothy A. Kent, a retired Bureau of Land Management cadastral surveyor, now teaching at Clark College in Vancouver, who spent long hours helping me locate and explore Burnett's 1846 Oregon land claim. Posthumous thanks are also due to William Elton Franklin Jr., whose 1954 dissertation at Stanford University provided valuable guideposts for my research. Among others providing major help were Patricia L. Keats, director of library and archives of the Alice Phelan Sullivan Library at the Society of California Pioneers, San Francisco; Stacy Bondurant and Bryan Young of the J. D. Williams Library at the University of Mississippi; Sacramento author and historian William Burg for a valuable interview and other assistance; and Kathleen Correia, superintendent of the California History Section of the California State Library in Sacramento, and her helpful staff.

Also, Robert Dreyer of the California Capital State Museum Association; Janette Tigner, director of the Hardeman County Library in Bolivar, Tennessee, who researched old newspapers for information on the shooting at Peter Burnett's Tennessee store—establishing there was none to be found, however; Todd Shaffer, reference archivist at the Oregon State Archives in Salem, who provided records of old donation land claims; Stephan Smith of Smith Creative Group in Portland for his generous work on maps; David Harrelson of the Confederate Tribes of Grand Ronde, who provided helpful background of the native tribes of the period; Oregon author and historian Stephen Dow

Beckham for providing records of Burnett's judicial career in Oregon; Mary Burslie Mertz Davis, a docent at the Surgeon's House at the old Fort Dalles, for her informative tour of the historic site; Scott Daniels and the hardworking staff at the Oregon Historical Society Library in Portland; the research staff at the Bancroft Library in Berkeley, California; Cheryl Hill of the West Linn Library in West Linn, Oregon, who patiently ran down books that were not easy to find; Dylan McDonald, deputy city historian and manuscripts archivist at the Center for Sacramento History, who helped with property locations in Sacramento and recommended additional reading; Nancy Brower and Lucy Sperlin Skjelstad of the Butte County California Historical Society, who steered me away from a mistake on the location of Burnett's mining claim on the Yuba River and helped in other ways; Frances Kaplan, reference librarian at the California Historical Society in San Francisco; and Erin Herzog, manager of the local history collection in the California Room at the San Jose Public Library.

At the Oregon State University Press, my special thanks also go to Associate Director Tom Booth, who provided wise counsel and suggestions for this book, prodding me to better explain why this book is important; Micki Reaman, who extricated me from computer briar patches into which I had stumbled; and Marty Brown, who ably assisted along the way.

Thanks are also due to my friend Robert Dobkin of Boynton Beach, Florida, a former Associated Press colleague in Washington, DC, who suggested a meaningful change for the title of the book.

And what would I do without the Internet and those anonymous folks who post historical documents, saving me the expense of extra trips to California. Among these records were the debates in the 1859 California Constitutional Convention, the proceedings of the 1849 and 1851 sessions of the California Legislature, Governor Burnett's annual messages to the legislature, early rulings of the California Supreme Court, records of the *Alta* newspaper, and on and on. For someone who started his career using a typewriter and carbon paper, it was amazing.

Index